PENGUIN BOOKS

TRIAL AND ERROR

"When first published in **1986**, this penetrating book ... played a significant part in the development of the campaign to establish whether or not these convictions were safe or satisfactory. Many people have a good reason to be grateful to Robert Kee for his careful and painstaking research" – Cardinal Basil Hume, October 1989

"A very fine job indeed, both for justice and journalism" – *Independent*

"Comprehensive and disturbing reassessment" – Ludovic Kennedy in the *Spectator*

"Continues that tradition of journalists who are prepared to fight for justice where injustice has been done and in doing so preserve the very fabric of justice itself" – *Sunday Times*

"This sensitive, thorough and compassionate book" – *Irish Times*

"A reasoned, dispassionate attempt to expose an alleged miscarriage of justice" – *Scotsman*

D0892915

An author, journalist and broadcaster, Robert Kee has worked for many years for both ITV and BBC television on current affairs series such as *Panorama* and *This Week* and on other programmes, including a number of documentaries. He has been a special correspondent for the *Sunday Times* and the *Observer* and was literary editor of the *Spectator*.

He is the author of *The Green Flag*, a monumental history of Irish nationalism in three volumes, which has been published by Penguin. Robert Kee made a thirteen-part series for BBC television based on *The Green Flag*. Entitled *Ireland: A History*, it received great critical acclaim and was widely shown both in Britain and in the United States. His other books include *1939: The World We Left Behind*, *1945: The World We Fought For* and *Munich: The Eleventh Hour*, published to commemorate the fiftieth anniversary of the Munich Agreement.

TRIAL
and
ERROR

The Maguires, the Guildford Pub
Bombings and British Justice

ROBERT KEE

PENGUIN BOOKS

For Alastair Logan

PENGUIN BOOKS

Published by the Penguin Group
27 Wrights Lane, London W8 5TZ, England
Viking Penguin Inc., 40 West 23rd Street, New York, New York 10010, USA
Penguin Books Australia Ltd, Ringwood, Victoria, Australia
Penguin Books Canada Ltd, 2801 John Street, Markham, Ontario, Canada L3R 1B4
Penguin Books (NZ) Ltd, 182–190 Wairau Road, Auckland 10, New Zealand

Penguin Books Ltd, Registered Offices: Harmondsworth, Middlesex, England

First published by Hamish Hamilton 1986
Published with a new Preface by Penguin Books 1989
1 3 5 7 9 10 8 6 4 2

'Accusations of the most appalling kind have been made against the police during this trial. If true, there has been a really gigantic conspiracy between two police forces – the Surrey Police and the Bomb Squad – through officers of all ranks, including Commander Huntley of the Bomb Squad, the Head of Surrey C.I.D., Detective Chief Superintendent Walter Simmons, and Surrey Assistant Chief Constable, Christopher Rowe. If the allegations are true there has been a most appalling perversion of justice."

Sir Michael Havers,
October 15, 1975

"As far as any of the persons convicted for the Guildford and Wool-wich bombings, they had no connection whatsover with it . . . I was in charge of the operation."

Brendan Dowd,
H.M. Prison Albany, Isle of Wight October 26 1976

"I didn't do what I'm supposed to have done, I can sleep peaceful at night with a clear conscience, can the cops and judges? . . ."

Gerard Conlon
H.M. Prison Manchester
December 30, 1977

"The Home Secretary is empowered under Section 17 of the Criminal Appeal Act 1968 to refer a case to the Court of Appeal (Criminal Division) but it would not be right for him to do so unless significant new facts or considerations of substance had come to light . . ."

Home Office letter to the author
March 27, 1985

CONTENTS

PART II: ARGUMENTS

PART III: CONCLUSION

Preface to the Second Edition

On the morning of Thursday, 19 October 1989, Mr. Roy Amlot, Q.C., stood up on behalf of the Director of Public Prosecutions in a packed No. 2 Court at the Old Bailey before the Lord Chief Justice and two other Lords of Appeal. In the dock were three Irishmen and one English girl, all in their early thirties, who had been brought to the Court, handcuffed, that morning. They had been in prison for nearly fifteen years, having been convicted in 1975 of the crime of the Guildford pub bombings described in this book. This time, however, they were not really in the dock at all. It was British justice itself which was being arraigned.

For what Mr. Amlot revealed on behalf of the Crown that morning was that "confessions" to that crime – the only evidence there had ever been against the Four – were the product of fabrications on the part of the Surrey Constabulary of the day. They were set free that afternoon. The innocence which they themselves had so long protested had been recognised at last. If this book, first published in the autumn of 1986, was of some help to others who helped bring about this dramatic event, it will have been the most satisfying achievement of my professional life to date. But the matter is not over.

As recounted here, seven other people from the household of a London Irish family named Maguire were sentenced and have served long terms of imprisonment in consequence of the Guildford Four's "confessions", which are now known to have been false. The measure of legal hypocrisy which made it possible for the Maguires to be tried on a charge technically unconnected with the Guildford bombing has continued to this day. For although the recent Home Secretary, Douglas Hurd, dismayed by the Guildford revelations, had to institute an enquiry into that scandal which will also include the Maguire case, he consistently refused over many years to have the Maguire case reviewed by the Court of Appeal. He maintained this refusal in the face of pressure from the very same people who long urged him to refer back the Guildford case itself. But then he consistently refused to take any action over that either over many years.

It has been my purpose in this book to unfold as dispassionately as possible the disturbing web of improbability and lurking doubt which continued to surround these two cases even after they had been dealt with by all the normal due processes of law – that is, jury trial and Appeal hearing, though the Maguires were actually refused leave to appeal. Having, perhaps, like Patrick Maguire (see page 5), always had too easy a respect for British justice, I was in no way early in finding these cases a matter for concern.

It was an Irish priest, Father Faul, a man of known integrity, who first pointed me in this direction in 1984. But Father Faul is also known as a man of strong republican views, and this naturally made me wary that his sympathies might possibly have distorted his judgement. However, it was someone of very different political views, my old undergraduate friend, the Conservative and strongly Unionist M.P. the late Sir John Biggs-Davison, who further drew my attention to disquieting details of the Maguire case. He had himself originally been strongly impressed by the fact that one of those convicted in that case, a devout Catholic who had died in custody in 1980, had continued with his last breath to protest his total innocence. I then learned that the Cardinal Archbishop of

Westminster, Basil Hume, had been impressed and disturbed by this man's protestations of innocence even before his death. The Cardinal had even spoken to Mrs. Thatcher on the matter in 1979, soon after she took office. She had properly expressed her own concern that anything that looked like a possible miscarriage of justice should be examined.

The trouble – and it is one with which, after Guildford, the legal system will have to concern itself – is that there is a gap between what politicians in office and some lawyers tend to regard as a possible miscarriage of justice and the view taken of such matters by other human beings, including archbishops, some lawyers and some politicians (usually out of office).

After long interviews with the Maguire family and documentary research made possible by some of those mentioned in the preface to the first edition, I became convinced that, at the very least, the convictions in both cases were unsafe and needed to be looked at again. It was greatly encouraging to find on publication of *Trial and Error* that such a view was shared not only by Cardinal Hume but also by two distinguished Law Lords, Lord Devlin and Lord Scarman, and by two former Home Secretaries – the two, in fact, who had been in office when the trials had taken place – Roy Jenkins and Merlyn Rees. Naively I hoped that the Home Office could be persuaded to agree with them that the cases should be looked at again. The Home Secretary, after all, has the statutory right, "if he thinks fit", to refer any case back to the Court of Appeal even though all the normal, regular processes of law have been completed. No other criterion is provided by the statute. It was difficult to see how anyone could read the material presented here and not think at least that the whole matter should be reconsidered on the existing evidence. The book was sent to the Home Office and politely acknowledged.

The handling of the Maguire case by the Government up to that moment is summarised in the book's concluding pages. Then, in the House of Lords on 4 November 1986, Baroness Ewart-Biggs asked what action the Government proposed to take, in both the Guildford and the Maguire case, in the light of *Trial and Error*. She referred to the need "to remove something which has nagged at, and will continue to nag at, the conscience of British justice". Lord Fitt, who together with a number of other noble lords expressed a sense of urgent concern, asked for representations to be made to the Home Secretary (Douglas Hurd) "telling him very clearly that this case is not going to go away, however much he may attempt to keep defending the perimeter". Lord Scarman reminded the Government that if the Home Secretary referred these cases back to the Court of Appeal, as he was empowered to do, that Court had the right to "look into the whole case again in order to ensure that justice, however belated, is done".

Such pleas fell on technically deaf ears. Lord Beaverbrook, in the Lords for the Government that day, made clear the gap which separates the concerns of officials from the concerns of other human beings: "There must," he said, "be some factor for the court to look at other than evidence which the courts have already considered."

In other words, however mistaken a previous legal decision may seem to be on informed and mature reflection by respected people, it can never be revised until some reason other than such reflection be found for doing so. The absurdity, quite apart from the potential inhumanity, of this complacent attitude is compounded by the paradox that, as Lord Scarman had pointed out, once new evidence has been found the whole case can be re-argued on its old merits. It was to be three years almost to the day before Gerry Fitt's words were to come home to roost to the discomfiture of the Home Secretary, Douglas Hurd, and to the detriment of the reputation of British justice, which for those three years had been in his keeping.

On 20 November 1986 David Mellor, then Hurd's junior minister at the Home Office, told John Biggs-Davison in the House of Commons that the Secretary of State was "looking carefully" at *Trial and Error* "to determine whether it raises new points which require further investigation or which may affect his earlier decision that he would not be justified in referring the Maguire case to the Court of Appeal". The same day also in the House of Commons John Biffen answered another question from John Biggs-Davison about whether the Home Secretary had studied an all-party motion urging him to act on Guildford and the Maguires, in view of the doubt about both cases felt by Lords Scarman and Devlin, two former Home Secretaries, Cardinal Hume, the Editor of *The Times* and others. He was told that his "courteous persistence in these matters" was "admired" and that the Secretary of State's attention would be drawn to his request.

We then waited to see what effect the material in *Trial and Error* would have on Douglas Hurd. He had the reputation of a humane and liberal man. The relevant statute, the Criminal Appeal Act of 1968, placed no further restriction upon him in its clause 17 than that he should "think it fit" to send the cases back to the Court of Appeal. Would he not, reading what is presented here, think at least that the cases should be looked at again?

In the meantime Gerry Fitt and I had been courteously and separately received by the present Commissioner of Metropolitan Police, Sir Peter Imbert. He listened at length to our strong expressions of doubt particularly about the Maguire case. He had been a detective superintendent in the Bomb Squad in 1974 and had conducted interviews with some of the Guildford Four about the Woolwich bombing. He himself seemed particularly concerned about the Maguire case. He appointed a young detective inspector, Roger Pearce, to make an internal enquiry about the Maguire case. I was introduced to Roger Pearce, who impressed me with his assurance that he would be determined only to get at the truth, whatever that might be. On 20 January 1987, before in fact that internal enquiry had been fully completed, Douglas Hurd reported to the House of Commons. He told Members at some length that he could see no grounds on which it would be right for him to refer either case back to the Court of Appeal. He was honest enough to spell out clearly the basic flaw, if a Home Secretary should think it fit to look for one, in the entire present mechanism for looking at suspected miscarriages of justice.

"It is hard to see," he said, "how the Court of Appeal could fail to dismiss any reference to it based simply on the proposition, argued without fresh evidence, that its predecessors and the jury got it wrong."

He added that what was perhaps more important was that the public would "rightly" become deeply suspicious of "a convention which enabled politicians to throw a verdict into doubt simply because they had developed, without any fresh evidence, a view that the verdict may have been mistaken".

This reasoning, of course, side-steps the point that had already been made by Lord Scarman, in November in the House of Lords, citing a respected judgement, to the effect that once a case had come back to the Court of Appeal the *whole* of it could be argued again anyway.

Now, in response to Hurd's decision, Roy Jenkins said in the Commons that he would have been better advised "to have set up a special enquiry under a very senior judicial chairman to consider whether there was something in the climate of the time conducive to any unsafe verdict".

When himself Home Secretary Jenkins had in a famous case (the Confait case), which rested only on confessions, sent it back to the Court of Appeal not on new evidence but on what he described as "a consideration of substance", specifically a reconsideration of previous scientific evidence. Three young men who had been sentenced to life imprisonment on the basis of their confessions were consequently set free.

One further contribution to the debate on Hurd's decision on 20 January 1987 is worth noting. It struck what was to prove a prophetic note.

David Howell, the Member for Guildford itself, sought a categorical reassurance from Hurd that in reaching his decision he had "found not the slightest trace of new evidence". Hurd replied: "I am satisfied that in the Guildford case there was no new evidence or new matters of substance . . . not before the original court or the Court of Appeal."

But, of course, vital new evidence – which was eventually to free the Guildford Four – was sitting in the Surrey Constabulary's headquarters at Guildford all the time. It had not been found, and was not to be found, for almost another three years because the urgency to look for it was not there. The Home Secretary felt satisfied that without new evidence there *was* no urgency. It is a classic illustration of the way in which a Home Secretary, "if he thinks fit", can apply Catch 22 to make nonsense of British justice.

The nonsense was further compounded four days later by

Hurd's junior minister, David Mellor, when in a letter to *The Times* he wrote that the Secretary of State "did not say or imply in the House of Commons that he had no doubts about the rightness of the convictions". But that is, in fact, precisely the definition of "lurking doubt" which obliges a jury to acquit.

Mellor added in his letter that it was not the Home Secretary's function to "second-guess the Courts on the basis of evidence which they had already considered". But that is precisely what the two memoranda which Hurd now presented to Parliament on these two cases proceeded to do. Apart from containing a significant number of minor factual errors, they "second-guessed" the evidence which the Courts had already considered in a manner that confirmed the alleged correctness of the original verdicts.

Not for one moment did any of this deflect the now dedicated determination of Cardinal Hume that convictions which looked to him likely to prove neither safe nor satisfactory should be reviewed. Certain details of new evidence – though principally confirmatory of old evidence – came his way, and in July 1987 a deputation consisting of himself, the two Law Lords, Devlin and Scarman, and the two former Home Secretaries, Jenkins and Rees, went to the Home Office to put their arguments to Hurd and his new junior minister, John Patten. They were listened to courteously and at length, but neither Hurd nor Patten then showed any sign of being convinced that there was anything wrong with the two cases. However, in the following month the Avon and Somerset police were appointed to undertake an enquiry into the new evidence being presented.

In April 1988, after Hurd had seen Avon and Somerset's first report, which was not shown to Cardinal Hume's deputation, there followed considerable further correspondence between them and the Home Secretary, after which he finally agreed to refer Guildford back to the Court of Appeal in January 1989.

It may be noted that Mr. Roy Amlot, in his historic speech for the Crown on Thursday, 19 October, stressed that had the new evidence on behalf of those convicted been only that with which he had been presented up to that date, he would have felt confident in contesting it. However, the very proper rigour with which the new Crown Prosecution Service now set about its task of preparing for the Court of Appeal required that the Avon and Somerset police should try harder. It was their renewed investigation that resulted in the discovery of the documents, which had been at Guildford all the time, that showed that the confessions of the Guildford Four were fabricated and that the convictions had been, as Cardinal Hume and others had long maintained, neither safe nor satisfactory.

What are the conclusions now to be drawn from this terrible story?

First, that but for the persistence of Cardinal Hume and others like him, the Home Secretary of the day would, without new evidence, never have done anything about either of these cases. Second, that the necessary new evidence in the Guildford case would never have been found but for this persistence, which derived not from new evidence but from the belief, after mature study and reflection, that the original verdict might well have been unsound. Third, that therefore some new legal mechanism must be devised for ensuring that cases of possible miscarriage of justice can be re-examined even when new evidence is not available. It would not be difficult to build in safeguards to prevent waste of time by frivolous applications. As Guildford has shown, it is far too dangerous to leave miscarriages of justice to a mechanism by which it is so easy for a politician to stick to a formula for doing nothing.

Meanwhile the Maguires and others convicted with them fight to have their case re-examined and their names cleared. Meanwhile, too, readers of this book can decide for themselves whether, if they had been Home Secretary, they would have "thought it fit" that these cases should be reviewed.

November 1989

Preface to the First Edition

All the dialogue in this book is taken either from official police records or from accounts given by those arrested to their solicitors and others. None has been invented by the author.

Details of the judge's summing-up in both trials and of the judgments of the Court of Appeal are from the transcripts supplied by the Court Official Shorthand Writers. Details of the interviews with the Balcombe street active service unit are from verbatim transcripts.

Where the names of police officers have been omitted these are known to the author. Where police officers are named in allegations in the context of court proceedings, the words are cited principally from the summing-up of Mr Justice Donaldson as reported by the Court Official Shorthand Writers, though occasionally an account is taken from newspaper reports of court proceedings or from defendants' statements to their solicitors. The latter of course were not made on oath; the police officers' denials of improper interrogation were made on oath. All the allegations here cited against police officers in whatever form have always been consistently denied by all of them and their denials were unequivocally accepted as the truth by the juries concerned and the Court of Appeal.

The book could not have been written without the generous and skilled collaboration of Alastair Logan, solicitor, whose tireless work for twelve years to uphold the highest standards of British Justice is an inspiration to all who believe in a fair and free society.

I am also much indebted to Derek Mash B. Sc. for patient and scholarly advice on matters scientific and otherwise.

Among others who have helped with advice, encouragement and consideration I should like to thank my agent Gill Coleridge and my publisher Christopher Sinclair-Stevenson, and, without in any way implicating anyone in the conclusions of this book, the following with whom I have been able to discuss aspects of these disturbing cases: His Excellency the Irish Ambassador, His Eminence the Cardinal Archbishop of Westminster Cardinal Hume, the Lord Fitt, the Rt. Hon. Jack Ashley M.P., the Rt. Hon. Reg Freeson M.P., the Rt. Hon. Roy Jenkins M.P., the Rt. Hon. Merlyn Rees M.P., John Wheeler M.P., Sir John Biggs-Davison M.P., John Hume M.P., Lisa Astin, Pat Cox, Liam O'Flanagan, Frank Johnson, Cynthia Kee, Sarah Kee, Maura Kelly, Tom McGurk, Grant McKee, Joe Mulholland, Chris Mullin, Frances Partridge, Christopher Price and Barbara Twigg.

Gerry Fitt has devoted to the cause of the Maguires both inside and outside Parliament that energy, courage and independence of spirit for which he has long been renowned in other fields. I am particularly grateful to Tom McGurk and Christopher Price for putting their earlier research on the subject at my disposal and to Frances Partridge for advice. Topsy Levan gave support as well as being a wonderful typist. Judy Mott helped nobly in an emergency.

I salute those more than 200 Members of Parliament of all parties who have signed Early Day Motion no 280 (Miscarriage of Justice) in the House of Commons for standing up and being counted.

My greatest debt is to the Maguire family whose faith, through long years of suffering, in the ability of British Justice to live up to its highest standards in the end has been an inspiration ever since I first met them early in 1985. Their bearing and constancy as a family are testimony to that true worth of human nature which makes it so necessary always to distinguish between right and wrong.

PART I
Events

1
Introduction

On February 14 (St. Valentine's day) 1975 an English girl of
17, Carole Richardson, on remand in Brixton prison for a
murder with which she insisted she had no connection whatever, wrote to her boy-friend, also on remand for the same
offence and equally maintaining his innocence:

"I feel so miserable and fed up and just sick of life. . . . Oh
well, I can always think of Texas and poppy fields."

Hallucinating drugs had played a companionable part in their
relationship when they were free. They play only a small part
in the reality of this story, evoked in this sad momentary
vision of one of its characters. But it is another part of the
story that more conventional characters can also seek refuge
in illusion, indulging in fantasies quite detached from the
truth for all their own certainty that their lives are ruled by
prosaic routine and unequivocal fact. The poppy fields of
Texas provide a metaphor for realms in which people see
what they want to see.

3

In dreaming of such a place Carole knew what she was doing. But the possibility has to be faced that, in 1974 and subsequently, others with what are normally regarded as responsible positions in British public life, seeing what they wanted to see, took from the poppy fields a sickness which infected society itself, laying low not just Carole and ten fellow human beings but one of the most revered of all Britain's institutions: its system of justice.

The specific proposition to be faced is that in sentencing four people to life imprisonment for I.R.A. murders at Guildford in 1974, and in sentencing seven other people to long terms of imprisonment on a charge which derived from those Guildford murders, of handling nitroglycerine unlawfully, British courts just over ten years ago were responsible for a miscarriage of justice on a scale unprecedented in Britain in this century.

Those convicted of the Guildford murders were:

Carole Richardson, by then aged 18,
Patrick Armstrong, aged 25,
Paul Hill, aged 21,
Gerard Conlon, aged 21;

Those convicted of unlawfully handling nitroglycerine were:

Anne Maguire, aged 40,
Patrick ("Paddy") Maguire, aged 43,
Vincent Maguire, aged 17,
Patrick Maguire, aged 14,
Patrick Joseph ("Giuseppe") Conlon, aged 52,
Sean Smyth, aged 38,
Patrick O'Neill, aged 35.

The Guildford Four are now in their twelfth year in prison and are serving life sentences. If a miscarriage of justice is to be redressed, obviously theirs is the more urgent case. Yet so strangely interlocked are the two cases, and so much more apparent, in spite of their convictions, is the innocence of the Maguire Seven, that it is by the clearing of their names first that faith in the good name of British justice, so dangerously weakened by the whole affair, is likely to be most quickly restored.

The Maguire Seven have all now served their sentences with appropriate remission, that of "Giuseppe"* Conlon being terminated by death in custody. The last to be released was Anne Maguire, in February 1985. Like her husband, Paddy, she had been sentenced to fourteen years in 1976 but because she with her two sons had been granted bail for most of the fifteen months before the end of the trial it was she who had to wait longest for the ordeal to be over. During her imprisonment, when she eventually applied for parole she steadfastly refused to express the desired remorse for a crime of which, like the rest of the Maguire Seven, she claimed to be totally innocent.

When, at the end of the Maguire Seven's trial in March 1976, the verdict of "Guilty" was delivered against them, Paddy Maguire turned to his two young sons who had stood in the dock with him for six weeks and said:

"Sons, I'm sorry, I have to apologise. I always told you that British justice was the finest in the world and that you should trust and respect it. I was wrong."

He and his wife Anne, both born in Belfast, had then been living in Britain for nineteen years; they settled in London after he left the British Army in 1957 and brought up a family of three sons and a daughter who speak with the accents of Londoners. He was a member of the Paddington Conservative Club. It is a mark not only of his character but of his identification with much that is traditionally British that even after nearly ten years' imprisonment for something of which, if he is to be believed, not only was he innocent but which never actually happened, he is not a bitter man and would still like to be able to say that British justice is the finest in the world. It may be possible to do something to help restore his faith in it.

Anne Maguire was carried screaming from the dock in

*Christened Patrick Joseph, he was known as Giuseppe because he had had an Italian godfather.

March 1976, protesting her innocence. But she too still refuses to be more embittered than to say that "some mistake must have been made". Sean Smyth, her brother, who in 1974 had been living in the Maguires' London house for some months while he worked in London, and Pat O'Neill, a London Irish friend who had called at the house on the afternoon of the day the police arrived there, find it impossible not to feel bitter. Both their marriages foundered as a result of their imprisonment. But their chief concern has always been, as it has been that of the Maguires, to assert their innocence and to ask for their case to be re-opened.

This can be no easy matter. The Maguire household was tried by the proper forms of British law and found guilty by a unanimous jury* – a verdict of which the trial judge plainly approved. Leave to appeal against it was refused by the Court of Appeal which found that the trial had been exemplarily conducted.

How then can the Maguires, Smyth and O'Neill – and this applied to Giuseppe Conlon too until he died – be so confident and persistent in asserting their innocence? Could such an assertion perhaps be part of a very subtle I.R.A. plot to discredit British justice? Were the Maguire Seven not only terrorists but, after conviction, dedicated I.R.A. "sleepers", conspiring to serve their cause again on emerging from the long years of imprisonment?

In fact the I.R.A. have never shown any public sympathy or support for the Maguires, either in their imprisonment or since, and such reticence is quite out of character with their otherwise forthright propaganda techniques. Nevertheless, like every possibility in this story, it is one to be borne in mind in the search for truth. For the searcher returns repeatedly to the same question: how can the accused in the Maguire case all be so quietly and impressively assertive of their innocence in the face of what happened in the law courts? It is a mystery story in reverse: one which starts with the verdict, and leads

*The jury was unanimous for six of the seven defendants. They found Patrick, aged 14, guilty by a majority of 11 to 1.

back through devious paths to that other list of accused: the Guildford Four.

The charge on which the Maguire household were arraigned was in itself a strange one. It was very carefully not related to any specific act of terrorism. Each member was accused that at some time on December 2 and 3 1974 they had knowingly "had in his or her – as the case may be – possession or under his or her control an explosive substance, namely nitroglycerine, under such circumstances as to give rise to a reasonable suspicion that he or she – as the case may be – did not have it in his or her possession for a lawful object." This was the only charge.

Each of the accused steadfastly maintained that they had not had any nitroglycerine in their possession at all. Clearly, however, if a British jury were prepared to convict on such a charge they must have had what seemed to them very convincing material evidence. And so, to them, and the judge, the evidence had seemed to be.

The material evidence consisted of tests for nitroglycerine made on swabs taken by the police on the night of the 3rd to 4th December from the hands of the accused or, in the case of Anne Maguire, from some plastic gloves out of 24 in her kitchen drawer medically prescribed for her dermatitis and removed by the police on the next day. These swabs were found by the Government's forensic science laboratory at Woolwich to reveal traces of nitroglycerine.

Though an exhaustive attempt was made by the defence at the trial to cast doubt on the validity of the scientific tests carried out at Woolwich, the jury preferred the authority of the Crown's experts to that of those who challenged them. Such concentration on the scientific issue caused other considerations to be largely overlooked. Among these was the possibility that the swabs as tested might not have been true evidence of the state of the hands or glove as swabbed. Equally obscured by the complex scientific arguments was the apparent unlikelihood, given the accepted movements of the accused over the period in question and other circumstantial evidence, that they could have handled nitroglycerine within that period even if they had wanted to.

There were factors at work in the trial other than those to which reference was openly made in the hearing between January 27 and March 4 1976. It is not necessary to look very far to discover what these were. The first page of the official documentation of the case runs:

"Before

THE HONOURABLE MR. JUSTICE DONALDSON

REGINA

v.

ANNE RITA MAGUIRE and others"

The Honourable Mr Justice Donaldson had only three months before presided at the trial of the four people found guilty of murder in the I.R.A. bombings at Guildford. One of them was a nephew of Anne Rita Maguire.

The nephew's name was Gerard Conlon. He and one of his co-accused had implicated Anne Maguire in "confessions" which said not only that she had shown him how to make bombs but that she had personally taken part in the pub bombings. On the strength of this the police originally charged her with murder together with the four, and she appeared with them on this charge at Guildford Magistrates' Court, her name being listed with them in papers like the *Sun* and the *Daily Express:* "Mrs Anne Maguire of Third Avenue, Kensington."

However there turned out to be no evidence at all against her on the murder charge other than these "confessions" which her co-accused retracted immediately they had access to solicitors. These were in any case inadmissible in law against Anne Maguire as hearsay. Moreover she was able to show that she had not been in Guildford at all on the night of the pub bombings. Thus in spite of strong opposition from the Surrey Constabulary the Director of Public Prosecutions dropped the murder charge against Anne Maguire in late February 1975.

But the memory of her association with the Guildford Four

was unlikely to have faded from the public mind. The very article in the *Surrey Daily Advertiser* which announced the Guildford trial – "Ten Weeks for Bombs Trial" – concluded with a paragraph which ran: "The murder trial will be followed by the trial of seven other persons accused of explosives offences", and these defendants were named individually, including "Anne Maguire". Reflecting the assumptions of such association at the time, the *Times* index for the quarter April-June 1975 was to appear with the entry which still stands to-day: "Maguire, Anne – Involvement in Guildford and Woolwich bomb attacks; see Irish Republican Army: British activities in: Guildford and Woolwich bomb attacks . . . " Anne Maguire was never in fact found to have been involved in either of these bomb attacks. The entry merely crystallises the wide publicity given to her name by the prosecution at the Guildford trial. Making use of her nephew's "confession" the prosecution had described her by name as a bomb-maker in action, ". . . with a long black tube, some sand and a watch-face", telling her nephew to note what she was doing, "because you might have to do it yourself one day". And now at her own trial, three months later, charged with handling nitroglycerine unlawfully, she appeared first in the indictment, though alphabetically Patrick Joseph Conlon should have been named first.

But what most explicitly seemed to confirm a connection between the two trials was the fact that the same Judge, the Honourable Mr. Justice Donaldson, as he then was, and the same Crown Prosecutor, Sir Michael Havers, the very man who had accused her of being a bomb-maker, officiated at the second trial.

Havers and Donaldson solemnly proclaimed that there was no connection between the two trials at all. It is difficult not to see in this a certain lack of imagination, and to ask why, however correct legally, they did not feel that it was at least morally wrong to officiate at the second trial. For it was only the "confessions" of her nephew and his co-accused which led the police to the Maguire household in the first place.

The Appeal Court was not troubled by this or indeed by any other aspect of the case. In refusing all seven of those convicted in the Maguire trial leave to appeal against conviction they stated that they saw no reason for disturbing any of the convictions "either on the basis that any of them is unsafe or unsatisfactory or that the learned Judge was guilty of any non-direction or misdirection or that his summing-up in any way was unbalanced".

To try to understand all this and appreciate the atmosphere in which these trials took place it is necessary to go back to the Guildford bombing itself, the 36th incident involving I.R.A. violence on the mainland of Britain in the previous twelve months and one of the bloodiest and most savage to date. For whereas the Maguire Seven were able to claim with some plausibility that the crime with which they were charged had never even been committed, what had happened at Guildford had been all too horribly real.

2
The Guildford Pub Bombings

The town of Guildford in the south-east of England on
Saturday nights in the early autumn of 1974 had some of the
atmosphere of World War II Britain without the black-out.
Young men and women from the army training camps in
Hampshire and Surrey would congregate there as the only
non-military town in the area in which to hunt the elusive
pleasures of ordinary life to which army discipline during the
week lent almost mystical desirability. In the town's cinemas
and public houses fantasies of well-being could be pursued to
the accompaniment of rounds of drinks which only sporadi-
cally led to trouble. The fact that, in contrast with wartime,
army personnel could wear civilian clothes and that a uniform
was hardly ever to be seen in the crowded pubs, heightened
the sense of release, while enabling camaraderie to be retained
through the sight of army haircuts and other corporate
idiosyncrasies recognisable in both sexes.

Julie Spooner, a seventeen-year-old Scots girl with the
Women's Royal Army Corps (WRAC) at Blackdown, had
come in to Guildford on Saturday October 5 with two other
Scots girls from her barracks and seen the film *The Exorcist* in
the afternoon. She knew at once when she went into the

ladies' lavatory at the Seven Stars public house just after eight o'clock that evening that the women waiting in there were "civvies". "You'll have to wait in the queue," one of them said to her nastily.

("The civvy women don't like WRACs and are usually nasty to us," she told someone a few days later.)

Civilians, however, were in the minority at weekends in the Guildford pubs popular with the Army.

Earlier that evening Julie Spooner and her friends had spent two hours in another popular public house, the Horse and Groom. The beer there was slightly cheaper, and a regular pattern of behaviour was to start the evening there and then move down the 200 yards to the Seven Stars where there was a disco from eight o'clock. There was a tendency to move backwards and forwards between the two pubs more than once in the evening; they provided at least some sort of focus to the rather desultory pursuit of happiness which otherwise characterised visits to the town.

Samuel Murphy for instance, an eighteen-year-old recruit to the Irish Guards, had been drifting about Guildford that afternoon with a seventeen-year-old fellow Guardsman, Andrew MacQuade, "not going anywhere particular, just walking around". They had looked into a Wimpy Bar wondering if they should have something to eat, but had decided not to "because it was too crowded and the prices too dear". They had wandered up the High Street as far as the Odeon Cinema and had turned there into another road where they met some fellow Guardsmen. "They told us as we passed that there was nothing up there so we turned back." Eventually they went into a pub called the Three Pigeons where the only thing of interest seemed to be "a young bloke with a white poodle". They moved on to the Horse and Groom at about ten to six.

There were already a fair number of people there. Earlier a dozen or so Welsh Guardsmen had actually been waiting outside for the pub to open when a WRAC driver, Gillian de Grys, arrived with some Scots Guards friends and sat down on a bench to wait too. Among the WRACs with whom she had come to Guildford earlier was a friend, Caroline Slater;

they had separated in the afternoon, agreeing to meet up later in the Horse and Groom. Two elderly men with shopping bags moved into the pub shortly after it opened.

The place gradually began to fill up. It was not until the record which Murphy and MacQuade had put on the juke box was halfway through that they could find a seat at which to drink their pints of bitter. They moved off down to the Seven Stars about an hour later, at around a quarter to seven.

By that time Ivan Allison, a seventeen-year-old trooper in the Household Cavalry in Knightsbridge, who had trained near Guildford and liked the pubs there so much that he still came down on Saturday nights, was again drinking in the Seven Stars having already been up to the Horse and Groom and back within the hour. He had originally intended to start at the Horse and Groom. He had made an arrangement the week before to meet a girl there, though he didn't actually know her name. But on arrival in Guildford he had changed his mind about her and gone straight to the Seven Stars instead. A fleeting thought that the Horse and Groom might nevertheless be the better place in which to be, had taken him there for a few minutes but on seeing no one he knew ("The WRAC I was going to meet was not there either") he had simply used the lavatory and returned to the Seven Stars.

He had however spotted in the Horse and Groom, without knowing who they were, a family party in the innermost and darker of the pub's two left-hand alcoves, close to which stood the juke box. These people were there to celebrate a birthday, or rather two birthdays. Carol the WRAC daughter of Mr and Mrs Robert Burns, a driver and a canteen assistant of Boreham Wood in Hertfordshire, was nineteen on this 5th of October, and a young family friend, Paul Craig ("more of a friend than a boy-friend" Carol called him) was to be twenty-two the next day. He was wearing a blue tie with the word 'bullshit' on it in squiggly writing to make it look like a pattern. Paul had driven her parents over in his white Cortina to collect Carol from her barracks with a WRAC friend Sheila Parrotte, known as "Sammy". They all got to the Horse and Groom about seven o'clock by the pub clock which, unlike many English pub clocks, was said to be accurate to within a minute. Mr Burns bought two Bacardis and Coke for his wife and "Sammy", a Cinzano and lemonade for his daughter, pints of beer for Paul and himself and they all sat down together in the darkened inner alcove by the juke box.

Most of the WRAC girls in the Horse and Groom knew that it was Carol Burns' birthday and many came over to wish her a happy one. Over the top of the partition which separated the two alcoves Gillian de Grys too called out "Happy Birthday!" There was to be some mystification in her alcove over a light grey man's jacket found lying on a chair. It seemed to belong to no one and Gillian's Scots Guard boy-friend was worried because he had found himself sitting on it and had flicked ash on to it; it was eventually hung over the back of a chair.

Gillian's girl companion of the afternoon, Caroline Slater, had by now come into the Horse and Groom with another WRAC friend, Ann Hamilton. Caroline had joined the WRAC on the same day as Carol Burns and she too shouted "Happy Birthday!" as they went over to the bar to get some drinks. They sat down in the inner alcove with the Burns family. After a while "Sammy" Parrotte, who had been moving around talking to people and playing "Honey Honey", "I Shot the Sheriff" and "Jailhouse Rock" on the juke box, asked Carol if she would mind if she and Caroline went off up to the Seven Stars as Caroline wanted to see what it was like. Carol, the birthday girl, had no objection, and they left.

It was now some time after eight o'clock and the Horse and Groom was becoming crowded. On the alcove bench on which Carol and Mrs Burns were sitting, Carol whispered to her mother that she rather liked the look of a young boy sitting opposite to her in a red shirt, and indeed "Sammy" Parrotte had caught her flashing her eyes at him before she went out. Consequently Mrs Burns took some notice of him. He had not been there when they first arrived. Slim and smart and with hair cut in a rather unsoldierly fashion, he seemed to be keeping himself very much to himself.

In this, certainly, if he were a soldier, he was different from most of those who had been in and out of the Horse and

Groom already that evening. Typical had been two young Privates from the Third Parachute battalion at Aldershot, Paul Lynskey and Johnny Cook, who had come into Guildford expressly "to pick up a couple of WRAC girls" and who before the Burns party arrived at about seven had been standing by the juke box with a light ale and lime and a Colt 45, "eyeing-up" the three Scots girls, Julie Spooner and her friends who had not yet moved up to the Seven Stars. These three girls, and two people who gave the soldiers the rather hazy impression of being "a courting couple", were still then the only occupants of that inner alcove. The two elderly men who had gone to sit there with their shopping bags when the pub opened had left, apparently to catch a bus, at about half past six. Now the "courting couple" whom one of the three Scots girls, Rosemary Mackay, seeing "the lassie's head on his shoulder", had carefully avoided staring at, themselves got up and left. Lynskey and Cook moved into their places and started chatting to the girls. Even so, when the Burns family came in Lynskey could not help contrasting the blonde Carol's full figure with that of her friend "Sammy" ("dark-haired and slim"). Observing though, from an exchange of birthday cards between Carol and Paul Craig, that this was a private party, he and Cook concentrated their attention on Julie Spooner, Rosemary Mackay and Helen Kettles sitting beside them. When these girls decided to go up to the Seven Stars the two paratroopers followed, pretending that they wanted to be shown the way though they knew it perfectly well, having had their first drink there at the start of the evening. Lynskey had taken a particular liking to Rosemary Mackay.

Moving in the reverse direction a bunch of young recruits from the Scots Guards at Pirbright had just come into the Horse and Groom from the Seven Stars. Two of them, Wally Forsythe and John Hunter, eighteen and seventeen years old, were, in their way, dressed to kill. Forsythe, who had a dent in his skull above his right eye and scars under his chin from a car accident, was wearing white trousers, a white open-necked shirt and a white pullover; Hunter had borrowed a check sports jacket from the barracks Corporal for the occasion. They were seen to spend some time talking to a blonde and a brunette, and Forsythe at any rate seemed to be having some success with the blonde because, sitting down beside one of his other mates after returning from the lavatory, he remarked to him: "I'm fixed."

By about 8.30 the Horse and Groom was packed. Caroline Slater and "Sammy" Parrotte came back from the Seven Stars to rejoin the Burns party. They had only been away about ten minutes. They would have done better to stay away longer.

Caroline sat down with her friend Ann Hamilton who had also just made the journey to the Seven Stars and back. People on the benches in that alcove were being squashed together. In Mrs. Burns' words, "everyone was pushing and shoving and larking about". Mr. Burns felt like a sardine, and had had such slow service the last time he went to the bar for drinks that he was becoming fed up with the place and would have been happy to move elsewhere. One of the last things he remembered in the crowded alcove was over-hearing a woman say to her companion: "Come on, it's time we got out of here."

The man who was managing the Horse and Groom that evening for the brewers, Courage, was thirty-five-year-old Alan Bristow, whose wife, Heather, was helping behind the bar. Bristow was in fact only the relief manager, there for two weeks while the regular manager was on holiday. He was gratified by the amount of trade the Horse and Groom was doing because business had dropped off noticeably during the week. This in fact was to be the last weekend of his engage-ment. His wife, Heather, judged that the crowd was composed largely of new recruits: they were mainly drinking pints of beer rather than the shorts which she had been serving the weekend before. She had just come back to the bar from a short breather taken up the road at another pub, the Surrey Arms, where the barman was a friend of theirs. "It's your turn now," she said to her husband, when she got back: and he too, after clearing some empty glasses off the tables, went up to the Surrey Arms.

It was 8.50 p.m. Carol Burns, who had just changed places

on the crowded bench with her birthday companion Paul Craig, had been showing Ann Hamilton some charms she had been given as birthday presents and had just noticed Ann return to her seat by Caroline Slater in the alcove after buying some drinks; Caroline Slater had just told Mrs. Burns that she was planning to go back to her home in Bradford next weekend even though she would have to find the fare; Wally Forsythe, slightly unexpectedly rebuffed by the blonde with whom he thought he was fixed-up, had just put his favourite record, "Long Tall Glasses" by Leo Sayer, on the juke box and this was playing as he walked back to his place beside John Hunter in the alcove. At that moment Carol Burns felt a buzzing in her ears growing louder and louder until she thought she had fainted.

An eighteen-year-old WRAC girl, Linda Cummins, had her hand on the door of the ladies' lavatory; Michael Bryan, a recruit in the Royal Transport Corps was at the bar holding up a five-pound note; one of the barmen, James Tinney, was bending under the bar flap with empty glasses in one hand; Heather Bristow was pouring out a Pernod; "Sammy" Parrotte had just put down her drink; an eighteen-year-old recruit in the Royal Engineers, Terence Bonner, had just picked up his – when everyone in the Horse and Groom experienced different split-second sensations of the same shattering event.

All the lights went out: Bonner felt a force which lifted him up backwards and hurled him to the ground with a deafening noise which he realised at once from his training was an explosion. The door of the ladies' lavatory was blown off in front of Linda Cummins; Michael Bryan crashed to the floor with his five-pound note; the barman smashed into the bar, blood pouring from his hand. There was a frenzied screaming and shouting. "Sammy" Parrotte felt an electric shock followed by total darkness, then saw a small light and, putting out a hand, touched somebody's head before being pulled out of a hole in the floor. Carol Burns, who found herself sliding through the same hole, realised she had fallen into the cellar. "Everything seemed to go daft and there was panic," said one Private. Another felt as if he had been hit over the head

17

with a bottle and another as if he had been hit by a table. A friend of Wally Forsythe and John Hunter, who had been standing half crouched as he got up from his seat in the alcove, felt a terrific heat and blast which took him off his feet and over the partition right out into the street where people frantically tried to pull off his burning clothing.

Alan Bristow, the Horse and Groom manager, had been in the Surrey Arms about five minutes drinking the pint which his friend the barman had poured out ready for him when he heard what someone afterwards described as "a large woomph" and, going outside, was staggered to see that the front of his own pub had been blown out into the road and that people were lying injured and perhaps dead in the glass and rubble strewn all over it. He rushed down to look for his wife Heather. He found her in the street to which she had been carried. She was shaken and cut by glass but not badly hurt. Five people were dead: Caroline Slater, Ann Hamilton, Paul Craig, Wally Forsythe and John Hunter.

A reporter of the *Surrey Daily Advertiser* who had been to a football match in the afternoon had been working late in his paper's office round the corner a hundred yards away, when a vivid blue flash had lit up the street outside, followed by the sound of the explosion. His first thought was that there had been a terrible car accident but on rounding the corner he saw that it was worse than that. ". . . It was horrible. People were running and shouting and screaming. Many were young girls, many clutching bleeding heads. People were scrabbling among the debris trying to pull people out. It was panic and chaos. Everyone seemed covered in blood. I couldn't tell who were injured and who were the rescuers. It was noise – shouting, screaming, girls crying and sirens wailing. People were running everywhere trying to escape the horror of that place . . . 'Bastards, the bastards!' came from everywhere."

The time of the explosion had been 8.50 p.m. Amazingly, in the Seven Stars, up a narrow lane two hundred yards away sheltered by other buildings, only those who at that moment happened to have stepped outside for a breath of fresh air heard it above the noise of the disco. One such was a sixteen-

year-old Scots Guards junior recruit who ran down at once
into North Street. What he saw made him burst into tears
and he found himself unable to stop crying as he watched the
injured being carried through the rubble. Inside the Seven
Stars the disco went on playing.

The disco was in the public bar separated from the saloon
bar through connecting doors, and run by a young part-time
barman and disc jockey, Tim Cummins. It had been in full
swing for an hour. Both Lynskey and Cook, the two paratroopers who had followed the Scots girls there on the pretext
of needing to be shown the way, had by now picked up other
girls and, while Cook was dancing with one called Jean in
the darkened disco, Lynskey sat out in the saloon bar with
another called Brenda. The three Scots girls had themselves
met up with a group of Scots Guards recruits but, when
someone rushed in to tell these that one of their mates was
being "jumped" outside, they all rushed out to his rescue and
the girls were left to dance by themselves.

After a few minutes, as the Guardsmen never came back,
the girls themselves decided to leave. Out in the lane they
met two other WRACs who told them that a bomb had gone
off in the Horse and Groom. They too ran down into North
Street to stare at the chaos and the ambulances. Turning
away from the upsetting scene, Julie Spooner wanted to go
back to the Seven Stars for another drink. But in the end they
decided to go and find a taxi in which to return to camp.
They were waiting in the taxi queue at the bottom of North
Street when, this time, they heard the explosion. It was the
Seven Stars being blown up.

Lynskey and Cook too had been lucky to leave with their
girls only a short time before. But quick thinking had played
as important a part as luck in what happened at the Seven
Stars.

Not long after nine o'clock, Nigel Rose, a plastic coating
operator of Farncombe in Surrey, who acted as one of several
part-time barmen, became aware of a hysterical girl in the
bar talking about an explosion at the Horse and Groom.
When another girl asked him if he knew anything about it,
he could only say that he did not and just went on collecting

glasses. But the manager of the Seven Stars, Owen O'Brien, discussed the matter with his wife and decided to go down and investigate after first stopping the disco and ordering all the lights to be put on. He was to be back within a few minutes.

Meanwhile a Scottish stoker in the Merchant Navy, who had seen what happened at the Horse and Groom, rushed into the Seven Stars, shouting:

"Any Irishmen in here?"

Sean McKeon, a local man, son of an Irish father and an English mother, drinking shorts in the bar with a friend who was more prudently sticking to lager, called out:

"Yes."

An altercation followed, in the course of which McKeon was heard saying:

"Well, we're better than you dirty little Scots bastards!"

The stoker flew at him and split his lip. But just as a fight was starting Owen O'Brien, the manager, now back from the Horse and Groom, intervened and turned him out, saying that they had enough trouble already there as it was. He ordered the bell to be rung for "Time" and told everyone to leave. McKeon's friend helped O'Brien and the barmen search the bar for any bomb that might have been planted there too, but nothing was found and he eventually guided a reluctant McKeon out of the pub towards a taxi. They had found one and were driving down North Street when they heard an explosion but, since the Seven Stars seemed to have been searched so thoroughly, thought it must be a gas main going up at the Horse and Groom.

A twenty-three-year-old Egyptian student, working as a barman, had looked behind the juke box and the fruit machine and had also been certain that the place was clear. He was sweeping the floor when he too heard the explosion but very loud indeed, and remembered nothing for the next ten minutes. Cummins, the disco barman drying glasses, was hurled to the floor with blood pouring from his hand; Owen O'Brien found himself lying half in the lobby between the two bars and half in the saloon. With help from others he was able to stagger out into the street with blood streaming down his face. Largely thanks to his foresight no one had been killed in the Seven Stars though ten people including himself were taken to hospital suffering from burns, bruises and shock.

The ambulance sirens could still be heard outside the shattered Horse and Groom. Some fifty people from there were admitted to hospital suffering from broken limbs, burns, shock, shattered ear-drums and deafness. Among them were the Burns family and "Sammy" Parrotte, all of whom, having been in the second alcove, were lucky to be alive. They were to be in hospital for weeks. Mr. Burns was in a critical condition for several days. Mrs. Burns, suffering from severe bruising and burning, had to have stitches in both armpits and in her forehead, and her rib cage was broken front and back. Carol Burns, whose last-minute change of place with Paul Craig had saved her life, was too badly burned, shocked and deafened to be interviewed by the police in hospital for five days.

The dead were taken the next day from the Royal Surrey County Hospital in Guildford to Chertsey mortuary, where they were photographed by the police. One of the dead girls had had her right leg blown off at the knee.

3

Surrey Constabulary in Action

The shock was felt across Britain. Messages of sympathy were sent to the Mayor of Guildford by the Queen, the Prime Minister, Harold Wilson, and the Leader of the Opposition, Edward Heath. The Home Secretary, Roy Jenkins, described the bombing as "a perversion of human reason and an act which can only cause the utmost human revulsion". A statement came from the Vatican condemning such acts as "menacing human dignity and society".

Britain was within five days of the second General Election of 1974. David Howell, the former Conservative Member and the Conservative candidate for Guildford, said, "We must hunt down the maniacs who did this thing." For a moment it even seemed that what had happened at Guildford might marginally affect the voting, as some individual Conservatives voiced a demand for the return of the death penalty for terrorists. Among these was the former Solicitor-General, Sir Michael Havers. Mr. Rhodes Boyson, the Conservative candidate for Brent North, urged capital punishment for anyone who made, carried or detonated a terrorist bomb, even if no one were hurt or killed by it. Lord Hailsham, subtler though no less severe, said that in his view bombings of this sort were treason, and he reminded the public that treason in fact still carried the death penalty. But political leaders made clear that the matter was still to be left to individual consciences in Parliament; capital punishment did not become a last-minute issue. The Election which took place on October 10 in fact rather diverted attention from the immediacy of the outrage. The hunt for its perpetrators was now the responsibility of the police.

The Assistant Chief Constable of Surrey, Christopher Rowe, had been out to dinner on the evening of October 5 and first heard of what had happened on his car radio while returning home. He drove straight to the Surrey Constabulary headquarters in Guildford, and arrived there about one o'clock on the morning of the 6th. He was at the scene of devastation half an hour later, and at 10 a.m. attended the post-mortems on the bodies in the mortuary.

Like his Chief Constable, Peter Mathews, Rowe had been in the R.A.F. during World War II but before that had been on the beat in London during the I.R.A. bombing campaign of 1939. This lent a certain personal intensity to what in any case was the gravest matter with which he had yet had to deal. He ensured that he took personal charge of the investigation, making Detective Chief Superintendent Walter (Wally) Simmons his second in command. Rowe was also determined that the Surrey Constabulary, rather than the Metropolitan Police Bomb Squad, should retain control of the operation.

The immediate steps taken by the Surrey Constabulary under Rowe's leadership were an example of routine police zeal at its most impressive. By eight o'clock next morning, Sunday, October 6, an incident room had been set up at Guildford police station and a Surrey "bomb squad" of 150 C.I.D. officers from all over the county had started to try and trace everyone who had been in the Horse and Groom and the Seven Stars the night before. By using polaroid cameras to photograph those who came forward they set about establishing a cross-reference system by which to identify witnesses' descriptions of people who might otherwise have seemed suspect. By October 8 they had already interviewed 450 people.

They were however working very much in the dark. Significant material clues were hard to come by after the devastation caused by the bombs. The Chief Constable Peter
Mathews' comment that it "was not the work of a scatterbrain, to put a bomb of that size in a crowded place like
that" was about the only conclusion it was safe to come to.
One of the first considerations was to try and establish
whether a new I.R.A. active service unit had arrived in
Britain or whether the bombers were the same as those
responsible for recent explosions at the Tower of London and
the House of Commons*. The discovery of a watch-spring
among the Guildford debris indicated similarity with the
mechanism used in the Tower of London explosion: but,
whether the attacks were carried out by the same active
service unit or not, urgency was lent to the investigation
when bomb explosions on the night of October 11 at an ex-
servicemen's club off the Edgware Road and at the Army and
Navy Club, St. James's Square, made clear that one active
service unit or another was still at work.†

In a search for the individuals who might compose it the
police had one pointer, if not exactly a clue. All police stations
had some time previously been put on the alert for a young
Irishman, Kieran McMorrow, and a young Irish girl,
Marlene Coyle, both known I.R.A. activists of whom full
descriptions and photographs were in police possession. There
even existed video tape of the couple recorded by a security
monitoring system as they tried to plant a bomb in a factory
making government intelligence equipment in Bristol; they
had escaped before they could be caught. Their names figured
prominently this October in the trial of a girl for the bombing
of a military coach on the M62 motorway earlier in the year.
Moreover there were special reasons to think that McMorrow
and Coyle might have been involved in the Guildford
bombings. McMorrow had himself been in 1969 a British

*In June six people had been injured in the Westminster Hall of the House
of Commons. In July a woman had been killed and 41 people injured in
the Tower of London.
†There were no serious injuries in these explosions.

soldier in the Irish Guards, from which he had deserted, and Coyle in 1971 had for a time been in the Women's Royal Army Corps training near Guildford like those in the Horse and Groom and the Seven Stars on the night of October 5. If not exactly giving the Surrey C.I.D. "something to go on", knowledge of the possible involvement of McMorrow and Coyle at least gave some sense of coherence to an otherwise seemingly intractable investigation.

In one respect Rowe's, and his superior Mathews', decision to take control of the investigation themselves, while reflecting professional zeal, carried a danger. Unlike members of Britain's Special Branch, which in any case in 1974 still had much to learn about the I.R.A. and its methods of operation, the Surrey C.I.D. knew next to nothing of them except what they had read in the newspapers or in their police bulletins and general information issued by the Home Office. The traditional C.I.D. approach, if a known suspect existed, was to work first of all on that basis and, if that failed, to fall back on whatever else might be available. It was in the last part of this traditional formula that the danger lay. For by that time sensitive police self-esteem was involved.

As might be expected from policemen as dedicated as Rowe and his subordinates, they spread their net wide and with great thoroughness. Particular attention obviously had to be paid, in view of the possible Coyle connection, to the questioning of all WRACs now training in the vicinity. But however inclined he might be to think that McMorrow and Coyle had been implicated, Rowe kept an admirably open mind. No possibility seemed too slight to be followed up. Information received at the incident room on the night of October 7–8 that four people with Irish accents had just been heard discussing the bombings in the Brush and Palette restaurant in Queensway, London, brought a telephoned request from Guildford to the Metropolitan Police to investigate immediately. Inspector Prendergast of Harrow Road police station went round at ten minutes to two in the morning. He found three young people: a Mr. and Mrs. Curran of East Barnet and a Mr. John Greene of the Irish Tourist Board, all of whom earlier in the evening had been

to see Irish Tourist Board films in Eaton Square. None fitted
the physical description of wanted persons given by the Surrey
police and none had any criminal or Special Branch record;
they at least could be eliminated from the enquiry.

There were other early leads which went nowhere. Two
girls seen running from one pub to the other between the two
explosions, who, the police said in a statement issued on the
October 7, "may have been responsible", were eliminated
almost at once. Photofit pictures of two other wanted girls, a
blonde and a brunette, were then issued. Rowe was quoted
as saying that they had been moving between the two pubs
and "were obviously spying out the land and appeared to
have waited until the maximum number of young people were
in them". He was wrong. The photofits turned out to be of
one of the girls who had been killed and of another who had
been seriously injured. But Rowe had soon opened up another
possibility. On October 10 it was reported that a hunt had
started for a man dressed in a black three-quarter length coat
"who police believe master-minded the Guildford bombing".
Rowe was quoted as saying: "The information we have pieced
together of this man is without doubt the best so far." The
wanted man had been seen in the Seven Stars with a brown
paper bag and a plastic holdall and in the Horse and Groom
with a plastic holdall. He was described as being aged 30 to
35, slightly built with a thin face, five o'clock shadow and
straight dark hair. Some thought that he might be the same
man as the car gunman who had shot at an army Colonel
the Sunday before.

Police work was made no easier by what appeared to be a
number of hoaxes which could never be safely treated as if
they were. Three separate anonymous telephone calls within
a few days warned of bombs in Guildford public houses,
cinemas and dance halls; the police had to distribute warning
leaflets round the town. Even a bizarre call to the office of
the Yorkshire Television programme "Calendar", delivered
from a public call-box in a precise educated voice which
claimed that the International Marxists and the I.R.A. could
reveal their responsibility "now that we are all clear", had to
be logged seriously.

Events

Then came the London explosions on the night of October 11. On October 14, while the key suspect remained the man whom the *Daily Express* called "the bomber in black", a new photofit and description was issued, this time of a middle-aged woman. The Surrey police said that she probably had no connection with the affair but she had been seen outside the Horse and Groom enquiring about a young couple who had come to stay the night with her, and they wanted to interview her. She was eventually traced, and their surmise was proved correct: she had no useful information to offer.

On October 22 a bomb went off at Brooks's Club, in St. James's Street in London, while Edward Heath, Leader of the Opposition, was dining at Pratt's Club nearby. On the night of the 24th a bomb went off at Harrow School in the cottage which until six weeks before had been occupied by the man in charge of the school Army Cadet Corps. On Friday, October 25 the evening television programme "Police Five" broadcast an appeal for help from the public in which Surrey's Detective Chief Superintendent Wally Simmons said the police were anxious to trace a couple seen in the further alcove of the Horse and Groom on the night of the bombings three weeks before. They were "strongly suspected" of being responsible for the bomb there. Photofit pictures of the couple appeared on the screen: a man, aged between 20 and 30, height 5 feet 10 inches; the woman, in her early twenties, height 5 feet 2–4 inches, with dirty blonde shoulder-length hair parted in the middle. Two, slightly varying versions of these photofits were published in the national press the next day.

The three weeks' intensive interrogation of witnesses had yielded at least this concrete result: two people, a man and a woman, present that night between about 6.30 and 7 p.m. in the alcove in which the bomb exploded in the Horse and Groom, were unaccounted for and were almost certainly the people who had planted the bomb. Exactly who they were, and where they were to be found were as much unanswered questions as ever.

Nevertheless even in completing this much of the jigsaw the Surrey Constabulary had performed a prodigious feat.

At first, in the witnesses' statements there had been much vagueness and blankness of memory, as always when people overtaken by an unexpected event try to recall details from a time just before it was signficant to remember them. Thus, for instance, in the first statements of Private Lynskey and Cook taken on the day after the explosions, October 6, one of them said that they had arrived at the Horse and Groom at 7 p.m., the other 7.30 p.m. Similarly, though both then identified the Burns family in the second alcove recognisably enough they were both at first very vague about two people who left just before they themselves sat down. Lynskey said on October 6 specifically: "I cannot remember who they were", while Cook said: "The only people I can really remember in the Horse and Groom were a family at the next table." Yet eleven days later, in a statement running to eleven pages, compared with his previous statement of two pages, Lynskey was describing these two people at length as "a courting couple", adding details of age, height, hair-styles and clothing, even to the extent of thinking that the top button of the man's shirt was undone. Cook, interviewed again more than three weeks after his first statement of one and a half pages, was able to produce one of ten pages. He now had himself and Lynskey arriving at 6.45 p.m. instead of 7.30 and he too remembered "a courting couple", describing them in detail very similar to Lynskey's, saying that the girl had "dirty blonde" hair of shoulder length which he too "thought" was "parted in the middle".

That there was a couple of some sort in that alcove in the earlier period of the evening had been established from other early statements as well as from Lynskey's vague one of October 6, though at that stage of course it was not known that they would not later come forward to be identified. One of the Scottish WRACs had been more precise than Lynskey when she was interviewed the day after the explosion, specifying them at least as "a man and his girl", and adding on the 7th that the man had long dark hair, the girl long fair hair and that they seemed between 19 and 20 years old. On October 9, an officer in the Royal Engineers who had also noticed the couple said he thought the girl had been a WRAC and the man a civilian of about 28. The same day a soldier in the Royal Engineers describing the couple said the man was aged between 23 and 24 and the girl was "21, dark with curly shoulder-length hair", and added that they were both English. Five days later a young Irish Guardsman described the man as being aged 26, height 6 foot 1 inch, and the girl as aged 25, height 5 foot 9 inches with long fair hair over her shoulders. Interviewed on the same day another Guardsman said of the couple that they were both about 22 and that the girl had black shoulder-length hair.

In this welter of scanty and sometimes semi-contradictory information it was understandable that the police should still find themselves groping for substance. The full descriptions of the couple which eventually emerged nearly a fortnight after Lynskey and Cook had found it so difficult to remember anything, in fact matched, on the great majority of points, the descriptions available to the police of McMorrow and Coyle. The pair were thought to have acted in the past as a courting couple, and that phrase which now entered both Lynskey's and Cook's statements received graphic independent confirmation next day when the WRAC Rosemary McKay recounted her wish not to stare at the pair because they were "cuddling", though she did describe "the lassie's" hair as dark.

Mr. Burns, not well enough until the middle of November to be interviewed in hospital at length by the police, also found himself using the phrase "courting couple". The exact wording of his statement reads:

"I would describe the young people as 1) male, 19 to 20 years, 2) female, 19 to 20 years. I cannot possibly remember anything else about them except I have the feeling they were an ordinary young courting couple."

The slightly stilted flow of language, common to all the other statements, serves as a useful reminder that such depositions taken by the police are often inevitably the product of question and answer. An answer "Yes" to the question "Do you feel that they were an ordinary young courting couple?" might thus finally appear in the more positive spontaneous form above.

Trial and Error

In the end it has to be said that masterly as had been the technical side of the police operation, involving the taking, checking and collation of several thousand individual statements, it turned out to have no immediate bearing at all on the arrests eventually to be made for the Guildford bombings. Indeed, perhaps the most useful contribution of this mammoth investigation to the solution of the mystery lay in such light as it shed on the manner of taking police statements, and on the suggestibility of the human mind under even the most benevolent prompting.

4

A Kilburn Sub-culture

In the summer and autumn of 1974 there existed, in the small area of north-west London bounded by Cricklewood and Kilburn on both sides of the Edgware road, a self-sufficient twilit sub-culture, housed often in squats and sustained by drugs and petty crime, in which immigrant Irish of both sexes from Northern Ireland and the Irish Republic, sometimes in work and sometimes not, played a noticeable social role. In cheap flats and squats in rundown late-Victorian houses like those at 14 Linstead Street and 14 Algernon Road to which this story now turns, and in public houses like the Memphis Belle and the Cock in Kilburn High Road where denizens of these places spent much of their time, a world with its own wonders and difficulties flourished in its fashion, temporarily compensating many young people, Irish and British, for the emotional or economic inadequacies of the environment from which they had drifted. In the case of those who had drifted from Northern Ireland, and particularly from the Catholic and Republican areas of Belfast, in search of work, a welcome respite was also to be had from involvement in the tensions and hazards of the daily under-cover war there between Crown forces and the Provisional I.R.A. Though sentimental

Irish Republican ballads would be heard from time to time in the squats and seedy flats, as in more conventional homes both Irish and even British, and conversation would sometimes turn to events in the North, featuring sympathy with the Catholic population and often dislike of the British Army presence there, the general tenor of such talk seems to have been basically a-political and averse to cruelty and violence. Inasmuch as the occasional individual might hope to seek personal status by a claim to knowledge of the inner workings of the IRA this seems to have excited only a certain wariness tinged with some scepticism in view of the claimant's prevailing involvement in the Kilburn scene.

In the early summer of 1974, two very young English girls, each unhappy in her family home, found themselves drawn together into this, at times rough, but at other times curiously gentle milieu. There together they began to experience something of the strange glories of life often denied to the more conventional, and to relish these against a background which, if by conventional standards often squalid, was also free and their own. The experience was to have for them a terrible climax.

When in the following year Carole Richardson sat down to try calmly to give some account of what had happened, her way of beginning was to say that she had absolutely no knowledge of her father: "I cannot even recall seeing him." She thought he had died when she was a baby, but according to her mother he had been a labourer who deserted her even before Carole was born. She had brought Carole up in her own parents' home in Kilburn, where her mother was a Sunday School teacher and her father, Carole's grandfather, secretary to the Kilburn Evangelical Church. Carole attended this church fairly regularly on Sundays throughout her childhood until she was about thirteen. Living conditions in the grandparents' home were what a social worker was later to describe as "cramped . . . which made normal adolescent problems more difficult to cope with". However, in the early 1970s, Carole's mother moved with her to a house at 88, Iverson Road, N.W.6 where she started to live with an Irishman from Co. Wicklow, an electrician by trade, a non-practising Catholic, whose name was Alan Docherty, and whom she eventually married. Long before that, though, Carole had been developing her own restless pattern of existence.

She had played truant from local Kilburn schools intermittently from the age of seven, when she first began to hang around a riding school in Grosvenor Crescent Mews, being allowed to help with the mucking-out of the stables and being rewarded with occasional rides. Fascinated by horses, she began to think of spending her life working with them, though as she grew older and played truant from school more and more persistently her interests widened. Though her mother apparently never knew about her truancy, Carole only attended for three weeks in the whole of her last year at school. She finally left altogether when she was fifteen, by which time she had already taken to staying out all night with friends; on Fridays she would go dancing at the Lyceum in the Aldwych until 7 o'clock in the morning. When she was fourteen a boy-friend had introduced her to drugs: cannabis and amphetamines ("speed") at first, from which she graduated to LSD, cocaine and morphine. In 1972 she was convicted of breaking and entering premises and placed on probation under a supervision order for a year.

None of this did anything to improve her relations at home with her step-father, Docherty, whose strong disapproval and attempts to be strict with her seem to have had only the effect of committing her more and more irreconcilably to her own wayward life-style. However, she did feel an attachment to her mother, and she took a number of jobs, a fact which seems to indicate that despite the drugs her attitude to life in general contained, as her social worker might have put it, some positive motivation. A job as a shop assistant in Kilburn lasted a week when the manager found out that she was on probation, but after answering an advertisement in *Horse and Hound* she got a job as a groom at Chipping Norton which she held for two months, after which she felt homesick and returned to Iverson Road. She became an office assistant in a firm of solicitors at Cricklewood and somehow held this post for three months before going to work with horses again at a riding school at South Molton in Devon. One of the girls with whom she worked there remembered afterwards that she had "seemed to crave attention and be a bit on the wild side".

Carole returned to the solicitors' office after six weeks but was soon away again working with horses, first in London, and then at Newmarket where she stayed two and a half months, returning home every third weekend. On one of these weekends she did something which, by a bizarre coincidence, was to contribute to her later misfortune, though no step taken so far in her career can have seemed more innocuous or could have been presented as more praiseworthy at the time. In April 1974 she went to the army recruiting office in Edgware and put in an application to join the Women's Royal Army Corps (WRAC), hoping eventually to be able to work there with horses. Her term of service was to be for a minimum of three years with a liability to be posted to the British Army of the Rhine after September 1974. She gave two references: her social worker who attested to "fairly close contact during the period of the supervision order" and the Cricklewood solicitors who, however, wrote back bluntly to the Army Careers Information Office to say that they were afraid that they were unable to assist. (Carole later said that there had been an understanding between her and the firm that she could leave the job and return whenever she liked, but it is possible that the understanding was not recipro-cated.) Nevertheless she was given the normal recruiting test and interview, but found by Captain Antoinette Harrison of the WRAC to be "unsuitable for service in the Corps".

Her life at Iverson Road was continually disturbed by differences with her step-father. One source of his disapproval was her frequent visits to a pub in Kilburn High Road called the Memphis Belle, a well-known haunt of Irish supporters of Sinn Fein with whom he had no sympathy. Carole, who was still not quite seventeen, was technically under the legal age to be served alcohol, but it was in this pub that she first made friends with an English girl a year younger even than herself, called Lisa Astin, who was also in trouble at home.

Lisa had been brought up in Burnley, Lancashire, and had gone to a Catholic school there but in 1971 her family had moved to London. Her father had died when she was only nine months old; her mother had married again, had a son and daughter by her second husband but was now divorced from him. Lisa could not get on with her mother and, like Carole, continually played truant from the London school to which she was sent, a Catholic one in Maida Vale.

In June 1974 Carole started going out with a Scots boy whose mother ran a pub in St. John's Wood. A party organised by him in the upstairs snooker room of the pub, while his parents were out, now not only brought Carole and Lisa closer together, but marked the beginning of another friendship which was to alter the entire course of her life. For when the boy's parents returned to find the party in progress they were furious and his father threw him out of the house. Someone from the party knew of a squat where they could stay at 35 West End Lane, and Carole went with him "out of conscience because it was partly my fault that he had been thrown out". Among those then living at this squat was a 24-year-old young man from Belfast, Paddy Armstrong.

Paddy Armstrong had paid his first visit to Britain in search of work in 1972. After six months he had gone back to Belfast to help his mother, who was having trouble with a younger sister playing truant from school. But he had returned to London at the end of 1973. In Belfast, Paddy had lived in the Divis Flats, a Republican stronghold, and, like many young Catholics of that area, had been picked up from time to time by the army for questioning, an experience he had always found rough and frightening, but after which he had always been released. For him as for many of his age and background a certain mythological aura surrounded some of the hard men of the Provisional IRA, whisperings of whose identity and activities – often speculative and exaggerated – were part of the normal occasional currency of everyday life in those areas of the city. In London such mythology had little relevance though Paddy, for instance, when under the influence of drugs or drink – and both played a consistent part in shaping his consciousness – had been known to boast, while playing darts in a pub, of driving a petrol tanker with a bomb on it into Royal Avenue, Belfast. In fact he was known in the Kilburn area as a man who did not drive, having got no further than a provisional licence for a motorcycle.

Certainly Paddy's activity in Britain had been on an unheroic scale. Such work as he found was largely in pubs as a part-time barman, collecting and washing up glasses, or as a labourer on building sites, but other interests had got him into serious trouble in March 1974 when he was arrested for burglary and held on remand for three months until acquitted at Middlesex Crown Court in May. After his release he had gone to live for two months at the squat in West End Lane. There Lisa had stayed with him for a few days after meeting him at the Cock public house in Kilburn. And now, on the night on which Carole's boy-friend had been turned out of his home, Carole too met Paddy Armstrong.

Lisa's stay at West End Lane was short because the police picked her up one evening in the Cock public-house for being under age and took her home. But she continued to see Paddy in the Memphis Belle and on visits to West End Lane where she became the girl-friend for a time of another of its inhabitants. After this liaison had ended, she called there one day, to find the squat deserted. Only several days later did she learn that Paddy had moved to another squat at 14 Linstead Street.

Carole meanwhile had been drifting from squat to squat in London with her boy-friend, although she called once at her home in Iverson Road but found no one there. She had a nasty surprise, however, when waiting for her boy-friend in a café called the Copper Spoon in Kilburn High Road one day. Alan Docherty walked past and spotted her through the window. He came into the café and began remonstrating furiously with her for leaving home, and finally ending up by saying: "If you're not home in five minutes, don't bother to come back."

She did not go back, but spent the next three weeks in a squat at King's Cross, telephoning from time to time to her mother who worked at the Regent Street Polytechnic to tell her where she was and that she was "all right". Once indeed she went back to Iverson Road but found Docherty there. He told her to take all her belongings out of the house and demanded back the latch-key which in fact she did not have.

However, a shifting impermanence attached even to her break with home. After moving back from the King's Cross squat to a squat in Kilburn she then went back to Iverson Road for a fortnight until, as she put it, Docherty's disapproving attitude to her made it impossible for her to stay any longer.

On September 6, 1974, Lisa Astin celebrated her sixteenth birthday in the Cock public house and, when it closed, Paddy Armstrong, whom Carole had met a number of times in the past fortnight, suggested that they continue the party at Linstead Street. That night Carole and Lisa moved into the Linstead Street squat with him. They were all to be based there for over a month.

The life they led during that time is by definition difficult to bring into focus with much precision, since drugs and drink and a carefree attitude towards conventional routine were, for them, the principal attraction. The opening and closing of pubs and bookmakers, the starting and ending of pop concerts, the movements of those, like Carole's mother, who had normal jobs, gave some optional structure to their existence, but the means of supporting this existence, by street "tapping" (begging), pilfering, odd part-time jobs, or clumsily-executed small-time burglaries, made no very rigorous demands on a sense of order in any case alien.

That it was in fact a sort of sub-culture, however ill-defined and inferior to the level at which orthodox society rated itself, requires acknowledgment. Personal ties of a rough and ready nature bound it from squat to squat and from squat to cheaply-rented rooms, and through the ill-coordinated detail of drugs and sex and petty crime there ran a thread of aspiration to happiness occasionally fulfilled. It was not the sort of life to leave memorials. The roughest records of incidents from everyday experience alone survive to give glimpses – and no more than hazy glimpses – of what it was really like to live in places like Linstead Street. And yet, because, in this particular little corner, the sub-culture was to be so swiftly and overwhelmingly eclipsed by the moral juggernaut from which these people had voted themselves free, such glimpses reveal, in retrospect, if not exactly dignity, at least the pathos of all human beings trying to make something tolerable of their lives.

For over a month Carole, Lisa and Paddy shared the downstairs front room at Linstead Street. Paddy and Carole slept together; Lisa's relationship with Paddy was close and friendly, but not physical – that of "a little sister" as they sometimes described it. Several other people were living in rooms in the squat. All were on drugs, mainly cannabis or LSD. One young man, Brian McLoughlin, was thought to be taking drugs to keep up with the others. His own chief contribution to the squat lay in his theft of food from supermarkets, which he brought back in shopping-bags to be shared among them all.

Petty crime of this sort was a normal part of the squat system of maintenance, though occasionally ideas were more ambitious. Such was an attempt one September night to rob an old man living in Abbotts Place, off West End Lane. Carole, Paddy, Lisa, Brian McLoughlin, and another inhabitant of the squat named Jimmy Goodall set out on the expedition. McLoughlin had got hold of a gun which, though it was not loaded – and indeed he had no ammunition – troubled Carole and Lisa, who thought it might give the old man a heart-attack. There was some discussion as to who should go to the basement door with the gun. Carole and Lisa went first. In Carole's words:

"It was my job to take the gun and point it at the man. Lisa and I went to the basement door. I was to hold the man up. Lisa was to get the money. Both of us were scared and I pretended to knock on the door. Then we both left and went to the corner of the road where Paddy, McLoughlin and the others were waiting. I told them the man wouldn't open the door. Then Paddy and McLoughlin went. I threw the gun at them and I think Paddy got it."

McLoughlin later said that it was with Goodall that he went to the door. They knocked and a man answered. They pushed past him into the living-room but the man took a picture from the wall in the hall and tried to hit McLoughlin with it. He pushed the man into a chair, and Goodall covered him with the gun, telling McLoughlin to go into the next room to find the money. At that moment people were heard coming down the steps and Goodall and McLoughlin bolted. Waiting on the corner, Carole and Lisa heard screaming and bolted too.

McLoughlin had been more successful on another occasion when he and Carole stole a suit from a house in Boundary Road, which they gave to Paddy Armstrong. But the scale of such crimes was small. Another time he planned with Carole and Lisa to steal money from the till in a fish and chip shop called Saffron's in West End Lane. Lisa and Carole were to hold the door open for him as he made the snatch. But the attempt ended in débâcle when the woman in the shop screamed and they all ran off.

McLoughlin was in fact unpopular in the squat and suspected of being a "squealer" to the police about drugs and burglaries. Here is Lisa's account of the way in which he finally took himself off from the Linstead Street squat:

"Brian was in his sleeping-bag pretending to be asleep and I said to Carole, 'Is the squealer listening?' I then said I was making LSD at my house and shouted out my mother's address, at the same time kicking his head so that he should hear and I would know that he had heard."

Later that day he left, taking Carole's Levi jacket and four pairs of trousers and tops with him. He eventually indeed went to the police, and among the offences which he asked to be taken into consideration against him was the theft of the suit he had given to Paddy Armstrong.

Jimmy Goodall's departure from the squat on the first stage of his return to Ireland was the occasion for a momentary shock for Lisa. He was arrested at the airport on a drugs charge and on September 29 the police came to check up on Linstead Street. All this time Lisa knew that her mother was trying to trace her and she was careful to avoid any contact with the police. On September 29, coming back to the squat she saw the police car outside and hung about in the street until it had gone. It could be seen as an omen that things were beginning to close in on her. The next day she heard that her mother had been to see the manager of the Memphis Belle to tell him that Lisa was under age. She found herself banned from the Memphis Belle in future.

But on Saturday, October 5 Lisa's and Carole's carefree life in the squat still seemed relatively unthreatened. In the afternoon they both went to see a 16–year-old girl-friend Maura Kelly who worked in the ABC baker's shop near Primrose Hill and in the evening both went with a new friend from Newcastle, Frank Johnson, to a pop concert at which a Newcastle group called "Jack the Lad" were playing. This was at the South Bank Polytechnic near the Elephant and Castle, where a photograph was taken of them by a member of the group.

On October 8 there was a knock on the door at Linstead Street and Carole Richardson opened it. It was the police.

"Are you Carole Richardson?"

"Yes."

"Can we come in?"

"Yes."

In front of Lisa they then began asking Carole if she knew where Lisa Astin was. She said she did not. They turned to Lisa and asked her who she was. She gave a false name but something about the two girls' attitude made the police suspicious. They took Lisa away, and she was placed in care for a month, first living at a hostel in Agamemnon Road and then with a schoolmaster and his wife.

This did not prevent her from continuing to visit Carole and Paddy in Linstead Street. But in the middle of October an incident occurred which revealed something of the incipient menace behind the happy-go-lucky life they were living. Late one night when Paddy and Carole were at Linstead Street there came a knock at the door of the house and a man's voice was heard outside. To Carole's amazement Paddy jumped out of the window and disappeared. The door of the room then opened and two men came in, waving a hatchet.

"Where is Paddy?"

Carole said she didn't know. "Tell Paddy," he said, "that

if he is not at the Memphis Belle tomorrow night we will be
back for him and we will use this." He added to Carole: "If
I didn't know you so well I'd use it on you."

When a few of the other squatters came in to see what was
happening the man went out into another room, shouting:
"Where's Paddy?" Finally he and his friend left, telling Carole
to make sure that Paddy "got the message".

Paddy himself came back about half an hour later and said
that it would be better for them not to stay that night at
Linstead Street. They went instead to friends of his who lived
in a rented ground floor flat at 15, Rondu Road, Cricklewood.

The next day, after collecting some clothes from Linstead
Street, they set off together on a hitch-hiking tour of the south
and west of England which was to last ten days. Paddy told
Carole to forget the incident and she went with him
"perhaps," she said later, "because I was about to get
engaged to him." In fact, the two men had given Paddy some
money a few days before to buy them drugs and he had
failed to deliver. It was a type of transaction, with awkward
outcome, with which Kilburn squatters were not unfamiliar
and to which Paddy Armstrong as much as anyone was
accustomed.

For some of the time Carole and Paddy's hitch-hiking tour
had a certain idyllic quality, and it was to be this which
would remain vivid in Carole's memory. Some weeks before,
on a visit to his friends in Rondu Road, Paddy had spoken
about getting married "to an English girl" and now he and
Carole made a plan to marry on New Year's Day, 1975. But
under the strain of each other's undiluted company for many
days something started to go wrong. Carole became gradually
obsessed with the thought that Paddy was talking more and
more about Lisa Astin. She grew more and more jealous and
resentful. Paddy denied that there was any cause for jealousy
but grew increasingly impatient with her resentment. By the
end of the tour the situation was to become too much for
them and Carole was to decide to break off the engagement.

Until then, however, perhaps to convince herself that all
was well, she had written normal holiday letters to Lisa and
to another friend, an Irish girl, Maggie Carass, from the

Linstead Street squat. The hitch-hikers settled briefly at least once, spending nights in Joseph's Guest-House, Dover, where the proprietor afterwards remembered them with a certain affection. While in Dover, Carole actually got herself a reader's ticket at the Lending Library though she did not officially take out a book. Only one incident was later, in retrospect, to acquire a certain significance. On October 25, Carole went into a telephone box at Sandgate outside Folke-stone to call her mother in London. She had been talking to her for some time when a man waiting to telephone opened the door and demanded to know how long she was going to be. She went on talking. A little later he opened the door and again demanded to know how much longer she would be. She replied that it was a public telephone; whereupon the man lost his temper, hit her and banged her head against the window. Carole ran to a nearby shop and rang the police.

A Panda car with two police officers arrived. Carole and Paddy got into the car and they drove around until Carole pointed out the man who had assaulted her. The police arrested him. Both the police officers described Carole as looking "scruffy". They drove her, Paddy Armstrong and the man to Folkestone police station. There she gave her full name and the address of her mother. Paddy Armstrong gave his name and address at Linstead Street, though the police had some difficulty with his Belfast accent. Eventually the police told Carole that they were not going to press charges but if she herself wanted she could prosecute the man. She felt she could not be bothered, and she and Paddy continued with their hitch-hiking tour. At the end of the month they separated. Carole went to visit an aunt in Newcastle. Paddy, first went to get money off his sister in Welwyn Garden City, and then to live with his friends at Rondu Road. Carole, on her return to London at the beginning of November, found that the Irish girl from Linstead Street, Maggie Carass, had moved to another squat at 14, Algernon Road to be with a new boy-friend, Paul Colman. Colman agreed that Carole could move in to Algernon Road too.

When Paddy moved with his haversack and sleeping-bag

into Rondu Road, there were three Irishmen living there whose names were about to be linked with his in dramatic form: Brian Anderson, John MacGuiness, and Sean Mullin. Because he was short of money, Paddy spent most of his evenings in the flat watching television, playing cards, and occasionally taking drugs.

In the Kilburn squat world the need for drugs and the illusion of wider dimensions which they offered continued to require intermittent pilfering from shops, supermarkets and, where easy, flats and private houses. Soon after moving into Algernon Road Carole went on a short visit to Dublin with Maggie Carass. Originally the plan had been for another girl from the squat to accompany them, but the burglary which Carole carried out the day before they left, in order to pay the boat fare, turned out to yield only enough money for two tickets, though the haul consisted of three suitcases containing clothes, a hair-drier, a stereo, a tape-recorder and two irons. They left on Friday, November 7, spending the weekend with nuns in Merrion Square, and returned to Algernon Road the following Tuesday, November 11. On the Friday of that week, November 14, Paddy Armstrong came to the door at about five o'clock in the afternoon. Paul Colman and Maggie Carass let him in and asked him what he wanted.

"It's OK," Paddy said, and went down into the basement where a young Irishman he had known in Linstead Street had moved in a day or so before. Carole was out but when she came back Maggie told her that Paddy was there. Carole's reaction was: "Oh, God, no!" But she spent the night with him there and he stayed, with Paul's reluctant permission, for the rest of the month. This did not please Maggie, who found him frightening. He seemed moody at first and discussed with Paul Colman a plan to rob a jeweller's shop using the girls as decoys. There was also talk of 'doing' a pub near Waterloo, where he had worked on a building site, and of guns that might be used. In fact the only successful robberies carried out from Algernon Road for the rest of the month were on a less ambitious scale.

That weekend Lisa Astin, still nominally "in care", went to Portobello Road with Carole and Carole stole a bag from one of the street market stalls. She had wanted one with her birth-sign, Gemini, on it but, as she put it, she "had to be quick" and so took one with a Scorpio sign. Her relations with Paddy were still not easy. She had missed a period while separated from him at the beginning of the month and had begun to worry that she was pregnant. She found herself a job for a week in a hostel and moved to another squat at 44, Kenilworth Road, where on December 3 she was able to partake of the proceeds of another theft.

On the night of Sunday, December 1, Paul Colman and two other inhabitants of the Algernon Road squat had broken into a nearby chemist's through the basement window and tried to force their way up through the ceiling into the shop itself. Finding this impossible, they went to an upper floor, and, breaking through the floorboards, dropped into the shop through the ceiling. There they helped themselves to all the barbiturates, amphetamines and other such drugs as they could find, together with the money in the till. From this haul Colman sold Carole, for £3, eighteen capsules of Tuinol, a brand of sleeping pills which she had used as a drug before. December 3, 1974 was thus for Carole as typical a day as any other, though it was to end very differently.

She got up late. When on Tuinol she liked to take about three capsules an hour, so that the effect, which she found rather similar to drink, would prolong itself; she found that they relaxed her, and that, though they made her drowsy, they also left her feeling aware of what she was doing. She began taking her normal dose of three capsules at about 2 o'clock in the afternoon, giving four to Lisa Astin who had come to see her.

Carole liked if possible to meet her mother in the evenings off the bus which brought her back from her work at the Regent Street Polytechnic. But it was not until about 6.45 p.m. that she left Kenilworth Road that day, which meant that she was too late to catch her. Feeling that she wanted to see her mother to let her know that she was "all right", she decided to go with Lisa to 88, Iverson Road. By the time they had left Kenilworth Road, she had taken about ten capsules.

When they got to Iverson Road they could see a police car waiting outside the house. Lisa, thinking that they might be looking for her, waited a few doors away while Carole knocked on the front door. Alan Docherty, her step-father, opened it.

"You'd better come up," he said. "There are a couple of policemen waiting for you."

Carole went upstairs. Two policemen were indeed there, and asked if she would go with them to Harlesden police station. She asked them why.

"It doesn't matter, we just want to ask you some questions."

"All right."

As they were leaving, Carole's mother asked if she could come with her.

"No," said Carole. "It doesn't matter, I'll either see you later on or meet you for lunch tomorrow."

When they were downstairs Carole asked the police if it was all right for her friend to come with her as they were going out for drinks afterwards. The police agreed. She shouted to Lisa that she had to go to Harlesden and told her to come too. Lisa shouted back:

"Why do you have to go?"

Carole said she didn't know but that they would find out when they got there.

The two police officers sat in the front of the car and Lisa and Carole in the back. On the way one of the policemen asked the girls if they had friends.

"Yes, why?"

He said he wanted them to look some friends up, and asked if Carole knew where Guildford was. She said she thought it was in Surrey.

When he asked if she had ever been there, she said:

"No. The nearest I've been as far as I know is Woking."

When he asked why she had been there she said it had been to see a friend in Coldingley prison, and at that point Lisa whispered to her not to tell him she had such friends.

"I didn't ask the officers what it was all about," she said later. "I knew I would soon find out when I got to the station."

At the police station Carole and Lisa were separated and taken into adjoining rooms.

The official police record of the interview with Carole which then took place differs little materially from Carole's own account given to her solicitors a few months later. Such differences as there are, appear to be, in the police account, those of compression.

Detective-Sergeant John Sutherland Donaldson of the Surrey Constabulary told her that he was a police officer from Guildford and that he wanted to talk to her in connection with the Guildford bombings. He told her that anything she said might be taken down and used in evidence against her.

"Do you understand?"

"Bombings? What the hell would I know about bombings?"

"How old are you?"

"Seventeen."

"Well, you are Carole and your boy-friend is Paddy Armstrong. I want you to tell me where Armstrong is, I want to see him."

Here, Carole says that she was shown a photograph and asked if it was of Paddy. She said it was, but that his hair was different and he was growing a beard.

She said to Donaldson:

"He's not involved in bombings, is he?"

"When did you last see him?"

"Some weeks ago."

Carole here says that her words were "a couple of days ago" and that she added that she had then had a row with him.

"Where is he living?"

"I don't know. Squatting."

Carole says that she was then asked if she had ever been to Guildford, and said, "No."

Donaldson then said to her:

"I think you have."

Carole's account continues:

"I said, 'Why?' and he said: 'Because you are going out with Paddy.' "

"I said: 'No, I am not.' He asked what the row was over.

I said: 'Nothing serious' and I asked why they wanted Paddy. He took the photo back and showed me the bottom bit which had previously been folded under."

This photograph was now revealed as part of an official police poster: "Wanted for Murder".

"I said: 'I don't believe you.'

"He said: 'You should because you were with him.'

"I told him it was a load of 'bloody rubbish' and he knew it."

Carole says that the reason why she did not give Paddy's address at first was that she wanted to know why the police wanted him. When she realised the seriousness of the charge she changed her mind.

The police account runs:

"Now listen carefully. This is a murder inquiry. I believe you are involved in it and your boy-friend Armstrong."

Carole burst into tears.

Donaldson said:

"I need your help. Where is Armstrong?"

Still crying, Carole replied:

"All right, if it will save lives. He is at 14, Algernon Road ... It's a squat. But for God's sake don't tell Lisa I told you."

Carole says that she first wrote the number of Algernon Road as 44, thinking of Kenilworth Road where she herself had been that day taking Tuinol. She corrected herself in this slip and then went on to admit that she had seen Paddy that day, after all.

She was asked:

"Will he be there now?"

"I think so. I told you wrong. I saw him tonight. . . ."

"Where was that?"

"Just outside Paddy Milligan's but he said he was staying in tonight and the last I saw of him, he went off into an off-licence to get some cigarettes."

Carole says that the police kept on insisting that she herself had been at Guildford.

The police record has her asking:

"When was the bombings at Guildford?"

"In October."

"If I can see my diary it will prove I wasn't at Guildford."

"I think you were, but we'll talk about that later."

The "accused" is described as starting to cry again and shouting, as Donaldson left the room:

"Then you'll have to prove it."

Carole says that this is not a phrase she would ever have used. What she says she said to Lisa Astin a few minutes later was probably a more likely expression for her in the circumstances.

For after Carole had been taken down to a cell she heard Lisa screaming in the cell next to her. Lisa, who had not been allowed to telephone the headmaster and his wife with whom she was then 'in care', had also been interviewed. She had at first laughed at the police when they told her she was being held for murder, and had been kicked by a C.I.D. man from Guildford for her insolence. It soon became clear enough that none of this was a joke. Carole told her to calm down, saying it was only the Tuinol that was affecting her, but Lisa then told her how she had been accused of murder.

"They have accused me of it as well," said Carole, "but they'll have to eat their words."

She kept trying to calm Lisa down. Then a policeman came past and said that if they didn't quieten down they would get more than 30 years apiece. "We then both shouted abuse at the policeman and kicked and banged on the door."

Lisa was released after twenty-four hours. Carole has remained in custody ever since.

Meanwhile the police had gone to arrest Paddy Armstrong in the squat at 14, Algernon Road. For it was from among the inhabitants of this twilit world that the Surrey police had decided they had found the perpetrators of the Guildford bombings.

5
Arrests

The arrests of Carole Richardson and Paddy Armstrong were the culmination of five days' intense police activity. By midnight on December 3, 1974 more than 40 people were under arrest in connection with the Guildford bombings, almost all from the Kilburn area. Among the others were the three Irishmen from 15, Rondu Road: Brian Anderson, John MacGuiness and Sean Mullin, together with Paul Colman and Maggie Carass from the squat at 14, Algernon Road.

What had happened?

Perhaps what had not happened is the more significant starting point. For the first three weeks of November, following the "Police Five" television broadcast, the Surrey "bomb squad" had appeared to make little progress. Their most ambitious project had been to commission an artist named Reynolds, a great-grand-nephew of Sir Joshua Reynolds, and one-time stand-in for the man who drew "Jane" in the *Daily Mirror* strip cartoon, to sketch impressions of the wanted "courting couple" from information supplied by witnesses from the Horse and Groom and Seven Stars. One such witness still in hospital was said by detectives to have become "very excited" and to have nodded at the sight of them.

This was circulated to police stations across the country on November 15 and issued to the Press on the 19th. But no arrests had followed. Meanwhile the I.R.A. had been continuing to strike.

At about ten o'clock on the evening of November 7 a Gas Board driver sitting in the back of his truck in Francis Street, Woolwich, East London, keeping an eye on a parked compressor beside a hole in the road while his mates were having a drink, noticed someone get out of a maroon Ford Cortina parked just by it. It was a young man who walked to the outside of the nearby King's Arms public house and came back almost immediately. Two others then got out and went up to the pub, after which they all ran back and got into the car which drove off quite fast without putting its lights on until it was some distance away. At that moment the Gas Board driver heard what he described as "a terrific bang". A bomb had been thrown in at the window of the King's Arms, killing two people and injuring several others.

A fortnight later in Birmingham on the evening of November 21 bombs exploded in two crowded public houses in the most savage act of terrorism ever experienced in Britain. 21 people were killed and 171 injured. Within hours of the explosions five Irishmen were arrested trying to board the Irish mail boat at Heysham in Lancashire. They were on their way to the funeral in Ireland of an I.R.A. man who had blown himself up in Coventry the previous week. A sixth man who had seen them off from Birmingham station a short time before the bombs in the pubs exploded was also arrested. On Monday, November 25 the six appeared in court charged with murder and were remanded in custody. Forensic tests were said to have revealed traces of nitroglycerine on the hands and/or clothing of some of them. Some of them had made statements admitting involvement in the bombings.

On the same Monday three I.R.A. bombs exploded in pillar-boxes during the London evening rush hour, outside Swan and Edgar's in Piccadilly Circus, at King's Cross and at Victoria Underground station. Passers-by were showered with flying metal and 14 were taken to hospital. On Wednesday the 27th another pillar-box exploded in Tite Street, Chelsea, hitting a man in the stomach with flying metal. After police and ambulance men had arrived on the scene, a second, booby-trap bomb went off injuring six of them. Bomb Squad detectives were reported as saying that widely spread attacks with larger bombs could well be the next move in the terrorists' campaign and Scotland Yard issued a statement:

"Information from the public is absolutely vital if we are going to trace and identify the bombers."

Their search both for the bombers and the bomb factory which supplied them intensified. There was increasing psychological pressure to secure results. On November 28, while a Prevention of Terrorism Act was being rushed through Parliament enabling police to hold terrorist suspects for up to seven days without charge, the Surrey police arrested a 20–year-old Irishman from Belfast, Paul Hill, in Southampton and took him to Guildford for questioning in connection with the Guildford bombings. The information which led to his arrest was said to have been bought from a Belfast informer for £350.

Hill had in fact been in Britain since August 23, having come over on that date apparently in search of work with his sister, and his girl-friend, whose own married sister lived in Southampton. An old school-friend of his from the Catholic area of Belfast, Gerry Conlon, had also come over earlier in the month to find work, also with a girl-friend, whom he hoped to marry, and was also living in Southampton where he met Hill apparently fortuitously one evening in a pub. The two men after a time got jobs as labourers in London with Robert Hart, building contractors.

At first they had both had difficulty finding anywhere to stay in London, even though both had relatives who lived there. They had stayed for a night with an uncle of Conlon's, Hugh Maguire, in the small two-room flat where he lived with his wife and a girl lodger at 25, Westbourne Terrace near Paddington Station. But, now in work, they found lodgings at an Irish hostel run by a priest in Quex Road, Kilburn. Hill would go down to his girl-friend in Southampton at weekends while Conlon would sometimes have his Sunday dinner with his Uncle Hugh and spend Saturday evenings playing snooker with him at his working men's club. (Hugh Maguire, a porter then employed by Phillips, the Auctioneers, was a member of the Paddington Conservative Association.)

Conlon also had another uncle in London, Hugh's brother Paddy Maguire, who lived with his wife Anne, three sons and a small daughter at Third Avenue, Harlesden. Conlon had actually hoped soon after his arrival in Britain that Paddy and Anne might put him up in their home. He had stayed there two years before when in London. But there had been unpleasantness then over money which he was suspected of taking from the Maguire boys, so that there could be no question of their having him. In fact when Hugh Maguire later took in Conlon with Hill for the night he warned him not to go near Paddy, who, he said, would "kill him" for "the bad things" he had done in the house when last staying there.

Based finally in their hostel in Quex Road, Hill and Conlon blended naturally into the Kilburn-Irish scene, going to pubs like the Memphis Belle and the Cock, taking drugs, even dealing in them in a small-time way and occasionally haunting the fringes of petty crime. They also enjoyed themselves and had both been to parties at 15, Rondu Road and 14, Algernon Road. Which was why when, on Friday, November 29 under interrogation by the Assistant Chief Constable of Surrey, Christopher Rowe, himself, and his assistant, Detective Chief Superintendent Wally Simmons, Hill began to give details of the part he said he had played in the bombing of the Horse and Groom and the Seven Stars at Guildford, people like Paddy Armstrong, Brian Anderson, John MacGuiness, Sean Mullin, Paul Colman, and Carole Richardson were soon to find themselves in police custody.

How was it that Hill came to say the things he now started to say? Were they the truth? Or did he have his own reasons for weaving a tale of fantasy?

When he had been found by Detective Sergeant Jermey of the Surrey Constabulary sitting in an arm chair in his prospective sister-in-law's house in Southampton on the morning of Thursday the 28th he had been told to get up and come into the hallway. There he was informed that he was being arrested on suspicion of causing explosions and cautioned that anything he might say could be used in evidence against him. The police say he made no reply, although he says he remarked: "You're kidding, it's not all that serious is it?" He was taken to Guildford police station. Just after half-past four, as he sat in the cells there, Jermey came in to see him again, this time with Detective Superintendent Underwood.

"I have reason to believe that you were concerned in the bombings of the pubs in Guildford."

"No, sir."

"You know what pub bombings I'm talking about?"

"Yes, sir, the soldiers' pubs."

"That's right. What do you know about it?"

"Nothing, sir, only what I read in the papers."

"I think you know a bit more than that."

"I don't, sir."

"Have you ever been to Guildford?"

"I only passed through on the train."

"When was that?"

"The day after the bombs. I was coming back from Southampton to London and there was a diversion on the line."

"So what you are saying is the only thing you know about these bombs is what you have read in the newspapers?"

"Yes, sir."

"We will see you tomorrow."

For nearly twenty-four hours Hill was left to ponder his predicament. But the first people to interview him the next day were not the Surrey police. They were two detectives from the Royal Ulster Constabulary. They had flown over from Belfast to question him about a murder by elements of the I.R.A. of a former British soldier Brian Shaw, suspected by the I.R.A. of being an intelligence source. Jermey and Detective Chief Superintendent Simmons of the Surrey police introduced the R.U.C. officers and then left. In the interview, though Hill today admits that he had had something to do

with Shaw's kidnapping, he at first denied involvement.*
According to him, he only agreed to talk when the R.U.C.
men told him that his girl-friend Gina Clarke who was also
under arrest would be charged with the Guildford bombing.
He says he made a deal with them: if he signed a statement
admitting involvement in the Shaw case they would release
Gina Clarke. He signed and was then interviewed by Simmons.

"I now wish to speak to you regarding the pub bombings
here in Guildford."

"I don't know anything."

"I think you can help us on this matter."

"I can't."

"Two bombs were placed in two public houses in this town.
I think you know something about this matter. That is why
you are here."

"All right, I'll tell you what I know."

The above dialogue is from the official police record. Since
this is the starting-point for the whole subsequent complex
history, involving altogether more than forty arrests to be
followed by two major State trials and long terms of imprisonment for eleven people, four of them for life, it is pertinent to
say something about the circumstances in which Hill now
began to talk about the Guildford bombing. He does not
today deny that he began to talk about Guildford very soon
after making a statement about the Ulster murder. He does
not say that at this stage physical violence was used against
him, a significant consideration since others who were to
make statements about Guildford would make such a claim.
He does say that the same threat was used against him as
had been used when he was interrogated about the murder
of Brian Shaw, namely that his girl-friend Gina Clarke, of
whom he had caught a glimpse crying in the police station
on his way to the interview with Simmons, would be charged
with the Guildford bombings if he did not talk. And he does
today still say what he said at his trial, namely that what he
told the police about it was nonsense.

He says that he was taken to the incident room at Guildford

*He was in fact to be convicted of the murder in a Belfast "Diplock" Court.

54

police station where there were plans and photographs on the wall of what had happened at the Guildford bombings. He used these, he says, as some basis for his subsequent statements, while the rest came from letting his imagination work among the people he knew in London. He believed that the people he named would have no difficulty in proving their innocence and thus his own.

"I picked them out of the blue," he says, "the first ones, anyway. Then it sort of took on its own momentum."

He maintains that he was led in his statements as he had been when he talked about Shaw. As he puts it:

"One would say: 'You went there with so and so, didn't you?' The statement was basically formed for me."

The police on the other hand maintained at his trial that he spoke entirely of his own free will and that the substance of his story was true. There might well be a natural presumption to believe them – and indeed the judge and jury plainly did so – were it not for certain internal evidence of his having been led in the statements themselves and, more importantly, if so much of the story he told had not turned out to be nonsense. Some explanation is however required for his willingness to talk relatively so soon after his first denials of involvement.

His own account is that he was impelled by fears for his girl-friend, Gina Clarke. He knew that on the strength of his admission to the R.U.C. he would now be charged with the Belfast murder. Of the Guildford charge, he says:

"I wasn't thinking logically at all. My mind was in complete confusion. I just kept telling myself that [what I said] would never stand up because when it came to it I could prove I was elsewhere."

It is known that Hill was also wanted at this time for questioning by the Provos in Belfast. They wanted to ask him about the disappearance of an Armalite rifle in circumstances which aroused a suspicion that it might have been handed either to the security forces or to the Official I.R.A. A wish to stay safely in Britain combined with the fact that he knew he was sought for the Belfast murder anyway may have induced him to make a confession about Guildford for his own sake as well as for Gina's. He seems to have been a man in whose mind at that time considerations of truth played a secondary role to an instinct for self-preservation. His least self-centred emotional drives seem to have been directed towards his girl-friend and also towards his mother in Belfast whose fears for him there and whose wish for him to get away to England were, he says today, the main reason for his move in August. His motives for talking as he did may well have been more muddled than precise. Speculation about them – which must include consideration of the police view that they contained an essential wish to tell the truth – is in any case less material to the development of this story than the consequences of what he said, which were precise.

The first consequences were the arrests in London of Hugh Maguire and his wife, and of the inhabitants of the flat in 15, Rondu Road, John MacGuiness, Brian Anderson and Sean Mullin, while, in Belfast, where Gerard Conlon had now been back at his parents' house in Cyprus Street for a fortnight, the Royal Ulster Constabulary called for him at about 5.30 a.m. on Saturday, November 30.

Like most young men from the Catholic and Republican districts of Belfast, Gerard Conlon had been picked up for random questioning by the security forces before and was apprehensive. He was taken to Springfield Road police barracks and placed in a cell. He stayed there until midnight when he was interviewed by Detective Chief Inspector Grundy and Detective Sergeant Jermey of the Surrey Constabulary who had flown over from England to see him. Many more such interviews were to follow.

Because eventually Conlon was to make statements on the strength of which he would be subsequently convicted, and which appeared to implicate, among other people, his aunt Anne Maguire in the bombing of the Horse and Groom and the Seven Stars, it is of interest to recall not just the content but the style of his first reactions to the charge that was being put to him. The following dialogue in the Springfield Road interview is taken from the official police record.

"I have reason to believe that you were involved in the

bombing incident in Guildford when two public houses were attacked and several people lost their lives."

"Not me, mister. I have never been to Guildford, I don't know where it is."

"Are you aware of which incident I am talking?"

"I think so. I read about it in the paper."

"The incident happened on the evening of Saturday, 5th October, 1974. Where were you at that time?"

"I would be down at the club in Kilburn where I went every Saturday with my aunt and uncle."

"If that is true it will be a simple matter to verify it. Is it the truth?"

"Oh yes, mister, you've only got to ask them."

"So you were in England then at that time?"

"Yes. I went over to get married but she called it off."

"Do you know Paul Hill, sometimes called Benny?"

"Yes. He's my mate."

"Paul Hill is in custody at Guildford and is admitting being involved in the bombings there, and he has said you are involved too."

"Not me, mister, may God strike me dead, I don't know nothing about it."

"You say this man is your mate, why should he involve you in something you say you have not done?"

"What can I say? I've never been there. I don't know nothing about it."

Grundy said:

"I don't believe that Hill would involve you in anything as serious as this without good reason to."

"I don't believe you've got Benny Hill in. I want to see him with my own eyes before I say anything and that's all I'm saying."

Grundy then told Conlon that he would remain in custody overnight and he would see him later during the day.

Grundy and Jermey indeed returned at 7 p.m. on the following day, Sunday, December 1, and Grundy began by saying:

"You have had some time to think about what we have

said to you concerning the Guildford bombings. Do you want
to say anything to me now?"

"Look, mister, you got to believe me, I don't know about
bombs and things. I was only over there for to get married
and to work. I was never in Guildford in my life."

"Were you with Benny Hill on the 5th October, 1974?"

"No. I spent Saturdays at the club like I told you."

"You will be able to tell us exactly what you did do in
England when Hill says you were with him in Guildford."

"I was never there. Anyway, Hill went down to
Southampton to see his bird every Saturday so how could I
be with him."

Grundy then produced a warrant which he read to Conlon,
cautioned him and told him he was arresting him and taking
him back to Guildford where further enquiries would be
made.

"You've got the wrong man," said Conlon. "I know
nothing about the explosions."

Grundy and Jermey took him from Springfield Road station
and flew with him to Britain, taking him to Addlestone police
station in Surrey at 11.30 p.m. that night. There he was
detained in a cell overnight and, on Monday, December 2
at 1.15 p.m., Grundy interviewed him again, this time at
Godalming police station with Detective Sergeant Jermey.
Grundy again cautioned him and said:

"You know the nature of our enquiry. Do you have
anything to say?"

"No, mister, I told you the truth. I was never in Guildford."

"Your friend Hill says you were concerned and that you
and he were shown how to make bombs."

"I don't know anything about bombs. The only thing I've
done here is smoke pot and take acid."

"Are you an addict, then?"

"No. I just take them now and again for the kick."

"You went to a house in Brixton with Hill, didn't you?"

"Where in Brixton, mister? I don't think I've been there
at all."

"It seems funny that you are denying everything that Hill
says is true."

"I'm telling the truth, sir. I don't know what this is all about."

Detective Sergeant Jermey then spoke:

"Do you know a girl called Marion? Who was showing you and Hill how to make bombs?"

"I don't know any girl named Marion. Honest to God, I wouldn't go near bombs. I'm frightened of things like that."

"Why is Hill saying these things, then? After all, he is your friend."

"I don't know, mister, but it's all lies."

Skilled writers of fiction can create character solely from dialogue. If such a writer had been commissioned to write dialogue for a rough young Catholic Irishman from Belfast accused of a crime of which he was not only innocent but also quite ignorant, it would be difficult to think of anything more convincing than the above section from the police record. At the same time it must be said that a guilty man is very likely to deny at first all knowledge of the crime of which he is accused, and that a very clever guilty man would be able to disguise his denial so as to make it sound as genuinely innocent as does that of Gerry Conlon. On the other hand it is known in what manner members of a Provisional IRA active service unit respond to questioning and an example appears later in this book. Certainly, they are talking about activities to which they have admitted, but both the style of the response and the revealed characters of the men responding seem very different from those evinced in these first interviews with Gerry Conlon.

However, the question which had been put to Conlon by Detective Sergeant Jermey needed answering: why, if he and Hill were friends, as they undoubtedly were, should Hill be saying these things about him if they were not true?

What in detail had Hill been saying?

6
Statements

Hill's first statement – he was to make six altogether – had begun as a fairly straightforward account of how he came to England in August, with his sister and his girl-friend, in search of work and how, after meeting his old school-friend Conlon who had come to Britain earlier, he searched with him for lodgings and work. But it quickly acquired a sinister ring.

"I came with my sister Elizabeth and my girl-friend Gina Clarke, neither of whom knew that I was coming over to do anything."

This could of course just have represented an answer "No" to the question: "Did either of them know that you had come over to do something?", while another earlier passage could equally have originated in a less sinister form than it finally emerged:

". . . I met Conlon at my aunt's house. He told me we had to go and meet a fellow. We met a chap called Paul at a pub called the Wheatsheaf in Camden Town. He told us that he had no stuff. I know he meant explosives."

This may have been the truth or it may have resulted from a willingness to please following the question:

"Did you know he meant explosives?"

There is one positive indication that Hill was at least partly helped by his interrogators. He was already launched on a graphic if often mysterious account of preparation for the Guildford bombings when he told how someone called "Paul" one day came to the hostel in Quex Road "with a guy who I now know to be Patrick Joseph Armstrong". In the interview which preceded the statement he had simply said:

"Paul came in with another guy I know, Paddy Armstrong."

In fact Armstrong's second name was not Joseph. Living in the Divis flats, Belfast, where Armstrong came from *was* a Patrick Joseph Armstrong, a senior member of the Official I.R.A. On a number of occasions in Belfast Paddy Armstrong had had his identity checked and had been mistaken by the security forces for this man who was prominent on their wanted list: Patrick Joseph Armstrong.

Nevertheless, whether led or simply encouraged by his questioners, Hill's imagination was soon taking wing on its own account. The gist of this first statement, discernible amidst a wealth of rather confusing detail about car journeys and people met in pubs (one man incidentally wearing a long black coat reminiscent of one of the early unidentified police suspects), had been that he and Conlon had been taken by "Paul" to a flat in Brixton where "a girl called Marion" had shown them how to make bombs; and that some time later four of them (Hill, Conlon, Paul and Armstrong) with "Marion" and another "older" girl had driven down to Guildford in two cars with bombs in the boots*. Armstrong who, in Hill's account, appeared very much to be the man in charge of the operation was described as driving one car and "Paul" the other. On another occasion Armstrong, this time driving "a small sports car", had come down to Hill's place of work and asked him to store some strange "yellow

---

*The use of the name "Marion" is possibly explained by the fact that the wanted IRA girl, Marlene Coyle, was known to have a sister named Marion.

liquid" in a container which Armstrong then came and collected off him the day before the Woolwich bombing.

Such were the details with which Conlon was now being confronted.

"Don't you remember the flat in Brixton? There was only two chairs and a table in it, and you were taken there by a man named Paul in an old Morris car."

"No. No. No. I swear to God I don't know what you're talking about."

"This Marion showed you how to make bombs in that flat. Paul asked you on the way back if you could remember what she had shown you and you said, 'Yes'."

"I swear on my mother's life, mister, I don't know what you're talking about. I never seen no bombs. I don't know Marion."

"Do you know a man named Armstrong?"

"Yes. I know Paddy Armstrong. Is he involved in this?"

"Did he show you any photographs?"

"What of?"

"Public houses or anything like that he said they were going to bomb."

"No, I've never seen any, mister. Honest."

In fact it was hardly surprising that, on one detail at least, Conlon should have been bewildered. In his assertion that he knew nothing of any flat for making bombs in Brixton, there was already some reason to think he was speaking the truth. For, in an interview with the Metropolitan Police Bomb Squad two days before on the evening of November 30, the full details of which had apparently not yet been absorbed by the Surrey police, Hill had formally changed his story that the bombs were made in a Brixton flat and was now saying that they were made in the flat at 15, Rondu Road, Cricklewood, where Anderson, MacGuiness and Mullin lived. He had had to change his story after he had been told by the police to take them to the Brixton flat and had proved unable to produce for them, after much hesitation, anything better than a flat in which were living two impeccably harmless old ladies. He was now saying that it was to the Rondu Road flat that "Paul" had taken him and Gerry Conlon, and that it was there they had met "Marion" who had displayed elaborate bomb-making equipment to Gerry while "Paul" had shown him a number of photographs of pubs at which soldiers drank which were to be blown up. Hill agreed to help in the operations. No one else, he added, had been in the Rondu Road flat at the time.

At the end of this interview with the bomb squad Hill had also revealed a number of other details. Asked to describe Armstrong's girl-friend he said he had not got one. Asked to describe "Marion" he said she was "nice-looking, long blonde hair, obviously dyed, with dark roots parted in the middle, age 18/20, nice build, modern dresser . . . " (A description issued by the police shortly after the bombing.) Asked if she had any mates he replied:

"Yes, a woman about 30, heavy make-up, same length, dark hair, with a sheen off it, medium build, same height as Marion, sorry a bit taller, wearing a dark coloured raincoat, a blueish colour."

"What was her name?"

"I don't know, I only met her once coming down to do the Guildford job."

He gave details of the cars used at Guildford. That which he said Armstrong drove was "a dark colour four-door car, with plastic sheets on the seats, like a saloon". The car used by "Paul" was "an old dark colour Morris 1100. It looked very dirty, two doors."

He said that the journey down to Guildford had taken place in the afternoon and that Armstrong had dropped him off at Waterloo after getting back to London about 5.45 p.m.

He also revealed for the first time who "Paul" was: "Paul O'Malley or O'Mallow."

When much later, at Hill's trial, Detective Chief Superintendent Neville of the Metropolitan Police Bomb Squad was asked about this man and whether he had been found, his reply was:

"He does not exist, or even if he does, no one of that name has been found."

Small wonder that Conlon sounded so convincing when he said he did not know what Hill was talking about. Eventually, pressed yet again to explain why, if he and Hill were such mates, Hill should say he was involved in the Guildford bombing when he wasn't, Conlon replied:

"I don't know. I don't think he would. If you've got him show him to me and I'll ask him why."

Jermey then left the office and came back a few moments later with Hill. He said to Conlon:

"Who is this?"

"My mate, Benny. Benny, what are you trying to do to me? For God's sake tell the truth. I wasn't invovled."

Hill said merely:

"I am saying nothing. I've cleared my conscience. I've made my statement. I'm not putting words into your mouth."

Hill was then taken from the room. Jermey said to Conlon:

"Hill has made a statement naming you as having been involved and you have failed to give any explanation for him saying this. A mate would not say this sort of thing if you were not involved."

Conlon jumped to his feet and said:

"All right, all right, I'll tell you. I'll tell you the truth – he hasn't."

"What is the truth?"

"I don't know how to make bombs. He does. He told me once that if three I.R.A. men had listened to him they would have been alive today and that I knew his crack."

"What do you mean by his crack?"

"It's the way we say, like, you know, the score."

"What was your part in the bomb attack on these pubs?"

This question skilfully deflected Conlon from the point he was trying to make. What he seems to have been saying was that though Hill himself may have been implicated he had not told the truth when he said that he (Conlon) was involved. Now he was being pressed to give some explanation of his own involvement as if he had conceded this.

"When he said we were going for a drive I thought I was going to get a head job."

"Why would you think that?"

"Because I had been taking dope and they don't like that.

Benny knew all about this, and about me shop-lifting, that's why I was frightened of him."

"Where did you drive to?"

"I don't know. Some place I'd never been before."

There then followed a confused description by Conlon of a drive in a car with a girl. Some details of this could certainly have derived in part from information he had been given by the police in the course of his earlier interrogation. Asked by Jermey if she was carrying a bag he replied:

"Yes, one of them plastic shop bags."

They went into a pub of some sort for a drink. The details of an evening emerged hazily. They reflected either a confused account of some specific reality mixed with details of what he had already learned or, as his questioners undoubtedly saw it, an account deliberately intended to mislead by vagueness. One thing Conlon at least made clear was that on the night of which he was giving an account some eight or nine people were out with him. But he said nothing about Guildford and the only mention of it occurred when he was asked:

"Did you read in the papers the following day about the bombing in pubs in Guildford?"

"Yes."

"Did you not think that was anything to do with you?"

"No. I didn't give it a second thought."

The impression was that what Conlon was talking about was a drive, probably while doped, in which visits to pubs were made with Hill, Armstrong and some other men and girls. No doubt the police were hoping to match this drive with the drive which the I.R.A. unit must have taken to bomb the Guildford pubs.

In this they already had a problem. For here was Conlon talking about a night expedition, whereas Hill had told them the expedition had been back in London by 5.45 and their interviews with the Horse and Groom survivors had the bombers leaving Guildford at about 7 p.m. These were only some of the many anomalies with which the statements they were gathering would present them.

At 2.20 p.m. on this day, December 2, Conlon wrote his first written statement, compiled with police assistance on the basis of this interview. It remained basically confused but help from the police had pulled it together considerably.

As with Hill's first official statement, Conlon's began with an innocent enough straightforward account of how he had come to England in August with his girl-friend to find work and how his first lodgings had been fixed up for him by a friend in Southampton, where he had accidentally run into his old mate Hill.

"At first," he said, "I thought Hill had been sent over from Belfast by the Provos to take me back as I had been shoplifting ... I had already been arrested by the Provos and beaten up for this ... [But] he just said things had got bad in Belfast and the soldiers were looking for him and I believed him because he got his hair cut short and it was dyed. I knew Hill was in the Provos as I had seen him shooting at soldiers ... He told me he was of D Company in the Falls where I live and how Martin Skillen [a school friend of both of them] got shot dead. Hill also told me that he fired the shot from a rifle at his funeral and he was told by the head man to come to England or to go down South as he was too hot in Belfast ... "

Conlon's account of early difficulties in finding somewhere to live in London again tallied with Hill's. He mentioned a failure to contact Paddy Maguire, the short stay with Hugh Maguire and the final lodging at the Irish priest's hostel in Quex Road. He then described how, soon after they had started work on their building site job, he "started smoking dope again". Hill, he says, "would not take any of it and said if the boys at home found out he was taking dope he would get done. I said, was he going to tell them that I took drugs, and he laughed and said no, but if he did I would get a head job like Brian Shaw got". It is at this point that what Conlon first describes as an offer from Hill to "do a little job with him" (we know that they were both involved in petty crime during this period) turns into "giving the English a little fright ... a bomb scare". Conlon goes on: "I was soaking dope and feeling high because of the dope and I said I did not want to hurt anybody. I am not into violence. That's why I came from Belfast. He just laughed and said I should not be taking dope because if he told the lads in Belfast it would be curtains for me . . . "

A few nights after this conversation, according to Conlon, "Hill said we were going to see some people. I had just taken a tablet of acid which is LSD . . . I later remember having something put over my eyes and I started to have a bad trip. I must have been screaming and shouting because they took it off . . . "

And it was, said Conlon, in this condition that he was taken to a flat where a number of other people were assembled and where, contrary to his earlier denial, he now said he was present at a bomb-making demonstration.

"I was sitting on a settee beside Hill and he said to me, 'This is Jim or John'."

This seemed to be the head tenant in the Rondu Road flat: John MacGuiness. In the hour which had elapsed between the preliminary interview and the taking of the statement the police had caught up with the fact that Hill was now saying the bomb-making demonstration had taken place in MacGuiness's flat in Rondu Road. Also in this flat was "someone called Paul. There were other people there, but I did not hear their names. I think one of them was Tucker Clarke [the foreman who employed Hill and Conlon at Robert Hart, the building contractors] but I am not sure. Also Paddy Armstrong could have been there."

(Hill's Rondu Road account said that, apart from Paul, the girl, himself and Conlon, no one else had been there.)

A description of a bomb-making lesson of sorts then followed – Conlon's version of what Hill had described to police in his opening statement. But, whereas Hill had given the girl a name, "Marion", Conlon simply said:

"A girl who I had never seen before put a box on the table. I think there was sand in the box and something long and black with what looked like a watch. Everyone was standing round the table and she was talking. But I did not understand what she was saying . . . "

Conlon's statement then proceeded to recount events on a Saturday a few days later – Saturday indeed being the day of the week on which the Guildford bombings had taken place on October 5. As Conlon had already said in the preliminary interview, Hill used to go down to his girl-friend in Southampton on Saturdays while he himself usually spent the evening with his Uncle Hugh at the Conservative Working Men's Club. But on this particular Saturday, Conlon's statement declared, after he had been down to Ladbroke Grove to buy some marijuana and LSD, had smoked some marijuana at the hostel, been to the betting-shop and the pub, and returned to the hostel to smoke some more, Hill made a sudden appearance and said they were going for a drive. The time was 6 p.m. Hill, said Conlon, took him to the Old Bell pub in Kilburn where after he had been sick in the lavatory, feeling, as he did, threatened by Hill for his indulgence in drugs, they were joined by Paddy Armstrong. They all eventually got into a car, with himself sitting in the back between Hill and Armstrong while a girl sat in front beside a man who drove. The confused drive he had already described in the preliminary interview then followed.

Somehow from the hazy background described by Conlon another car appeared with two or three other girls and two men in it, and the two cars drove off into the country, finally stopping at a pub. Hill sent Conlon into this with one of the girls carrying a bag, while two men went off with the other girl. After a drink, Conlon went on, he and the girl left the pub and drove back to London with Hill. In the course of this drive Hill told Conlon not to tell his uncle and aunt or his mother, when writing to her, where they had been. This particular account of the bombing of the Horse and Groom ends in something of an anti-climax:

"The next day when I read in the papers and heard of what had happened I did not know it was the place I had been to."

Gerard Conlon's statement, which according to the police record had taken five and a half hours to compile, was signed by him at 8.03 p.m. on the evening of Monday December 2.

Hill had by then made his third statement in which he gave some prominence in the planning of the operation to MacGuiness who, he said, had unzipped his jacket at one point and revealed a gun in his waistband, describing himself as Armstrong's "minder" and telling Hill not to get out of line, for in Belfast he had once "banged a big shot in the Army at his own door". Another colourful detail added by Hill was that the car driven by Paul on the Guildford expedition, which he had previously described to the London Bomb Squad as "an old dark colour Morris 1100" with two doors, had now become a four-door lemon or yellow XL Granada, to accompany the dark saloon with four doors driven by Armstrong. (Further difficulty was to arise for the police on this latter point, as it was soon to appear extremely doubtful that Armstrong had ever been able to drive.)

In this account of the putative journey to Guildford, Hill also described how Armstrong stopped the car just after passing a race-course and picked up "two birds . . . one of which was Marion I have mentioned . . . and the other bird was about thirty . . . both had carrier bags . . . I knew Marion but was never told the older woman's name . . . "

In the course of this statement he also gave a very detailed account which he had not given the London Bomb Squad of how he, Paul and Armstrong had driven down to Woolwich in a two-seater silver sports car this time and Armstrong had thrown a bomb through the window of a pub there.

On the afternoon of December 2, while Conlon was busy making out his own first statement, Hill volunteered yet another. This began, as had now become his custom, with a sentence to the effect that, while his previous statement had been true, he had not then told the whole truth. Now he merely made clear that, when they had got to Guildford, Gerry Conlon "and the old (30-year-old) bird" had composed one bombing team while "Paul" and Marion had been the other.

Then, some time after 2 p.m. on the afternoon of December 3 when he was being interviewed by two officers at Godalming, he said to one of them:

"You won't be mad at me if I tell you something?"

One of the officers said:

"What do you mean? Is it connected with the statement you made yesterday?"

"Yes . . . The girl Marion – that's not her real name. It's Armstrong's girl-friend, Carole. She's the one you want."

So, between 3.50 p.m. and 5.03 p.m., he voluntarily completed yet another statement. For Carole, as for the Maguire family, living at 43, Third Avenue, Harlesden, and others, it was to prove catastrophic.

Once again Hill offered a version of his standard preliminary:

"All I have said in my statements before this is true except that there are some people I have not mentioned . . . "

The first name was one that had in fact been mentioned the day before by Gerard Conlon, that of Tucker Clarke, the ganger-foreman at Robert Hart and Company, whom Hill now described as an important contact. And he now formally implicated Carole Richardson.

"In my other statement I said there was a girl called Marion, which is untrue. This girl is called Carole and I am not sure of her surname but I believe it is Linnberg or something like that, and that she is Armstrong's girl-friend and that she was squatting in Kilburn . . . Her description is the same as that I gave of Marion except that she has got an English accent and not an Irish one. And she was the girl who came on the Guildford bombing with us and went with Paul to plant the bomb. And the other woman which I said I did not know is a woman called Annie who I first met in a Maida Vale club and another time at the Carousel Ballroom in Camden Town and on both times she was with Hugh Maguire and his wife Kitty. She told me she was from Belfast and was from Abyssinia Street and she said she had a brother called Robert who was about twenty-ish and was retarded."

Anne Maguire, Conlon's aunt, was indeed from Abyssinia Street in Belfast, had a retarded brother called Robert and had met Hill at the Conservative Working Men's Club in Maida Vale and again only a short time before in the Carousel Ballroom at Camden Town, both times with Hugh Maguire and his wife Kitty.

"The next time I seen her," Hill now went on, "was with Carole and that was when we were on our way down to Guildford and she was also on the bomb pair with Gerry.

She said she was over in London for a good time and she was friendly with Gerry and Carole."

Anne Maguire and Carole Richardson say that until the events of December 3, 1974 neither had ever seen the other in their lives.

Ten minutes after the interview which had led to this last statement of Hill's, Detective Chief Inspector Grundy and Detective Sergeant Jermey of the Surrey police were back interviewing Gerard Conlon. They had already been at it for over an hour in the morning, trying to get some more precise detail into the very hazy account he had given so far of the car journey which, they maintained, was the bombing expedition to Guildford.

Now they began eagerly:

"Before lunch you told us that you knew nothing about the pub you went in?"

"That's right, mister."

"Right. We will forget that for the minute and talk about making bombs."

"I never made any bombs, mister, honest to God I haven't. You've got to believe me."

"Hill now says that it wasn't a girl called Marion who made the bombs at a flat in Brixton and that the flat wasn't in Brixton but somewhere else."

"I've never seen any bombs made. I've never made any bombs. I don't know what they look like."

"Hill says you were shown how to make bombs."

"No, mister, honestly. He knows – I know he does."

"How do you know he does?"

"He's told me often enough, mister. I thought I was going to get a head job. I was frightened that he was going to shoot me because I had been taking drugs."

"We are not talking about drugs. We're talking about bombs. You were shown how to make bombs."

"No, mister, may God strike me dead. I know nothing about bombs."

In view of Conlon's persistent denial on this point, the police record now has a rather surprising twist. After a short

71

digression on Conlon's shop-lifting habits, Detective Chief
Inspector Grundy suddenly asks:

"You have said you were shown how to make bombs."

Conlon had in fact just been constantly saying that he did
not know anything about bombs. Only in the statement he
had been brought to make the day before did he give a very
garbled account of a bomb-making exhibition. Nevertheless
Grundy persisted:

"Tell us again who was there?"

"Those persons who are down in my statement."

"Is there anyone else that you have forgotten?"

"No, mister, at least no one I know."

"Who was this woman who was making these bombs?"

"I don't know, mister, honest to God I don't know."

"What did she look like?"

"I don't remember much what she was like because I'd
taken a tablet of acid and I was having a bad trip."

"I think you're lying. They would hardly let you near
explosives if you were in that condition."

"It's the truth, mister, I'm trying to clear my conscience."

"Are you a drug addict?"

"No. I just take them from time to time."

"It seems convenient for you that when we ask you about
incidents and ask for details, you tell us that you are under
the influence of drugs."

"Benny kept telling them I was all right."

"I think you know who was showing you how to make
these bombs."

"What does Hill say?"

"It doesn't matter what Hill says. What do you say?"

This, it should be remembered, is the official police record.
If Conlon were being led on this point, it would not appear
in the record. He had just asked what Hill had said, which
might suggest that he had been told what Hill had said in
earlier instances. The police record continues:

"All right, it was my Aunt Annie."

"What was she doing?"

"Showing us how to make bombs."

"Where was this?"

"I don't know. It was in some flat where Hill took me. I was high at the time."

"Did you expect to see your Aunt Annie at this flat?"

"No. I was surprised. In fact she said, 'I bet you're surprised to see me here,' and I said, 'Yes, I am.' "

"What is your Aunt Annie's full name?"

"Annie Maguire."

"Where does she live?"

"43 Third Avenue in London."

This time, when Conlon was asked if he knew that the pub he went to that night "with the bombs" had been at Guildford, he answered:

"Yes, mister."

"How do you know?"

"Because I saw it in the papers next day . . . "

He went on to say more about the journey and visit to "Guildford". They were in two cars. Conlon, Hill and Armstrong were in the back of one car with a man driving and a woman in the other seat. Asked who the man and woman were, he said he didn't know. Pressed about the woman, he said, "Her hair was black, it was styled and turned up at the ends. I couldn't see her face." Asked if he knew the name of the driver, he said, he thought the driver's name was Paul. He again denied knowing anything about the woman.

"You are obviously trying to shelter somebody; who is it?"

Conlon answered:

"All right, I'm telling you the truth, mister, it was my Aunt Annie."

"You mean the same Auntie Annie who showed you how to make the bombs?"

"Yes, mister, it was her."

Very little of this appeared in the formal statement which Conlon now drew up. It began baldly:

"My Aunt Annie showed six of us how to make bombs. Annie is the woman in the flat I have spoken about in my first statement . . . Paul Hill and Annie did most of the talking on how they were made. They showed us a box with a long black thing and a pocket-watch – also sand was in the box. Annie said to me, 'I bet you are surprised to see me here.' I said, 'Yes, I am.' She said, 'I know Paul from long ago.' I did not know what she meant. She said to all of us that we might have to do this one of these days." He then recounted how "Annie" had accompanied him, Hill and others on a bomb-making expedition to "a town which I had never been to before".

Almost immediately after making these statements, subsequently at his trial and ever since, Conlon has maintained that he made them under the threat of physical violence. The police officers concerned strenuously denied this allegation.

It is clear enough from the police record itself that his formal statements implicating himself and Anne Maguire give a somewhat unreal impression of the lengthy preliminary interviews which preceded them. In view of the calamitous consequences for so many people of his statements, a short extract from his own account of the way in which he says they were obtained may be noted.

The account was written in 1986 when Conlon had already been in prison twelve years. It tallies with an account he gave his solicitor in 1975 to which he has not had access since. The police refute it today as in 1975.

". . . (G) started to shout and yell at me and he also slung me against the wall a few times.

"I was crying again by now, I couldn't believe this was happening to me. (J) came back and they started asking me questions, questions I couldn't answer because I hadn't done anything. This went on for hours, how long I don't know but it was a long time. I was hit . . . now and again, and all the time abused and threatened by them. I was called a cunt, a bastard, an animal, a murderer and more, over and over again. I was very frightened and crying. At about seven I told them I would make a statement, the truth, so I did.

"After I finished the statement which was after eight I gave it to one of them who read it. After he read it, he went mad, screaming at me, (J) hit me from the side as well. I said I was telling the truth. In the statement I denied the bombing and kept saying I was innocent. (G) said that if the statement was true then I better start telling lies and be quick about it. (J) who was behind me lifted me off the chair by the hair then let go. I was then put against the wall in the search position and they started all over again with the questions.

"I wasn't hit again that night, but I was scared and very, very frightened. I kept saying I was telling the truth, this only seemed to make them worse. (G) then ripped the statement I had written up and threw it in a waste-paper bin. About an hour later I was taken to the cell by the both of them, (J) said as he put me in the cell that they would be back in the morning to see me again and they would get a statement out of me one way or another, I was then locked up. I had nothing to eat that day again, only water. I didn't sleep much.

"Some time next morning I was taken upstairs again by (J). We went to the same room as before. (G) was sitting behind the desk. I was told to sit, I did. (G) said I had plenty of time to think and was I going to tell the truth about my part in the bombing. I said I hadn't done anything. I was called a liar by both (G) and (J). They started getting aggressive. I was being asked the same questions over and over again. This went on for about an hour before (J) hit me. (J) also came round the back of the chair and stood behind me. Now and again he would slap me across the back of the head. It wasn't really sore but it was frightening as I didn't know when he was going to hit me.

"Once he put his hands at the back of my neck and said he was going to show me an old R.A.F. trick, I thought he was going to strangle me. But instead he moved his hands to just behind my ears and suddenly dug his fingers in and picked me up from the chair by his fingers. I couldn't believe the pain, it was like getting an electric shock. One second I was screaming in pain, next second I was on the floor coming round. I must have blacked out. Next thing I remember is (G) leaning over saying something like:

" 'It doesn't have to be like this. Just make a statement like Hill has and everything will be all right.' "

Conlon alleges that there was a good deal more of this sort of physical violence, including the squeezing of his testicles and that "accidents" were threatened to his family in Belfast.

All this was denied by the officers at the trial. This is how, finally, he alleges that he was brought to make the statement which implicated his aunt, Anne Maguire.

"I was taken upstairs by (J) and taken to a room (G) was in. (G) said Hill had told them my Aunt Annie had showed us how to make bombs. I said:

'No.'

"(G) said he wanted me to make another statement saying my Aunt Annie had showed us how to make bombs. I said she hadn't and Hill was lying. (G) said his boss (S) believed Hill and wanted a statement from me saying she was involved and if I didn't he would have to tell his boss and I knew what his boss was like. I said all right, but I would have to see Hill's statement. (J) got it. I wrote what they wanted. I would have mentioned any name they wanted by now. After the statement I was put back in the cells."

Again, the officers wholly deny the allegation. Gerry Conlon's final comment:

"A short time later I was taken to Guildford to Court and remanded for a week in prison. I felt very relieved that I was going to prison and not back to the police station."

While he testified on oath to much of the above treatment at his trial, the police officers concerned, equally on oath, strenuously denied all such allegations. The jury – and later the Appeal Court – believed them rather than Conlon.

The writing of his second statement ended at 7.02 p.m. on December 3, 1974. But a telephone call had already gone through from Godalming to the Metropolitan Police in London. By 7 p.m. two police officers, Detective Sergeant Charles Hunter and Detective Sergeant Elbourn, were sitting in Detective Sergeant Elbourn's private car outside number 43 Third Avenue, W.10, where Anne and Paddy Maguire lived. Hunter got out of the car and walked past the house so that he could see into the front room. Through the net curtains he was able to make out several men and a woman there. He went back to Elbourn's car and after about five minutes saw one of the men leave the house and drive off in a dark-coloured Ford Escort, index number HBH220K.

7

The House on Third Avenue

In Belfast the previous Saturday, Giuseppe and Sarah Conlon, parents of Gerard, had called several times at Springfield Road police station to try to see their son after his arrest, but had been unable to do so. They spent the Sunday in a state of desperation. Giuseppe called again at Springfield Road to leave some cigarettes and was given a list of clothes required. They had been told their son would be taken to Guildford in Britain but that they would be allowed to see him before he went. However, when they rang up that evening they were told he had already left, and when they called again at the police station a little later with a solicitor this was confirmed. (Gerard Conlon says that he had in fact glimpsed his parents for a moment from a corridor on one of their visits but had not been allowed to speak to them.)

Giuseppe Conlon, a former Royal Marine, was a sick man, suffering from extensive tuberculosis in both lungs. However, after a telephone conversation with his solicitor, Ted Jones of the Belfast firm of Nurse and Jones, he decided to go to England to see what he could do for Gerard there. He went to Springfield Road police barracks and told them he was going. He called on a neighbour in Cyprus Street, James

Delaney, to ask if he would drive him to the Heysham boat the next day. He seemed in an extremely nervous and agitated condition. Both Delaney and his wife, knowing Giuseppe's ill-health, did their best to try and dissuade him from going, but he was determined to go.

Hugh and Paddy Maguire were the brothers of his wife Sarah. Giuseppe tried to telephone Hugh in London to ask if he could stay with him. He was surprised, however, to find no reply from the Westbourne Terrace flat either that evening or the next morning, Monday. He therefore decided to go to Sarah's other brother in London, Paddy, and arranged for his solicitors to send him a warning telegram. And on the evening of Monday, December 2 Mr. and Mrs. Delaney drove Giuseppe Conlon to the Heysham boat.

Paddy and Anne Maguire had been living in London for 17 years. They had come over together from Belfast on the day on which they got married in September 1957, a few months after Paddy had left the British Army. His military career had actually begun in the South of Ireland when in 1952 he joined the Irish Army, but he had deserted from it after 18 months and then joined the Royal Inniskilling Fusiliers in the North. He had served with them in both Egypt and Cyprus. In London after two years as a labourer and paint-sprayer, he got a job through the British Legion with the North Thames Gas Board. He became a gas fitter and held the job for 11 years until 1970, about which time he found he was beginning to drink more and more heavily. Looking back on this development a few years later, Paddy Maguire put it down, at least partly, to the start of the troubles in Belfast about the same time. Whether or not that is a rational-isation of something that was going to happen anyway is immaterial to this story, though the drinking itself is not. He left his job at the Gas Board. He says:

"I started drinking seven days a week. In the end it got so bad that I finished up twice in hospital over it."

He spent five weeks in Horton Hospital at Epsom in Surrey, receiving treatment as an alcoholic, before he discharged himself. Later he again went back and again discharged himself. He managed to get one job as a fitter for a firm making double glazing and another with William Press which he left "after an argument". He is proud to emphasise that he has never been sacked, but always resigned.

On December 2, 1974 he had been out of work for a month, having given up a job which he had held for nearly a year as an assistant caretaker at Willesden College of Technology. He was suffering from stomach trouble and what he calls "general alcoholic trouble". He was getting depressed, particularly, he thinks, about the situation in Northern Ireland and the dangers to which his mother was exposed there. He was then, he reckoned, "a nervous type anyway, although I didn't show it". But it is fair to say that he was also a spirited type, a man proud of his male dignity and not one to shirk his family responsibilities. He was scrupulous to see that his wife got the housekeeping money for his family of three boys, Vincent, John and Patrick, then aged 16, 15 and 13, and their little daughter Anne-Marie, aged 9. Most of the rest he spent on drink.

"I was certainly," he was to say ruefully later, "drinking heavily enough to give me D.T.s when I came off it!"

A friend with whom he was drinking fairly regularly in the days before Tuesday December 3, described him as "getting through 10 to 12 pints of Guinness at lunch-time" and "a good steady drinker".

Paddy Maguire's drinking did not make for an easy marriage. Ever since he had left his job with the Gas Board, Anne had found him unable to settle.

"He was drinking more and more indoors, whisky and wine and cider and then you had to leave him alone. He would get angry if you said anything, though he never hurt the kids. It's because of that that the trouble between us started."

He had not told Anne at first when he left the Gas Board. When he did tell her at lunch towards the end of October, he had already been drinking and a furious row followed. In reply to his statement that he had "resigned", Anne said words to the effect that he had better resign altogether or she would. His memory is understandably unclear as to what exactly he said, but he thinks he probably left the house saying he would not be coming back. In any event he went straight to the local Council Housing Officer and, in what the local Housing Officer described as an angry mood, demanded to have his name taken off the tenancy and to be given a separate bachelor flat. When told that this was impossible he left, telling the Housing Officer to look out, or he could well blow the house up. (He remembered afterwards that he was thinking of using the gas meter to do so.)

The inevitable ups and downs of all married life became embarrassingly exaggerated. He was to say later, honestly enough: "I'd say the rows were really my fault. She runs a lovely home. Nine-tenths of the time I was drunk and I could not hold a steady job. Most of the rows were over my not working . . . I would be very bad-tempered. I could be moody and just shut up and not speak for hours on end and would treat her with contempt or ignore her if I felt I had a grudge."

One day on her way back from one of her cleaning jobs, Anne went to the Citizen's Advice Bureau to ask for help in preventing the marriage from breaking down. She actually saw a solicitor and discussed separation and divorce but finally decided that she would wait until he came out of the mood into which he had got himself at the end of November and have a serious talk with him herself for the children's sake, "and if that didn't work I would warn him that I would leave him". At this time, in Paddy's words: "I had stopped talking to her except for the bare necessities." Indeed, they had hardly spoken to each other at all in the days preceding the afternoon of Monday December 2. Which is why, when something extraordinary happened in the early evening of that day, Paddy never told her anything about it.

He had spent the day in much the usual sort of routine into which he had lately fallen. He was last out of the house, long after Anne and Vincent had gone off to work and the other children had left for school. At about 11 o'clock he went to the local Tax Office to get a form on which to claim a rebate after four weeks' unemployment. He then went to the Labour Exchange to look at the cards advertising jobs on the walls, though he had already filled in three applications for jobs as a security guard – one with the British Legion in Eccleston Square. Having a drink with his old friend Jimmy Blaney at lunchtime, he gave him the impression that his failure to get a job was really worrying him. He went back to the house after closing time, read the papers and watched TV.

About 6 o'clock that evening there was a ring at the bell. The sons were back in the house and one of them went to answer it. It was a telegram. It read:

"YOUR NEPHEW GERARD CONLON ARRESTED AND HELD IN GUILDFORD LONDON STOP FATHER HAS INSTRUCTED US AS SOLICITORS NURSE AND JONES 7 LOWER NORTH STREET BELFAST STOP PLEASE TELEPHONE" (the number followed) "AFTER SIX OR" (another number followed) "BERNARD SIMON COMMA SOLICITOR 40 BEDFORD STREET LONDON STOP."

This was, as Paddy afterwards described it, "a shock and a half". He had known from Gerry Conlon's stay with the family two years before that his nephew was hardly a model character, but he had never expected him to be involved in anything as serious as now seemed to be the case. It seemed particularly disturbing in view of what he knew of Gerard's father's (Giuseppe's) state of health. Paddy, not wanting to spend the money on a telephone call to Belfast, rang the London solicitor's office and asked for Mr. Simon. A Mr. Walsh spoke to him. Paddy told him he didn't want to have anything to do with the matter. Since he was not speaking to Anne he told her nothing about the telegram.

Instead he tried to get in touch with his brother Hugh. He was not on the best of terms with Hugh but thought the solicitors might have contacted him too. He could not understand why he could get no reply from the Westbourne Terrace flat, though he rang several times. He did not tell Anne that he was doing this, either. The last call was around midnight and there was still no reply. He went to bed.

On Tuesday, December 3, he got up about 7, made himself some tea, called Vincent for work and, just after Anne had left for her cleaning job in the office of an accountant called

Morris Apple in Harrow Road, again tried to telephone his brother Hugh. Again there was no reply. He then thought of telephoning a man whom he knew to be one of his brother's best friends, Sean Tully, and after first having to look up his telephone number in the book did so.

Sean Tully's wife answered and said her husband had gone to work. When Paddy asked whether she knew if Hugh was all right, she replied that she had been trying to get in touch with him all the weekend. They had known that he was not working on Saturday and were worried. Someone had even been round to the house and got no reply.

Paddy then got Anne-Marie her breakfast, saw Vincent off to work and John and Patrick off to school. When Anne came back from her first cleaning job of the morning she took Anne-Marie to school while Paddy sat down with the newspaper to puzzle over the business of the telegram and the failure to get through to his brother Hugh. He finally decided that when Anne came back he would have to tell her about the telegram.

He was sitting in his chair in this state of mind when to his astonishment he thought he saw Giuseppe Conlon himself walk past the window. He could hardly believe his eyes. He knew that Giuseppe's tuberculosis was so bad that he had hardly travelled anywhere for a long time. He went to the door. Giuseppe came in carrying a little case which he put down in the living-room. He was plainly upset.

Paddy asked him about the telegram and after discussing the matter they again telephoned the London solicitor, Bernard Simon of Bedford Street. They were told to ring back about 3 o'clock. Giuseppe asked if Paddy would like to go out for a drink and Paddy at first declined because he had no money. "Otherwise," he said characteristically, "I'd have asked you out in the first place."

But Giuseppe had money, and they went out to a pub called the Grey Horse off Kilburn Lane, where they drank until afternoon closing time – pints of lager for Giuseppe and twice as many pints of Guinness for Paddy. Giuseppe gave Paddy £2 so that he could pay for some of the rounds himself. Paddy, becoming more expansive with the drink, felt bound to say that if Gerard had been involved in the Guildford bombing then he deserved everything that was coming to him. Giuseppe agreed but added:

"He's my son. What can I do?"

In the pub was Jimmy Blaney, Paddy's friend with whom he had been drinking there the day before, and he exchanged a few words with him.

Anne was now back at the house. After taking Anne-Marie to school she had gone to her second cleaning job of the morning, a betting shop in the Harrow Road. When she had finished there she went for a cup of tea with a friend of hers who worked in a greengrocer's a little further down the road, and after 12 o'clock accompanied her to a charity jumble sale. There she bought some curtains and attachments for a Hoover and a purplish coat which her friend took to the cleaners for her, while she went and did some family shopping. She bought some mince, sausages and hamburgers at a butcher called Pearse and some tea-bags, eggs, biscuits and a Christmas pudding at Tesco's. On her way back to the house in Third Avenue she met neighbours, a Mrs. O'Shea, a Mrs Roach and a Mrs Watt. They talked about getting ready for Christmas and how expensive everything was.

Anne was back at the house between half-past one and two, by which time Paddy and Giuseppe were sitting comfortably in the Grey Horse drinking their pints. Vincent was back early from his work while John and a friend of his from school were watching TV. In the living-room Anne spotted a little suitcase.

"Who owns that, do you know? Where's your Dad?" she asked Vincent. He said he didn't know.

"Dad wasn't in when I came back from work."

They looked into the case. There was not much in it: a jacket, some socks, and a few other personal oddments.

Anne decided it might have belonged to one of Paddy's friends from the hospital in Surrey.

"Whoever they are," she said, "they're not staying here."

They had lunch about two o'clock and afterwards she read the paper for a while before preparing a stew for the evening. She was mopping the floor, when around half-past three

Paddy came back in from the pub with Giuseppe. She was amazed to see Giuseppe, knowing, like Paddy, that he was seriously ill and hardly ever travelled. Paddy told her that he was there because Gerard had been picked up for the Guildford bombing.

She said she couldn't believe it.

Giuseppe said:

"We don't believe it, he's done many things but we'd never believe he'd do anything like this. That's why I'm over here to see his solicitor." He asked if he could stay for a few days until he'd got things sorted out with the solicitor. "I'm sorry, Paddy tells me he didn't tell you about the telegram."

She told him he could stay for as long as he liked. He then asked her where Hugh Maguire, his other brother-in-law, was because he had been trying to get in touch with him all weekend but without success; otherwise he would have gone to stay there. This was the first Anne had heard of the mysterious absence of Hugh from his flat and they agreed to telephone again after six o'clock when he was normally home from work. Giuseppe and Paddy then went into the living-room to ring Bernard Simon the solicitor. Paddy seemed to have some difficulty doing this, perhaps because of all he had to drink in the pub, and Anne told him to give the telephone to Giuseppe, who then got through to the number and made an appointment for himself to call at Bedford Street at ten o'clock the following morning.

Soon after this Anne-Marie came back from school with a friend of hers, Marie Baker. Anne made them tea and sandwiches in the kitchen. At about 5.30 Mrs. Roach, whom Anne had met in the street that morning, came in to ask if she had any Bisto. She had none but let her have an Oxo cube and Mrs Roach left again, saying how good the stew smelt.

It was about half an hour after that, around 6 p.m., that the husband of a friend of Anne's, Helen O'Neill, telephoned. Helen, who already had three small daughters, was expecting a fourth child and had been in hospital for observation. While she had been there the three children had been staying with her sister, who could no longer have them because her father was ill. His illness however fortunately coincided with Helen's

84

release from hospital due that Tuesday. Now, however, Pat O'Neill telephoned to say that Helen was not coming out of hospital after all and to ask Anne if she could possibly take the three little girls in for a few days. Anne, who had a spare bunk bed and a table bed, agreed at once. It is in fact a tribute to the underlying strength of her marriage that she was, she says, able to agree so readily because she knew that Paddy was at home and would be able to help look after the children. Pat O'Neill, who lived in Stockwell, said he would bring them round right away.

Meanwhile Paddy and Giuseppe had been sleeping off their lunchtime drinking session.

"I don't remember much detail of the afternoon," says Paddy honestly, "and I think I dozed off on the sofa. I recall my wife was making the dinner when I came to my senses."

It was now six o'clock and as agreed they once again rang Hugh Maguire but again there was no answer. Paddy went upstairs to put on a clean shirt because he thought he would be taking Giuseppe round to see Hugh. Anne then telephoned Sean Tully to ask if he had seen Hugh over the weekend. Tully was there and said he himself had been in Birmingham for the weekend and had just come back but when he had had his tea he would go round to the Westbourne Terrace flat to try and find out what had happened, and also go to the pub where Hugh usually drank to see if anyone there had seen him. Anne, then seeing that Paddy had his coat on, asked him where he was going. He wouldn't tell her, simply saying that he was going out on an errand. In fact his destination was one which, in the light of later events, assumes some significance. He went to Harrow Road police station.

As Paddy said: "If I had told Anne and the others this they would have tried to stop me because I was very angry and upset at the time and with a few beers in me I might well have got nicked, so they would have tried to stop me."

Harrow Road police station was only about ten minutes' walk away. When he got there a young policewoman asked him what he wanted and he said he'd come to make enquiries about his brother, Hugh Maguire. He told her about the continued telephoning to the Westbourne Terrace flat and how there was never any reply. He said he was worried that Hugh, who had a bad knee, might even be lying dead on the floor. Then a funny thing happened.

The policewoman said that someone had already been making enquiries about Hugh, someone called Maureen Hughes. Paddy, who knew that Maureen Hughes had been a lodger of Hugh and Kathleen Maguire's, then asked if a policeman could come with him and if necessary help him break down the door of the flat. The policewoman said, as if she knew more than she was prepared to tell:

"There's no need for that."

Paddy got the impression that the matter was somehow in hand, and this upset him still further because he felt that his role as a senior member of the family was being usurped. The true explanation of Hugh's disappearance never occurred to him. In this state of mind he arrived home some time before 7 p.m.

There was a short period of considerable activity in the house. First of all, Sean Smyth, Anne's brother, had just arrived back at his usual time from his work as a tractor driver for a firm called Fitzpatrick, a subsidiary of Tarmac Limited, at a site at Wembley Stadium.

The front door was open at this time as is often the case with families which have children continually going in and out of the house. Sean Tully walked into the sitting-room. He had shattering news. He had been round to Hugh Maguire's Westbourne Terrace flat and the woman who lived in the flat above had told him that Hugh and his wife had been picked up by the police on Saturday morning and taken to Guildford for questioning and that no one had seen them since. They were all shocked, unable to understand why Hugh and his wife should have been arrested.

Pat O'Neill arrived with his three little daughters – Jacqueline aged 8, Sharon, aged 6 and Jean, aged 4. Anne asked them if they had had anything to eat.

"Tea and biscuits."

"Well, that'll fill them. Would you like some stew? Would you like some chips?"

"Chips and eggs."

86

Their father told them not be be cheeky. Anne said they could have what they wanted.

Sean Tully wrote down his telephone number on a sheet of paper.

"You've got my number. If there's anything I can do to help don't hesitate to phone me."

He left the house, got into his Ford Escort, the number of which was duly noted by the police on watch outside and drove away.

A British jury, and subsequently the Court of Criminal Appeal, were to find that it was in the course of the day described above that Anne and Paddy Maguire, their sons Vincent and Patrick, Giuseppe Conlon, Sean Smyth and Pat O'Neill had been unlawfully handling nitroglycerine in the house on Third Avenue, Harlesden. The judge summing up at their trial was to say that, if they had done so, they had probably done so in the afternoon or evening of this day.

The detailed account of their movements is their own. Some of the timings could be confirmed by independent witnesses. Sean Smyth's return from work, for instance, at around 6.30 was confirmed by one of his work-mates. Sean Tully, never to be charged with any offence, testified on oath to the movements of himself and, within a few minutes, those of Pat O'Neill. The judge did raise in the jury's mind a question as to whether the defendants' memory of the timing was in fact as precise as they claimed. But his own assessment of the probability that if nitroglycerine had been handled it had been handled in the afternoon or evening suggests – and he did at one point specifically so suggest – that their timings could be more or less accepted. Since Smyth and O'Neill were both to be convicted, nitroglycerine must have been somehow handled and totally disposed of in the half-hour between Smyth's return and Sean Tully's leaving the house. For thereafter the police had the house under surveillance, and no trace of nitroglycerine or any other bomb-making equipment was ever found there, though evidence to imply its presence was nevertheless soon to be forthcoming.

There was of course a theoretical possibility that Sean Tully could have taken away the nitroglycerine which they were supposed to have been handling, and indeed any other bomb factory equipment, when he left in his car at five minutes past seven under police observation. But this possibility was eliminated when, as shortly happened, Sean Tully and his car were tested for nitroglycerine and the tests proved to be negative.

Tests however made on some medical plastic gloves of Anne's and on the hands of Paddy, Vincent, Patrick, Giuseppe Conlon, Sean Smyth and Patrick O'Neill would appear to show something positive. Sir Michael Havers, prosecuting for the Crown was to say that they showed that the Maguires, alerted by the news from Belfast of the arrest of Gerard Conlon, had been disposing in a panic of the nitroglycerine used in the recent series of London and other bomb explosions. This was, he said, a question of "all hands to the pump": there had been a "gathering of the clans" for the purpose. What he never successfully explained was why one clan member, still suffering from the effects of a long lunchtime drinking session, should have left the proceedings to draw attention to himself at a police station in the middle of the most crucial hour of all.

8
More Arrests

While Detective Sergeants Hunter and Elbourn kept watch on 43 Third Avenue from the latter's car, activity in the household continued with what anyone taking a suspicious view might view as peculiar normality. Anne, with Jacky O'Neill and her own daughter Anne-Marie, went out to a shop called Jason's in the Harrow Road at the bottom of Third Avenue to buy the chips which the O'Neill children had asked for. Vincent had left the house some time before to go to the college where he studied in the evenings. John and Patrick were already out with friends by the time Anne got back with the children. She went into the kitchen and started frying the eggs, while Pat O'Neill sat beside his four-year-old daughter Jean at the kitchen table. Paddy Maguire came in and asked Pat if he would like to come out for a drink. Pat said he wanted to wait for a telephone call from his wife Helen, who had said she would ring about 8 o'clock. The telephone duly rang. It was Helen, and Anne went to reassure her that it would be no problem for her to look after the children.

"Paddy's not at work and will keep his eye on them. I could take a week off work if the worst comes to the worst."

After Pat had spoken to his wife the four men, Paddy, Pat, Sean Smyth and Giuseppe, decided to go off for a drink in the local pub, the Royal Lancer, as the start of Pat's journey home. He said goodbye to his children and told them he'd be back to see them at the weekend.

Anne-Marie then got out her pencils while the O'Neill children put on their night-dresses. Anne left them playing on the carpet in the living-room while she went out into the kitchen to sort out some laundry for the washing-machine.

The four men walked off through the new flats which had just been built opposite number 43 to the entrance to the Royal Lancer in Lancefield Street some 500 yards away. They were shadowed by Detective Sergeants Hunter and Elbourn who watched them enter and then returned to 43, Third Avenue. The pub was crowded and the four went up to the bar and ordered pints. Giuseppe was drinking lager again. Paddy said "Hallo" to a man with crutches, an old drinking crony named Harry Crawford, well-known in that pub. He made a mental note to go over later and buy him a pint. The talk, such as it was, was of Hugh's arrest and what lay behind it.

They were just into their second pint when Paddy was surprised to see his son John come into the bar. His first thought was that Anne must have sent for him. Then he noticed the two men following John.

They said they were police officers and asked them all to come outside.

"What's it all about, then?"

"We want you to help us with our enquiries."

"Will I be back to finish my pint?"

"Outside."

Outside there were police officers in uniform and a number of cars including a van with a dog in it. The four were lined up. Paddy says he said to the others:

"They are police officers, it's all right."

He was afraid that Smyth and Conlon, being more used to the R.U.C. in Belfast, would be jumpy. (The police account of what he said ran: "They are police, do as they say but tell them nothing.")

Paddy was put into a car with John and three police officers. It drove off to 43, Third Avenue, where John was taken out. One of the police officers followed him into the house. Another then got into the car which drove off to Harrow Road police station. Paddy was not to be free again for almost ten years.

About a quarter of an hour earlier Anne Maguire had been putting a couple of shirts into the washing-machine when the doorbell rang. The door was in fact open. Looking through the little window from her kitchen into the hall she saw some men and thought for a moment that the four had come back from their journey to the pub. Then a policeman opened the door into the kitchen.

"What is it?" she asked. She got no reply.

Standing in the hall was a police officer she was to come to know as Detective Chief Inspector David Munday.

"Do you know who we are?"

"You're the police."

"We are the Bomb Squad."

He asked her to put the children into a room at the back, because he didn't want them to be frightened. She lit the gas fire and told them to stay there and be quiet.

Munday said he wanted to search the premises.

"Certainly. All you'll find is a rubber bullet. I'll get it for you."

But he told her to sit down in the living-room. (When she had last been to see her family in Belfast she had brought back a rubber bullet found in the street, as a souvenir.)

"Do you know why we're here?"

"Is it because of Gerard Conlon?"

"What makes you think that?"

"Because his father arrived here today to get solicitors for his son. He's been picked up for the Guildford bombings."

"Yes, we know."

He asked if her husband was in and she told him he was over at the pub. It was then arranged that John, who had just come in from his youth club, would go over with the

91

police officers to fetch him. Anne told Munday who Paddy's companions were, explaining that her brother, Sean Smyth, had been in England for some months because the uncles for whom he had been working in Belfast had been assassinated by Protestant extremists. Vincent came into the room, back from his evening classes. One of the police officers asked him to come with him while he searched the house.

Munday's and Anne's accounts of the conversation that followed between them more or less agree.

"What do you think about these bombings?"

"It's terrible, killing innocent people. I have lived in this country for years. I don't want anything to do with these terrible people."

He asked her if she had anything to do with the I.R.A.

"Goodness, no, sir. I think they're terrible people."

"Have you had any explosives in this house?"

"No, sir."

"Have you ever handled explosives or assisted in the manufacture of bombs?"

"No, sir."

She was beginning to become agitated.

"Is my husband coming?"

"You'll see your husband in our time."

Munday asked her to get the children ready for bed, which she did. When she came down again Munday said to her:

"Get your coat. We are going to the station."

She was now very upset. John was back from his errand to the pub. Munday told her that the boys were coming to the police station too. She was worried about leaving the small children. Munday let her send John to fetch Mrs Roach, the neighbour. Anne had noticed a policeman backing out of the kitchen with the drawer which contained among other things some plastic gloves which she used when having to put on her hands cream medically prescribed for her dermatitis. She said to him:

"What are you taking that drawer for? There's nothing in there."

He did not reply.

A policewoman said to her:

"Are you ready?"

Someone said something about the boys' coming and Anne cried out:

"These children are innocent!"

Theresa Roach, her neighbour, came in and she told her what was happening and asked her to look after the small children. She turned to the policewoman:

"Will I be long? I'm so worried about the children."

"Don't worry about the children. They'll be all right, and you won't be long, love. You'll be back soon."

The eldest Maguire son's, Vincent's, account of the day is the frankest and most human. He had got back early that afternoon from his work as an assistant gas fitter with the North Thames Gas Board and found only John and a friend of his from school at the house. But he also noticed a small suitcase in the front room. (His father, Paddy, and his Uncle Giuseppe – though he didn't know this – were out at the pub by this time.) John didn't know whose the suitcase was so they opened it and saw only clothes, underwear, socks and a sponge-bag. "It smelt a bit," he said.

They had something to eat and went into the back room where Sean Smyth's bed was, to play cards. It was a room which Anne-Marie sometimes used as a playroom and some of the cards were on the floor. Looking for them there, Vincent found a long stick of chalk under the bed which he threw back again. In the end, he, John and his friend did not play cards but went upstairs to play records. When his mother came back they discussed the possible owner of the suitcase and Vincent remembers Anne's speculation that it might belong to an alcoholic and even possibly to Giuseppe, in which case she didn't really want him there because of his illness. Later, after his father and his Uncle Giuseppe had come back from the pub, his mother came upstairs to tell him what had happened but he did not go down until John came to say Giuseppe wanted to see him.

"I went downstairs and shook hands with him. It hurt. My Dad was a little drunk and was yapping on about something. Then Giuseppe said there had been no word from Hugh or his wife over the weekend. Dad was a bit upset at this and they phoned Hugh's house to find out what happened . . . Then Dad phoned the solicitors and tried to do everything. Giuseppe was getting a bit annoyed because he wanted to do the talking. Dad's a bit like that when he's had something to drink. The solicitors apparently said they'd phone back and Dad kept telling Giuseppe to rest himself. Giuseppe said could he phone his wife in Belfast, and he did that. Then Dad spoke and he was all upset about Hugh and Gerry and started crying. Then him and Giuseppe were arguing about solicitors. Eventually Giuseppe said: 'Oh, I'm going, I can't stay here with you, Paddy.' My Mum walked in and she persuaded him to stay and not to be so stupid.'' (This telephone conversation with Sarah Conlon in Belfast was placed a little later in time in Paddy's memory, which in the circumstances may not have been so reliable as Vincent's.)

Vincent left for his evening class on gas-fitting at Paddington Technical College just after half-past five. He got there at six and left again at 8.30. After getting off his number 18 bus, he walked up Third Avenue and noticed two black police vans and a couple of small cars outside the house. A man was standing outside and there was a small crowd there. "I thought there must be something up."

He walked up to the front door and saw men standing in the passageway and caught a glimpse of a dog. "My mind went blank and I could not think what was happening."

One of the men in plain clothes outside said: "All right, mate, walk on."

"What do you mean? I live here."

The man then shouted in at the doorway:

"Here's another one of them."

When his mother saw him she said: "Look at this," making a gesture towards the search that was going on. She had looked stunned and worried.

"What are they looking for?"

"Bombs."

"It's a joke, isn't it?"

Then he was asked to go upstairs and help the officers search. He spent about three-quarters of an hour going through all the rooms with them. One had "a sort of detector" and another a black labrador dog.

When he came downstairs again he could hear his mother crying in the kitchen. A policeman in the hallway said to him:

"Get your coat, son, and your two brothers."

Patrick had left the house just after six to go to a Youth Club run by a Mr. Crotford. He liked to get down there early and hang around the entrance with his mates until a Mr. O'Leary came to open the door. Inside they played snooker or cards or table-tennis and listened to records. He left again about eight with several of his mates; Vincent, on his way back from his evening class, spotted them in a group on the corner of Farrant Street and Third Avenue. They were standing there when they saw a line of police coming up the road and Patrick's first instinct was that they were coming after them. At that moment he noticed a car drive up to the house, and was surprised to glimpse his father and his brother John inside. He turned and ran to the house. The door was shut and he had to knock on it. A policewoman opened it and said:

"Yeah?"

"I live here."

She pulled him into the kitchen. He sat down at the table, at which John was already sitting. Another policewoman came in and, a little later, another police officer. After a while Patrick said:

"What the fuck's going on? What are you doing with my Mum?"

"She's in the front room with other officers," said the policewoman.

"What are you doing here anyway? Why are you searching the place?"

John said: "Have you got a search warrant?"

The police officer replied: "One of the others has a search warrant."

The policewoman, obviously puzzled by their London accents, asked:

"Are you English or Irish?"

Patrick said: "Oh, that's it, is it? You think we are bombers? Well, I'd like to blow up Harrow Road Police Station and Scotland Yard."

Patrick, who was then only 13, says he said this because he was becoming so annoyed at the way the police were carrying on. "They were going on as if they owned the house. Before this, too, she'd made tea for all the police, and toast and biscuits, and not until she'd given it to them did she ask us if we wanted anything. Also, when I asked her for a drink of water and tried to get up, she said: 'Sit down, you little bastard.'"

John too was getting riled.

"I've got some money upstairs," he said to the police. "I hope it's still there when you go, 'cos if it's not there'll be some fucking trouble."

Patrick said: "It wouldn't surprise me if these cunts planted something in the place."

In the laconic language of a routine police report: "Nothing of relevance was said after that by the two youths."

Soon afterwards their mother was brought in crying. Told that the boys were being taken off to the police station, she cried out:

"Don't touch them. They're English!"

She and the three boys were then taken off to Paddington Green Police Station.

There the police conscientiously applied themselves to the task of interrogating suspect terrorists.

Young Patrick stoutly kept his end up with Detective Sergeant Hunt.

"Are you a Catholic family?"

"Yes."

"What do you think about these people throwing bombs?"

"I don't know."

"When these bombings occur, what happens in your house, do you all talk about it?"

"No."

"Have you any idea why we have come to your house?"

"Because we're Irish, I suppose."

"But there's hundreds of Irish round where you live."

"I don't know."

. . . "Do your parents talk about bombing?"

"Mum and Dad think it's bad, all those people being killed for nothing."

"Do you know what explosives look like?"

"Yes, I've seen it on the telly."

"There was a reel of black tape in the lounge, who does it belong to?"

"It's mine, I brought it from school to stick things up on my wall."

"Do your Mum and Dad ask you to take parcels to anybody?"

"No."

"Where did your brother get the coin with the hole in it?"

"I don't know, I've never seen it before."

He was asked about the tape again. "I stick things on the wall with it, sometimes when parcels come, I open them by mistake, then I re-seal the parcels using the tape."

"Do many parcels come to the house?"

"Quite a lot from John Moore's."

"What is in them?"

"Toys and things."

Detective Sergeant Hunt then applied himself to Vincent. "Have you any idea why we came to your house?"

"When I arrived home and saw all the policemen there, I thought Mum and Dad were having a ruck."

"Do they argue a lot?"

"Not a lot, but when they do, we get the squad cars and all that."

. . . "What are your personal feelings about these bombs being thrown?"

"It hasn't affected me yet, I only know what I've read in the papers. I wouldn't like it to happen to my relatives."

Asked if he had known that Giuseppe Conlon was coming, Vincent replied:

"I didn't. Nobody did. He just arrived."

Asked if he knew Gerry Conlon, Vincent replied:

"Yes, I've known him about thirteen years."

"Do you know he's been arrested?"

"Yes."

"Are you surprised?"

"Yes, I am, really."

"Does he strike you as the kind of person who would lob bombs through windows?"

"I don't know, maybe he was pushed into it. He could have been threatened. That's how they operate."

"How well did you know him?"

"He was my older cousin. I used to look up to him."

"How would he come to get involved?"

"You have to be involved when you're in Ireland and once you're in, you can't get out. You know as well as I do there are I.R.A. all over the country. You can't ban them because you can't tell who they are. That's why the soldiers are being troubled."

"Do you know what explosives look like?"

"Not really."

"Have you seen any explosives or bombs in your house?"

"No."

"So it follows, you've never handled any explosives?"

"No, I never have."

John answered similar questions in a similar manner, coming out quite openly with such details of family life or his own activity as he was pressed for, but displaying a certain off-hand confidence and puzzled indifference towards the fact that such questions were being asked at all. Asked what he thought of the bombings in London, he replied:

"I don't care much. I'm not really interested."

Talking about Giuseppe's arrival that afternoon, he said:

"I ain't seen him since the summer. He just come over from Ireland. I saw a small check suitcase in the living-room. Me Mum was in the kitchen. I didn't stay, I shot out, me girl was waiting outside. I went down the shops and got back about 6 o'clock. I didn't go in the front room, but shot out again. I didn't get back till half-eight just as you arrived."

"Whose are the rebel records in your house?"

"Me Mum's, she's had them a long time. We like the words to them."

"Does you Dad play them?"

"Not much, me Mum does."

"What would you like to see happen in Ireland?"

"We think the troops should be brought out."

"Have you ever taken part in any demonstrations in Ireland?"

"Only on Internment Night. We all ran into the streets. The young kids frightened lorry-drivers by holding their hands in their coat pockets as though they had guns."

"Have you ever taken part in anything like that over here?"

"No."

"Has your family?"

"Not that I know of."

"What are the clear plastic gloves used for? They were in the kitchen."

"I don't know."

"Have you seen them?"

"Yes, I suppose Mum uses them for cleaning the floors."

"Have you ever used them?"

"I used a pair once. I made a water-bomb out of it."

The first questions to Anne were more specific. Certain items found in the house at Third Avenue seemed to the police to require explanation. The rubber bullet brought back from Belfast had already aroused their interest. Anne had now told them its exact provenance. Her sister had given it to her when she went over to Belfast for a week's holiday that summer. It was a mildly grim reminder of the sort of thing people had been living through there. During a riot some time earlier Anne's sister had seen her small boy run into the street and had run out after him to snatch him back, but she had been hit on the thigh by this rubber bullet which she had kept and, this summer, given to Anne as a souvenir. Other souvenirs found in the house were some leather wallets which had puzzled the police. These had been given to her by her brother-in-law on the same holiday: sold originally for the Prisoners' Dependent Fund in Long Kesh and given to her as, in his view, interesting souvenirs of troubled times for her children in London. But more specifically still the police were interested in the plastic gloves which they had found in a drawer in Anne's kitchen.

"Whose are they?"

"Mine. I use the plastic gloves around the house as I have a skin disease and use ointment on them and the gloves stop me getting ointment around the house."

"When did you last wear them?"

"I wear them every day."

"Does anyone else wear them?"

"No, only me, for my hands."

"Are your hands still bad, then?"

"Not now."

"Do you use them for washing up?"

"No, just for making beds and things like that, to keep the ointment off the sheets. I've got some rubber gloves for washing up and heavy housework."

"Have you got any of the ointment left?"

"Yes, it's in the kitchen somewhere . . . "

"Where did you get the gloves from?"

"I don't know the name of the place, it's a cut-price shop in the Edgware Road."

The skin disease from which Anne had suffered intermittently for years was dermatitis. The cream for it had been prescribed for her by a doctor at St Mary's Hospital, Harrow Road. An affidavit exists to this effect.

Munday had also had his attention caught by some fingertips which appeared to have been cut off a pair of black woollen gloves. Patrick had done this to make mittens some time before. Some black insulating tape and two wigs found in the house also seemed of interest. There had been a time in the '60s when the occasional wearing of wigs had been a sort of fashion, but police attention was perhaps particularly directed towards these because of a notification circulated to police stations that Marlene Coyle, the known I.R.A. terrorist, was thought at times to have worn a wig. In fact

Anne's answer to Munday's question as to whether she wore them often had been:

"No, I never wore them – one belonged to a friend's girl-friend and the other one I gave to Anne-Marie to play with."

"Mrs. Maguire," Munday asked outright, "have you ever handled explosives?"

Anne replied, according to the police record:

"Oh! Jesus God, sir. I would never touch anything like that. I would never do anything like that. We are not people like that."

In Harrow Road police station to which the four men had been taken, similar questions and answers were registered.

Paddy was asked:

"Are either you or your wife a member of any political organisation?"

"I have nothing to do with anything like that. I am a member of the Royal British Legion."

"Are any of your household involved in politics?"

"No."

"Do you ever have friends in the house?"

"I haven't got any friends."

"Why is that?"

"Well, I'm a loner."

"What about your wife?"

"The only people would be women. Who they are I don't know."

Paddy added that he was not at the moment speaking to his wife. Asked how long this had been going on, he replied:

"This has been going on and off for the past two years or so. We have a row one month, and then it gets better. We haven't been speaking for the last couple of weeks."

Asked how often he or his wife went out, he replied that they very seldom did so, though Anne occasionally went to Bingo.

"So there's nothing that goes on in your house that you would not be aware of?"

Here the police record has Paddy replying:

"Well, I suppose not."

Paddy, however, is keen to reject what he regards as the implication of such a reply. "As far as I can remember," he says, "I said, 'Definitely no' giving the emphasis that I am the governor. That's what I like to show."

Asked if he ever discussed the present political situation concerning the I.R.A. with his wife, he replied, according to the police record:

"I've just told you I don't talk to my wife about anything and certainly have nothing to do with anything like that."

He maintains that what he said was: "We never discuss any politics or religion in the house."

This whole interview with Paddy had lasted about an hour and a half. Not long afterwards, about 1 o'clock in the morning, Detective Chief Inspector Munday himself arrived from questioning Anne at Paddington Green station. He said to Paddy:

"Mr. Maguire, you must realise that we did not pick your house out of all the houses in the area without good reason."

"No, I'm sure you didn't, but I haven't handled any explosives, and never had any in the house."

"Mr. Maguire, what would you say if I told you that I have information that a member of your household was involved in these bombings.?"

"Well, sir, I can tell you it has nothing to do with me."

"What about your wife? What are her views on these bombings?"

"She is sick of it, the same as everyone is."

Munday records himself as saying to Paddy:

"I get the impression that you think your wife may be able to help us more than yourself in this matter."

He records Paddy as replying:

"I am not saying anything of the sort. If that's what you think, you can, but I don't know everything she does, do I?"

Paddy denies categorically that Munday said this to him about Anne. However, Munday might well have been at least thinking it because he would have been told by the Surrey police on the basis of Hill and Conlon's statements that Anne had definitely taken part in the Guildford bombings. Paddy simply records that after he had been asked about the presence of Giuseppe Conlon in his house that night, and had explained it, Munday had stood up and that he, Paddy, had said to him:

"Well, what's going to happen now, then? Am I here for the night?"

"You'll be here for a while yet until we finish these enquiries."

"What about my wife and children?"

"They're in Paddington Green."

"Who is looking after my daughter and Pat O'Neill's girls and the house?"

Paddy says that Munday showed some understanding for this question, and replied that a policewoman would be spending the night there. Paddy felt relieved.

It was about the only cause for relief for any of those being held in Harrow Road, with the exception of Pat O'Neill. While the police were going through the routine procedure of taking his "antecedents", O'Neill burst out:

"I haven't done anything. I came over for a drink."

He was asked:

"Have you ever been involved in the handling of explosives?"

"No. I don't believe in them."

The apparent absurdity of continuing to hold him, given the circumstances of his presence in the house, seems to have struck the police. After completing the prescribed procedure for the swabbing of his hands and subsequent test for explosives – a procedure applied to all those being held in both police stations – they let him go home. Sean Smyth was not to be so lucky. He too was asked:

"Have you ever been involved in the handling of explosives or manufacturing of bombs?"

"No, never."

But he was to be held overnight, and indeed for many years to come.

The most unlucky of all was Giuseppe Conlon, father of Gerard. Cautioned in the charge room at Harrow Road police station about 11.30 that night, he was asked:

"Do you know why you are here?"

He replied:

"Look, I've only just arrived here. I come over from Belfast to see my son. He's down in Guildford, you probably know all about him. I suppose that's why you roped me in."

A little surprisingly, perhaps, the policeman who was interrogating him, one of those who had had 43 Third Avenue under observation since 7 o'clock that evening, said:

"To be honest, I didn't know your son was at Guildford, but acting on information we raided that address looking for explosives and you were there. Now I must ask you a few questions."

This irritated Giuseppe for a moment.

"Don't tell me you didn't know anything about my son. That's why you've arrested me. Anyway you must do what you think right so go ahead."

He too got the now routine question:

"Have you ever handled any explosives?"

"No, I've got nothing to do with that sort of thing."

"Do you have any access to explosives?"

"No, of course not. I don't know what my son's done, but I have nothing to do with that sort of thing."

"Why did you come here?"

"I told you: my son's solicitor asked me to come over because he thought I might be able to help."

Giuseppe too was to be held that night. He was never to be released.

The required procedure for the subsequent testing of the hands of all those held in both Paddington Green and Harrow Road police stations that night was as follows: each hand was first wiped with a dry swab of cotton wool to test for explosive traces on the skin and then with a swab inpregnated with ether to test for the presence of explosive traces beneath the skin; fingernails were scraped for further traces; the resulting swabs and scrapings were placed in separate plastic bags which were labelled with the name of the person from whom they had been taken, and sealed in their presence. An unused swab of the cotton wool applied was retained as a control. The hands of Anne and her three sons in Paddington Green police station were swabbed and scraped by Detective Sergeant Kenneth Day of New Scotland Yard. The hands of the four men at Harrow Road were similarly swabbed and scraped by Detective Sergeant Lawrence Vickery. All eight sets of swabs were then conveyed to New Scotland Yard and handed-in at 2.30 in the morning on December 4 to Police Constable David Farr of the Central Office there. Four and a half hours later they were conveyed to the Government Research Laboratory at Woolwich where they were handed over to the Principal Scientific Officer, a Mr. Douglas Higgs. At 8 a.m. of that same day Detective Sergeant Vickery returned to the house in Third Avenue, Harlesden to search the garden and dustbins for anything suspicious. He returned with nothing more intimidating than a roll of insulating tape, a transistor radio battery and the black woollen gloves from which Patrick had cut off the fingers to make mittens. But he was back there again at 2 o'clock that afternoon, when he collected from the kitchen Anne's disposable plastic gloves. These were brought back to New Scotland Yard where, that same day, December 4, they were "locked in a cupboard". Five days later, on December 9, they were handed by Detective Sergeant Vickery to Detective Sergeant Lewis of New Scotland Yard who "later that day" took them to the Government Research Laboratory at Woolwich. But a lot more had happened by then.

On December 4 Anne and Paddy Maguire, Giuseppe Conlon, Sean Smyth and Pat O'Neill had been taken down to Guildford. John, Vincent and Patrick had been temporarily allowed to go home.

9

Forensic Science at Work

By the afternoon of Thursday December 5 the official results of the tests made on the hand swabs had come through from the Government Laboratory Woolwich. They indicated positive traces of nitroglycerine on the hands or under the finger-nails of Paddy Maguire, Giuseppe Conlon, Sean Smyth, Pat O'Neill and two of the three Maguire sons, Vincent and Patrick.* Only John and Anne Maguire's hands were clear. But Anne in any case found herself being held for murder on the strength of Hill's and Gerry Conlon's confessions. She was in fact the first to be confronted with the swab results. At Guildford, throughout the afternoon of Wednesday and again on this Thursday morning she had been consistently protesting her innocence.

*The detailed results were curiously varied. Giuseppe Conlon and Sean Smyth were said to be the most heavily contaminated. All Giuseppe's swabs and nail scrapings were positive with the exception of the dry swab of his left hand. All Smyth's swabs and scrapings were positive. All O'Neill's nail scrapings were positive, all his swabs negative. Paddy Maguire's nail scrapings and the dry swab of his right hand were positive. The rest were negative. Vincent and Patrick were positive on their right-hand nail scrapings only.

Events

"You," Detective Inspector Powell of the Surrey force had said to her the day before, "were one of a number of people who came to Guildford on Saturday October 5, 1974 and planted the bombs in the Horse and Groom and Seven Stars public houses and caused the death of five innocent people."

"No, sir, I don't know what you mean, sir, I've never been to Guildford till you brought me here."

"Then why would Gerry Conlon, your nephew, make such an evil accusation against you?"

"I don't know, sir. He's lying, sir. Gerry Conlon's got no reason to say that."

"Why has Hill involved you?"

"I don't know, sir. They're both lying. My conscience is clear."

At this point on the Wednesday afternoon Hill himself had been brought in to confront her by Detective Chief Superintendent Simmons. Simmons said to Hill:

"When did you last see her?"

Hill replied: "The last time I saw her was in Guildford."

Anne Maguire protested:

"He didn't see me."

"I'm telling you the truth," said Hill and was taken from the room by Simmons.

Detective Sergeant Robinson, who was helping Inspector Powell with the interview, then reminded her that Gerry Conlon too had said that his "Auntie Annie" had shown him how to make bombs and been on the bombing expedition.

"You are his Auntie Annie. Does he have another Auntie Annie?"

"No, sir. I am his only Auntie Annie."

Anne says that in this the police record is inaccurate and she is almost certainly right since she knew that he had another Aunt Ann living in Manchester.

"Well, how do you explain that?"

"I can't, sir. He's lying. I don't know anything at all about it. I don't know why he should mention my name."

Detective Chief Superintendent Simmons then came back into the room, bringing Conlon himself this time. Conlon

107

looked at Anne Maguire and said in what the police record describes as a "raised" voice:

"I was not the first to mention your name."

"Gerry, I have got four children."

Conlon repeated: "I wasn't the first to mention your name."

Simmons said to Conlon:

"When did you last see her?"

"I've already told you, it's in my statement."

Conlon's own account of what happened at this meeting sounds slightly more realistic than the police record and an amalgamation of the two probably conveys a fairly truthful picture of what happened.

"Grundy said to me we are going to see someone who I know and I was to say what I said in my statement. I was taken by Grundy and Jeremy to another room and pushed inside. In the room was my Aunt Annie, she looked at me and said:

" 'Gerry, tell them I haven't done anything.'

"I said: 'I know.'

"Grundy said to me: 'Tell her she did it.'

"I just said something like: " 'I'm sorry, Annie, I'm sorry.' "

(Anne Maguire says that he did not apologise like this, but simply said: "You tell the truth.")

Simmons and Conlon then left the room. Anne's interrogation that day had ended after five hours, with a police officer's removal of her wedding ring which had split but had not been off her finger in seventeen years.

The following day they had this new shock for her: the results of the hand swab tests from the Government Laboratory at Woolwich. Detective Sergeant Robinson suddenly said to her:

"Members of your family, your husband and two sons have got traces of explosives on their hands. How do you account for that?"

"I can't, sir. I can't believe it, sir, I've never had explosives in my house or garden."

"Then how can you account for traces of explosives being found on the hands of your family?"

"I can't, sir. None of us are involved in anything, that's the truth, sir."

"When did you last go to confession?"

"In October."

"Are you a practising Catholic?"

"I'm a Catholic, but I don't go to church too often."

"When did you go to confession prior to October?"

"About a year ago."

"So after coming to Guildford and murdering five innocent people you later went to confession?"

"No, sir. It's not like that, sir. I didn't murder anybody. My conscience is clear. I'm innocent."

"Do you know anyone by the name of Armstrong?"

"No, sir. I don't know anyone by that name."

"He is one of the bombers and he says you were in Guildford with them."

"No, sir, it's all lies, they are all telling lies."

And the interrogation which proceeded intermittently throughout that day concluded in the evening with Detective Inspector Powell saying to her:

"Look, Annie, we've got children involved now. What possible explanation can there be for them having traces of explosives on them?"

"I don't know, sir. They're innocent. None of us are involved."

"It could be they may be charged. These are your children."

"Then they'll be innocent, sir. We'll all be. If this is my punishment I'll have to accept it."

"Punishment for what?"

"For nothing, sir – God's."

Anne Maguire's own account of this last reply differs slightly from the police record. She maintains that what she said was: "If this is what happens to innocent people then God help us." The inference is substantially the same.

It was on the following day that Paddy Maguire, who was also now in the cells at Guildford police station, received the news of the test results. Told that certain questions were now going to be put to him in the light of the laboratory findings, he replied simply:

"You can ask me what you like."

Told that it was nitroglycerine which had been found on his hands, he said:

"That's the liquid stuff, isn't it?"

"Yes, nitroglycerine is a liquid but it is also the constituent of the normal gelignite-type explosive."

"Well, none of it means anything to me. I've never seen explosives."

"Have you ever to your knowledge handled any explosive substance?"

"No, never. Well, yes, in the army. I was in the Royal Inniskilling Fusiliers. I was taught to throw grenades."

"We're talking about the recent past, not your army days."

"Well, no, sir, you must know I've never done such a thing."

"I know nothing of the sort . . . We are saying that traces of explosives have been found on your hands, which to us means that you have handled some explosives in the recent past."

"I can't help you, sir. I've never touched the stuff."

Sean Smyth, Anne Maguire's brother, had his first formal interview with the Surrey police just after the results of the tests had come through, but these were not at first communicated to him.

"You know, of course," Detective Chief Inspector Horton had said to him, "your sister has been arrested for being involved in the Guildford bombing incident?"

"Jesus, mister, she's a dear girl, she wouldn't do anything like that."

"But other persons admit their part, and say she was there as well."

"I don't believe you."

A short time later Horton was back again.

"I have now in my possession a copy of the forensic report which proves you and a number of other people where you live have been handling nitroglycerine."

"That's not true, sir."

"Do you know that nitroglycerine is an explosive?"

"Yes, I've heard of it."

Horton showed him the report but, since Smyth could not read, it could, as he remarked, say anything.

Horton assured him that the contents were what he said they were, adding:

"How come you had this substance on your hands?"

"I have not got it on my hands."

"Have you recently had any reason whatsoever to handle explosives?"

"No, only oil . . . I came over here to work, and I have not touched the explosives."

"There is positive evidence that you have."

"No, not on my hands. It must be that oil."

"I have given you every opportunity to give an explanation to the report which said you have handled the explosives; do you have any explanation?"

"None, sir. I wish to God I had."

That afternoon Horton came back to Smyth yet again:

"I have given you a couple of hours to think over what you have been told. Have you any explanation?"

"On my children's life, sir, I know nothing about bombs and neither does my sister."

Giuseppe Conlon too was to be asked throughout the day for an explanation. From the first he said simply:

"There is no explanation. I've never had anything to do with explosives."

"We have certain evidence that you were in possession of explosives on or about December 3."

"It can't be right. I only got here that day."

Asked over and over again if he had ever handled explosives he answered over and over again:

"No, I haven't. I don't even know what they look like. I've never handled any explosives in my life."

And he continued to repeat that answer as the questions continued to be repeated to him that afternoon and on the following morning.

It was only on the following morning, Saturday, December

7, that Pat O'Neill, who had been set at liberty after his hand swab test early on the previous Tuesday morning, was arrested. He had after all only been in the Maguire house a very short time when the police got there, and must have seemed such an unlikely suspect in these circumstances that, even with the powers of the Prevention of Terrorism Act at their disposal, the police saw no risk in letting him go free. And, if justification of the rightness of this decision had seemed necessary, the fact that he had done nothing suspicious in the interval or tried to abscond during his four days at liberty would have seemed to provide it. Now it was he who was in for a shock. He was asked at Brixton police station:

"You remember when you were taken from Maguire's address last Tuesday?"

"Yes, sir."

"You remember at the police station your hands were swabbed and scrapings were taken from under your finger-nails?"

"Yes."

"Those swabs and scrapings have been examined by scientists and they say that those swabs and scrapings show a positive reaction to explosives."

"What, what? That's impossible."

"Have you ever handled explosives?"

"No, I don't know what it looks like."

"Do you accept what I say, that traces of explosives were found on your hands?"

"Yes, sir. If you say it's there it must be, but I don't know how it got there."

After giving a detailed account of how he had come to the Maguires' house with his three children on the evening of December 3, he was brought once again back to the awkward fact of the laboratory findings with:

"So we come back to where did these traces of explosives, which were found on your hands, come from?"

"I can't explain that. I wish I could."

"Would it surprise you to know that practically all the

adults and some of the children who were in that house had traces of explosives on their hands?"

"Not the children, surely?"

"My information is that they were positive. That's why I'm asking you if you picked up anything in the house."

"No, I'm sure I didn't."

"Did you see any explosives in the house?"

"No, I wouldn't know what it was anyway."

"Look, there is no doubt that traces of explosives were found on your hands. That means that you must have handled it. The question is, did you handle the stuff knowingly or not?"

"Honestly, I didn't handle any explosives."

"Had anyone given you a package or anything like that, to take somewhere and you didn't know the contents?"

"Oh, I see what you mean. No, I've not done that."

"Are you sure, you might have carried something quite innocently, not realising it was explosives."

"No, honestly, no one has asked me to take anything anywhere for them."

"Have you been threatened at all or maybe your family has been threatened? That's why you handled explosives?"

"No, honestly, I've heard that people may be threatened but honestly I haven't."

"So we come back to the original question, how did these traces of explosives get on your hands?"

"I just don't know. I wish I did, but I don't."

O'Neill was then taken to Guildford where he continued to give the same answers to the same questions.

". . . But you have still not explained how explosives came to be on your hands."

"I don't know. I haven't touched any explosive . . . I haven't seen any explosive . . . I've never had any of that stuff on my hands."

He spent the weekend in his cell, pondering what appeared to be the inexplicable. Then on the following Monday afternoon he asked to see Detective Sergeant Jeremy of the Surrey police. It is difficult not to find pathos in what he had to say.

"I've been racking my brains down here, and the only

thing I can think of is that I did use the toilet. Whether it was before I had a cup of tea or after I can't remember. But I washed my hands after and dried them on a towel there. That's the only thing I did. Whether I could have got it off the towel or not I don't know."

Both Vincent and Patrick who, like O'Neill, had not been held after their initial detention on the Tuesday evening were now, like O'Neill, taken down to Guildford.

It was on the car journey down that Detective Inspector Harvey told Vincent that traces of explosives had been found under his nails. Vincent's reply was:

"Can't be. I don't know anything about it."

A Detective Constable Bray, also in the car, said:

"You must know something about it if traces of it have been found under your finger-nails."

"What's it look like?"

"What's what look like?"

"The explosives."

"I can only tell you that traces of explosives were found under your finger-nails."

"How do I know that?"

"Because when you reach Guildford I will show you the report."

And at 6.15 p.m. that day Vincent was indeed shown the report and told that it also implicated his brother Patrick, his father, his uncle William (Sean) Smyth and Pat O'Neill. (The name of his other uncle was omitted.)

Vincent said:

"I don't know. I can't understand it."

He kept shaking his head.

Detective Constable Bray asked him:

"Is there anything you can remember touching?"

". . . The only thing I can remember is a candle thing I found under Sean [Smyth's] bed . . . about eight inches long and smooth like a sort of wax. I could get my fingers right round it. I don't know what it was, it had bits broken off one end. It was like a big candle really."

"What were you doing under the bed in the first place?"

"I was looking for the cards. Most of them were on the

table at the bottom of the bed and some were on the floor. I sort of swept my hand about under the bed and pulled this thing out. Bits came off it as I was holding it."

"What hand did you have it in?"

"My right hand, I would think. Yes, my right hand."

"Did you tell anyone or show anyone this item?"

"No, I put it back."

"When was it that you found it?"

"It must have been about 2 p.m. on that Tuesday."

"It seems a bit strange to me. I have asked you if you touched anything unusual and you have been denying touching anything. Now you tell us about this."

"It slipped my mind. A lot has been happening."

Thirteen-year-old Patrick's first response when asked at Carter Street, South London police station, that Saturday afternoon, if he remembered the tests carried out the previous Tuesday was:

"Yes, with the smelly stuff."

"Do you know why the tests were made?"

"To see if I had been touching bombs or something."

"Well, that test has proved positive in your case. Nitro-glycerine has been found under your finger-nails."

"That's stupid," said Patrick.

He was driven down to Guildford. On the way down he was again asked for an explanation and replied:

"Well, it's daft. I never touched any nitro-whatever it is. They must have made a mistake. The police are not always right."

He was reminded that it was not the police but a civilian scientist who had found that he had touched nitroglycerine. He was further told that when he got to Guildford he would see from the report that not only he but members of his family and friends had been in contact with explosives.

"Who?"

"Your Dad, old Mr. Conlon, your Mother" (this was not then true) "Vincent and Mr. O'Neill."

"That's impossible. There is no explosive. What does it look like?"

"I am sure you would know if you handled explosives."

"I have nothing more to say. I am not a liar. I have been brought up to tell the truth."

At Guildford, Patrick was shown the report compiled by a government scientist named Elliott at Woolwich. His comment:

"I just don't know what to think but the man must be wrong."

Eventually he too, desperately began to try and find some explanation for what otherwise appeared to be inexplicable:

"I don't know, maybe I got it in Murphy's hut."

"When was that?"

"About a month ago. Me and my mates went in there to make some tea."

"Stuff as dangerous as that wouldn't be left in an unlocked hut. Where else do you think you could have touched it then?"

"Might be at school in chemistry."

"I am sure they wouldn't let young boys play about with nitroglycerine. You must have touched something in the house."

"Well, I haven't."

Later that evening, Patrick asked one of his interrogators:

"What's happened to my Mum and Dad?"

"Your mother has been charged with murder and your father with handling explosives."

"I don't believe you," he said. He then began to cry. But he soon stopped and, when asked if he knew what the stick of white material was that Vincent said he had found under Sean Smyth's bed, he replied at once:

"Yes, chalk. I got it from school. The gym master gave it to me."

The next day he and Vincent were freed. No charge was in fact to be brought against either of them for over two months. By that time something had begun to go wrong with the picture of the truth about the Guildford bombings which the police had imagined themselves to be successfully reconstructing.

The dialogue in all the above exchanges has been taken from official police records. What has been omitted is what is by definition likely to be missing from any such police records, namely the complaints of those interrogated that they were in varying degrees and at intervals subjected to physical humiliation, intimidation and occasional actual violence.

The complaints in this case could seem to be particularly convincing since, though every one of the Maguire Seven alleged improper duress in some degree, none ever admitted or could be brought to fabricate a story to the effect that they had unlawfully handled nitroglycerine. The complaints were quite unnecessary except as a statement of the truth. There can have been no self-interested motivation for them in making them. Indeed they were if anything to count against the defendants at the trial for the judge was in one instance to suggest that they were an attempt "in a rather stupid, muddled sort of way to discredit the police . . . You have seen the officers . . . Are they," he asked, "the sort of officers that you think would behave in this fashion?" In the second half of the 1980s such reliance on the overt respectability of the police might carry less weight with a jury than it did then.

Sean Smyth stated on oath in court:

"Hughes smacked me about the face. Hughes pushed me in the ribs and punched me every time I did not answer a question. Mr Simmons hit me on the face very hard. Hughes and Simmons hit me very hard on the cheeks. I had no marks of injury or bruises. I did not complain about violence to the magistrates."

The officers concerned denied on oath that they had done such things.

At one point Smyth says, he was picked up and told he would be thrown out of a window. (This is a threat which other people interrogated by the Guildford police were to record independently.) He alleged that one of the police officers said that if he did not answer a question they would telephone the British Army in Belfast and get them to inform the I.R.A. and he (Smyth) knew what would then happen to his family.

Again all such allegations were denied on oath.

Paddy Maguire and Pat O'Neill both testify quite calmly, to this day in exactly the same terms as they did then to beatings and abuse of a similar sort. Vincent gave the following account in Court on oath of what happened to him:

"I was hit and threatened. I heard Patrick screaming. I was threatened in the car going to Guildford, I was beaten in the police station. It was upstairs I was threatened with violence by Harvey in the presence of Bray and Standon. I was threatened that I would get a beating from Harvey. Standon was there when I was hit. Harvey ran at me with his forearm against my throat up against the wall. He twisted my head. He hit me in the stomach. It hurt and I cried. There was no other violence. I decided to tell the story about the candle when I heard Patrick scream."

All these officers denied the allegations on oath, just as Vincent had asserted them on oath.

Vincent's is the only instance in which it might be said that pressure allegedly led to an admission, but the only admission was that he had found this candle-like object which he later, on being returned to his home after interrogation, actually showed to police officers to be a piece of chalk.

Thirteen-year-old Patrick's screaming was because, as he alleged, he was also being hit.

"They kept on asking me about the nitroglycerine," he says, "and every time I denied it the bloke hit me. He slapped me round the face and cuffed me at the back of the neck and on the head. I did not fall over, I gripped the table . . . I did tell them about the chalk. In fact the gym master had not given it to me but I got it from the class for my sister, Anne-Marie."

Anne Maguire's account of what happened to her runs as follows:

". . . They kept telling me to tell the truth. I kept saying, 'I am an innocent person you are picking on' and I remember one big tall man saying, 'You're a blooming liar,' and he started shouting at me and then went out again . . . It was the second day when it started to get worse. They kept telling me I was in Guildford and in the pub. They made me take my socks and shoes off when I was in the cell. Without socks

and shoes and a very heavy period which I had at the time.
I was terribly uncomfortable. They made me stand against a
wall with the tips of my fingers on the wall and my feet right
back and apart. There was a hand-basin in the room and
they turned it on and made it drip. The fat one did this. He
made me stand there for half an hour or more and kept saying
things like:

" 'Tell us. Are you going to tell us?' "I said: 'I don't know
anything about anybody at all. I go to work and I do my
jobs and look after my kids and my home.' "

"I asked if I could go to the toilet and they said no. My
legs were weak and I kept falling down, and they kept telling
me to get up. Then a policewoman came in called Babs or
something. She was well-built. She kept saying:

'Here's Auntie Annie who makes the bombs.'

"One of them said: " 'We've been too lenient with you.' "

"After lunch the two women took me to the cell and said,
pointing:

" 'Walk down towards there.' "

"As I walked, the woman lifted her foot and gave me a
kick hard on the backside. I put my two hands out and hit
the wall which stopped me from falling. They brought me
into another cell and the woman said:

" 'Are you going to tell us, because we're going to get it
out of you?' "

"I said: 'I am an innocent person that you are picking
on.' "

"The woman then hit me a slap across the face. I was so
shocked that I did not even cry. She said to the other one:

'Look at the hard bitch, she doesn't even cry.'

"And she dragged my two arms behind my back and threw
me down on the bed.

"I still did not cry. I was just too shaken. And she said:

" 'Get out!' "

"She picked me up and pushed me out and brought me to
the other cell again. They kept on and on at me and I was
completely confused and horrified at the end of it all."

But Anne stuck to what she insisted was the truth.

"What really upset me was when they said Vincent and

Patrick had traces on their hands and that they would be taken to a Juvenile Court and put away and that Anne-Marie would be put in an orphanage. That's when my mind really went blank. I said:

" 'I don't care what you say about my kids and my husband, there was never anything in my house.' "

The charge against Anne herself at this stage of course was not that she had been handling nitroglycerine. Her hands had been found by the tests at Woolwich to be uncontaminated. On the strength of Hill and Conlon's statements which said that she had actually taken part in the planting of the bombs at Guildford, the police were presumably convinced that she was part of the bombing team. However, despite the pressure put upon her they had not obtained any admission from her. They knew that the evidence of Hill and Conlon was inadmissible, as hearsay in a court of law. The subsequent fortuitous discovery in the following week of nitroglycerine on a glove which belonged to her enabled the police to maintain the charge of murder against her as well as supporting a general conspiracy charge in relation to the Guildford bombing. Anne remembers them saying to her:

"If we don't get you on the murder charge, we're got you on the gloves."

It should be repeated that all the Maguire Seven's allegations of improper interrogation were strongly denied on oath by all the police concerned. Since this in fact led to no confession of guilt, and since the Seven's protestations of innocence carry such a curiously artless ring of truth, such allegations may perhaps be given secondary importance. More immediately relevant is the fact that further searches of the house in Third Avenue, and of the surrounding neighbourhood, including derelict houses on the banks of the local canal, were made by the police but failed to produce any trace whatever of nitroglycerine or bomb-making equipment such as was known to have been used in the recent wave of I.R.A. bombings. Between the arrival back from work of Sean Smyth at 6.30 p.m. and the observation of the house by the police at 7 p.m. they would have had exactly half an hour in which to get any such material clear of the area, clean up the house and themselves and be back in the front room, by the time the police arrived.

One wonders indeed how the police could at this stage be so confident that they had in fact penetrated to the heart of the operation which had brought about the Guildford bombings.

10
More Statements and Some Conundrums

If the by now elaborate and fully detailed confessions of Hill and Conlon were the basis for the police faith that they had cracked the mystery of the Guildford bombings, some of that elaboration and detail was in itself already providing a problem. The arrests for instance of John MacGuiness, Brian Anderson, Sean Mullin and Paul Colman, inhabitants of the flat at 15, Rondu Road or of the squat at 14, Algernon Road, simultaneously with Gerard Conlon's in Belfast on November 30, soon led to more embarrassment than corroboration. For it became clear that the information that the bombs had been made at Rondu Road was as much rubbish as the original misinformation that they had been made in Brixton. Searches at Rondu Road, as indeed at Algernon Road, failed to reveal any incriminating material whatever to suggest that the police had at last found the London bomb factory for which they were so desperately seeking.

A cross-check with routine police files could in fact have indicated that this would be a likely outcome. For, only a fortnight before, MacGuiness himself had sent for the police to come to 15 Rondu Road after discovering one afternoon that the flat had been broken into and the gas meter robbed.

Two other Irishmen had been present when Police Constable 153E James Barlow arrived to investigate. He afterwards said that he had found their demeanour "not particularly concerned, not frightened or agitated, slightly jokey. They were not in a bad mood about it, slightly fed up that it had happened . . . I told them another officer would be down to see them. I asked them when they would be available. They couldn't tell me. I took their telephone number . . . "

He had brought the matter to the attention of the police station officer and entered the event in the Crime Book.

Another officer did indeed go down to 15, Rondu Road a few days later, Police Constable 463E Andrew Forbes, who found MacGuiness's demeanour "a bit annoyed about the theft . . . but not frightened". Forbes's movements about the flat had been in no way restricted. Asked whether on that occasion he had had any cause to suspect that the flat was being used for any illicit activities of any sort, he replied: "No."

The contention too that MacGuiness, Anderson and Colman had actually taken part in the Guildford bombing was before very long to look equally thin. All strenuously denied any sort of involvement in any sort of illegal terrorist activity, although all alleged a certain amount of physical violence from the police to induce them to admit to it.

Nor had the arrests of Hugh and Kathleen Maguire supplied encouraging results. They admitted straightforwardly enough that they had given Gerry Conlon Sunday dinner now and again and had taken him to the Conservative Club on Saturday nights but they had nothing relevant to add except that neither Gerry nor Hill, whom Hugh Maguire referred to as Benny, ever spoke to them or talked together about the I.R.A. or planting bombs. Hugh Maguire's hands were swabbed for nitro-glycerine – by the Surrey police, not the Metropolitan Bomb Squad as was to be the case with his brother and family – and the results were found to be negative. He and his wife were released after a week in which Hugh had been kept in a cell with nothing on but his trousers and a vest for six days, seeing no one. His interrogation had yielded nothing in spite of talk of telephoning Belfast to reveal that he had been acting as an informer.

All of this made it increasingly important that some effective corroboration of Hill and Conlon's statements should be obtained from the two major series arrests made on the evening of December 3 namely those of the Maguire household at Third Avenue, Harlesden, and those of Paddy Armstrong and Carole Richardson.

Before examing the confessions of guilt which Armstrong and Richardson were in fact to make over the next few days, it is instructive to learn something more of the Surrey Constabulary's methods of interrogation from one of the other suspects already under arrest, who was before long to be completely cleared of all charges. Brian Anderson of 15 Rondu Road was originally charged with murder on the strength of Hill and Conlon's statements. He thus recounts how he very nearly made a confession himself.

As a preliminary he describes some of the attendant circumstances. He says he was questioned for about two hours on each of four days, being kept in a cell at nights in which he was only once given a mattress, once a pillow and never any blankets. He refers to being "slapped about". These details, however, seem of minor significance compared with the psychological pressure to which he testifies. He thus described it:

"They kept going on at me telling me that I had to admit that I was one of those who went down to Guildford and planted the bombs and I wouldn't do so. Eventually it got to the state where I was ready to say that I had planted the bombs at Guildford. I just couldn't take any more. What happened was the police officer brought me out from the cell and said that he was going to give me a last chance to tell the truth or else, and if I didn't tell the truth it would be the worse for me. He told me that I had to tell the truth about what part I had played in the Guildford bombings. I was so tired and confused by this time that I thought that the only way that I would get any peace was to say what he wanted me to say. Just as I was about to tell him, someone came into the room and told him he had a telephone call and he told me that he was going to put me back down in the cell to think about it for an hour and then he would ask me again. I went back down to the cell[1] and during that time I managed to recover control of myself and when I was brought out of the cell about an hour later to see the same officer I told him exactly the same as I had told him before, namely that I had nothing to do with it and didn't know anything about it."

Anderson was nevertheless charged with murder of those killed in the explosion at Guildford, and taken to Winchester Prison.

Armstrong, arrested at Algernon Road on the evening of December 3 was first taken to Harlesden police station where for a time Carole Richardson, Lisa Astin and Maggie Carass (Paul Colman's girl-friend from Linstead Street) were also being held. Lisa, high on the Tuinol which Carole had given her, was screaming her head off after an interview in which officers had told her she had been "fucked" by Conlon, Armstrong and others. One had kicked her and torn the crucifix and chain from her neck with the words: "God won't help you now!" (She got the crucifix back the next day, but never the chain.)

Lisa first denied knowing Paddy altogether because, well aware of the sort of petty crime in which he might have been involved, she had wanted to protect him. But back in her claustrophobic cell, screaming and shouting, she had started hallucinating and hearing Paddy's voice. Maggie Carass eventually persuaded the police officers to let Lisa out to sit on a bench in the corridor with her. Lisa could hear Carole Richardson somewhere asking over and over again for a solicitor but being told she could not have one. Then suddenly Paddy Armstrong was brought out of a room and she could see him in the entrance hall of the police station while his escorting detectives stood about talking. Maggie Carass shouted at him:

"Look at this trouble you've got us into."

He shouted back:

"Why do you say it was me? I haven't got anybody into trouble."

He was to do so soon enough, for, although Lisa Astin,

Maggie Carass and other inhabitants of the Kilburn squats who had been rounded up that evening were to be released the next day, Paddy and Carole Armstrong were taken down to Guildford the same evening.

As already noted, some of those who had known Paddy Armstrong in his Kilburn Irish world of drugs, pubs and petty crime (he was sometimes known there as "Belfast Paddy", probably because of his very strong Belfast accent) remembered him boasting of unverifiable activity in Belfast, an activity with which as a resident of the Falls Road he would certainly have been very familiar in 1974 whether innocently or not. Maggie Carass told police that he had talked of carrying gelignite, of shooting and killing people and of blowing the kneecaps off drug-pushers. However credible or incredible such boasts, or that of driving a tanker with a bomb on it, might seem, his claim to have taken part in robberies in Belfast had a certain plausibility in the light of his known proclivities in London and the burglary charge on which he had spent three months on remand that summer.

Brian Anderson, who lived with Armstrong at Rondu Road, said he had no reason to suppose that he had been a member of the I.R.A. and had never discussed politics with him or heard him discussing politics. Paul Colman, Maggie Carass's boy-friend, thought to be the "Paul" of Hill's statement and thus also held on a murder charge but soon to be cleared, said that Armstrong never mentioned the I.R.A. though he did once suggest robbing a jeweller's shop in London. A Linstead Street squatter, Paul Guerin, who saw Paddy nearly every day for four months after his acquittal in the stolen goods case in July, said that, though he had "known him as well as I got to know any person", he had never heard him talk politics and that he had shown no interest in the Irish situation at all. Primarily he saw him as an expert backer of horses. "He was a happy-go-lucky bloke who lived from one day to the next . . . quite incapable of doing what the police say he has done." This was also the view of a young Belfast man who had lodged in the Quex Road, Kilburn, hostel, and had been pulled in by the police as a result of one of Hill's statements. He thought that in Belfast Armstrong would have been inclined to the Official I.R.A. (the more moderate wing from which the Provisionals had split). "But I would have known if he had been involved in any I.R.A. activities, because of course news travels fast within the area in which we used to live."

Nevertheless there was obviously something unpredictable enough in Armstrong's general demeanour to make even those who were close to him sometimes uncertain of who he really was and how he might always behave. Lisa Astin thus summed him up after his arrest:

"I had been pretty close to Paddy over this period of time. I cannot say positively that I know he never went to Guildford but I can say I know him well enough to know that he would never do the sort of things that he has been charged with. He used to brag a bit, sometimes he was not very nice. He was never the sort of person who would do this sort of thing."

However, in the circumstances of Hill and Conlon's statements, the police could hardly be blamed for taking a less charitable view of that zone of his behaviour which was obscure. Moreover they were able to find almost immediate justification for their strong suspicions from the way in which he seemed so quickly prepared to concede, whether bragging or not, his membership of the IRA and to concur with the picture the police were building up from the statements of Hill and Conlon about the way in which the Guildford bombing had taken place.

His first interview took place at Guildford at 11.50 a.m. It got off to a rather shaky start. Not only did he insist on referring to Conlon as Connolly, but, though he had obviously become aware somehow that an auntie of sorts was scheduled to have taken part in the expedition, he was uncertain of the name she was to go by.

"Yes, sir, there was Connolly, Carole, Auntie Ethel or Edith and your man next door, Hill. I think he is a Lieutenant in the IRA, as well."

"Now let's take it slowly. Who contacted you over here?"

"Well, sir, I thought I had been forgotten about. It wasn't until I went into the Old Bell in Kilburn on a Saturday morning just before the bombings that I saw Connolly in there. I knew him from Ireland, he was my Lieutenant in C. Company. He told me that he would see me next week in the same pub. He lived by himself . . . "

Next week, he said, he went to the same pub and met "Connolly" who showed him photos of the Guildford pubs and told him that they were going to be bombed. In reply to Detective Chief Inspector Style he said "Connolly" had told him he was to keep watch and that he, "Connolly", would put the bomb in the pub.

"Who else was involved?"

"Your man downstairs."

"Who do you mean?"

"The bloke with the ginger hair and the beard, he was living with me at 14, Algernon Road." (This was a reference to Paul Colman.)

"What was his part in it?"

"He was the driver."

"What you are saying is that the five of you came down to Guildford and done both pubs."

"No, sir, there were two cars. Me, Connolly, Carole and Paul were in one. Your man Hill, Auntie Ethel or Edith and two other Belfast boys were in the other. I don't know who they were. I think they were brought over specially for the job."

Style then left the room. He soon came back and asked Armstrong to change his position to face the door. The door then opened to reveal Colman, standing in the doorway with Detective Chief Inspector Horton.

"Who is that?" asked Style.

"That's Paul, the one that drove us to Guildford," said Armstrong.

Colman was then taken away.

The police were convinced that these men of whose involvement in the Guildford pub bombings they were more and more certain had also carried out the bombing of the King's Arms pub at Woolwich on November 7. Armstrong further confirmed them in this belief. He said Hill had driven them down to Woolwich in an E-type Jag.

The interview did not always follow a very coherent

pattern. There was some digression while Armstrong told them about five robberies in Belfast. Occasionally Detective Chief Inspector Style had to say:

"Armstrong, will you talk a little slower because my colleague is writing this down."

Armstrong waxed quite garrulous about his I.R.A. activity in Belfast.

"I was out shooting at soldiers and Protestants at night on occasions, but only at Protestants if they sniped at us. Only about three times and I emptied my chamber and ran. I don't know if I killed anyone, it was always in the dark. I've shot at the army post at the corner of Albert Street."

When they got back to Guildford, he had much colourful detail to offer. He described Carole Richardson's clothing on the Guildford bombing expedition as "a pink coloured trouser-suit with a light coloured blouse". Asked about the cars used he said that the one he had been in looked like a Ford, and that the other had been a lot older.

"It was there when we drove to the café because we parked right behind it. When the others came out they got into it and drove away to do their pub . . . It was light coloured, the bonnet opened up from the windscreen and the clips from the bonnet were down by the side. I think it was like a Ford Anglia? I don't know much about cars, because I don't drive. I'll tell you what: MacGuiness has a car like it."

The interview had now lasted over two hours. After a ten-minute break in which Armstrong was given some rolls and, though offered coffee, drank only water, Style left the room again and came back before the interview was resumed. Style said he wanted to be certain that "Paul" whom Armstrong had identified as the one who drove the car to Guildford really was that man. Colman, he said, was not admitting responsibility and said he couldn't drive.

"Now, be certain," said Style, "because this is very important."

"That's him, so it is," said Armstrong. "I wouldn't put an innocent man in that position. He was there, I'll swear to it in Court."

"It would be a real evil thing to do to say he was there if he wasn't. Are you sure?"

"That's him, so it is."

He then launched into an account of something which had unquestionably happened: the burglary of the chemist's shop by Colman the previous Sunday which had yielded the drugs supply on which Carole and others had got so high the day before. He said he knew Colman could drive because on that Sunday he had asked him to do the chemist's shop with him, saying he was going to steal a car.

As a result of all this Armstrong made his first formal statement admitting to the Surrey police a part in the Guildford and Woolwich pub bombings.

It opened very differently from the way in which he had first greeted the police as they burst into 14, Algernon Road the day before. Then, when told that he was being arrested for the Guildford pub bombings in October, he had merely said: "I know about them but I never had anything to do with it." Later at Harlesden police station he had said he did not know either Hill or Conlon – which could have accounted for why he kept calling him Connolly – but had admitted straightforwardly enough that he had known Carole Richardson for a couple of months.

Now he began:

"I was pleased I've been caught. It's nice to tell someone all about it."

He detailed how he had joined the Official wing of the I.R.A. in 1969 because the Falls Road where he lived in Belfast was then being attacked. He had then moved on to the Provisionals when the Officials called their truce in 1971 or '72. He said that it was agreed that he should come to London and that he was told that Conlon would be coming later. (The name "Connolly" which he had actually used in the interview had now been ironed out into the one the police wanted.) Armstrong apparently reported back to the I.R.A. in Belfast which pubs he was visitng in Kilburn High Road, but his potential terrorist career received a setback when on March 5, 1974 he was arrested and charged with two offences of burglary and two of receiving stolen goods. Tried with four other Irishmen, he was finally acquitted months later. "This," he added modestly, "was not connected with the I.R.A."

He eventually met up in a pub with Hill and Conlon. It was Conlon, he now said clearly, who showed him photographs of two pubs which were to have been military targets. He was picked up for this job two Saturdays later at about 3 o'clock and took his place in a grey four-door Ford Capri driven by a man called Paul and with a girl called Carole sitting in the back seat.

"It was the first time," said Armstrong, "I had seen either of these people."

This was an odd statement, since he had already admitted that he had known Carole Richardson for a couple of months.

They drove for about an hour and pulled up at a café in Guildford in which Hill and two other men and a woman were already sitting at a table. These people's car – a light-colour Ford Anglia – was parked outside just in front of theirs.

The plan was for Conlon and Carole to plant a bomb in one pub while Paul sat in the car and he (Armstrong) kept watch for the police outside. He asked Conlon the name of the girl in the other group and was told:

"It's my Aunt Edith or Edna."

They stayed in the café from about half-past four until about 7 o'clock. Then the two groups drove to the respective pubs they had selected as targets. Conlon and Carole took a parcel-bomb, which had been in the back of the car during the drive, into one of the pubs which had a picture of a horse outside. They emerged about a quarter to eight without it. They then drove straight back to the Old Bell and Kilburn.

A fortnight later, Armstrong said, "Paul" and Paul Hill took him on a photographic reconnaissance of a pub in Woolwich and he saw on television a few days later that this pub too had been bombed.

This statement ended with an unflattering description of Conlon: "Conlon is a cunt."

The next day Armstrong was again confronted with Paul Colman.

One of the police officers asked:

"Is this the man that drove the car when you were engaged on the Guildford bombings?"

"Yes," said Armstrong, "there is no doubt about it."

"Have you any doubt at all?"

"No, that's definitely him."

Armstrong looked directly at Colman and said:

"Why don't you admit it and tell the truth? You were there and you know you were."

Colman replied:

"Why are you doing this? You know it wasn't me. We didn't even know each other until three weeks ago."

"Yes, you did, you came around to the house one night and spoke to me."

"Yes, you answered the door, but I came round to see somebody else."

Armstrong, who seemed to be developing some of the technique of the police who had been interrogating him, replied. "How did you know it was me if you hadn't seen me before?"

Colman said nothing. He was before long to be completely cleared of having driven to Guildford.

At 1.15 p.m. according to the official record, on Wednesday, December 4, 1974, simultaneously with the first interrogation of Armstrong, Carole Richardson was being interviewed too.

"Do you know why you are here?"

"The bloke said it was for the bombing, but I weren't here."

"Do you know which bombings?"

"The Guildford bombings? But it's nothing to do with me."

"Where were you on Saturday the 5th of October?"

"If you let me get my diary, I can tell you."

"Do you know a man called Pat Armstrong?"

"Paddy, yes."

"Do you know a man called Paul Hill?"

"I know a lot of Pauls but I can't think of a Paul Hill."

"Do you know a man called Gerry Conlon?"

"Gerry, Gerry, I don't think I know a Gerry Conlon."

"Do you know a woman called Anne Maguire?"

"No."

"I do not believe that you have never been to Guildford before."

"The first time I was here was when they brought me down."

"Paddy said you have been here with him."

"He's a bloody liar."

"Paddy says you came here and helped plant a bomb in a pub."

"He's a bloody liar trying to put me in it. I wasn't here. I had nothing to do with it. I told them where to find him so how can I have anything to do with it?"

"Why should he try and put you in it if you weren't anything to do with it?"

"They showed me his picture and told me they wished to see him about a murder. I didn't know what murder they were talking about. Do you think I would tell them if I had known anything about it or had anything to do with it?"

"The two men I mentioned before, Hill and Conlon, have both put you here as well."

"Well, they're fucking liars. I don't know anything about it. I always meet my Mum from the hairdresser's on Saturdays. Ask her. She'll tell you."

"What time do you meet your Mum?"

"In the morning."

"Carole, we are talking about the afternoon and evening, not the morning."

"Let me get my diary, that would tell you."

"Carole, from the enquiries that have been made I don't think your diary can possibly help you. I believe you were in Guildford and that you were a party to planting a bomb in one of the pubs."

"You can think what you fucking well like. I weren't here. They're all liars. Why would I want to blow my own people up?"

"Carole, it has been said by the other people that you have been present on at least one occasion when bombs were being made."

"What lying bastards they are. What are they trying to do to me?"

"Have you ever been anywhere with Paddy when people were making bombs?"

"You must be joking. Of course I haven't."

After some description of the way in which she parted her hair (she did sometimes part it in the middle as did the long-sought I.R.A. girl Marlene Coyle, and the girl circulated as "wanted" in the Reynolds artist's impression*), the same point was put to her again:

"I don't accept that you were not in Guildford on the 5th of October. I can't really understand why you, an English girl, should be with these mad Irishmen, but I don't think you are telling the truth."

She made no reply but, according to the police report, "sat with her eyes lowered".

But Carole's own account of this interview records uncompromisingly: "I started to smile when he said 'mad Irishmen' and (M) hit me with the back of her left hand. It hurt and I went: 'Ouch!' "

The police account continues:

"Carole, you are not telling the truth, are you?"

"In my own mind I know I didn't do it. Think what you like. I know in my own mind I wasn't there."

"Carole, you have shut your mind off from it. What has happened has happened."

"I know I wasn't there."

The official report now merely states that after three-quarters of an hour of this Carole burst into tears and said:

"Yes, I was smashed out of my mind on barbs. I don't know what happened. I was out of my head."

But Carole's own account is rather different. She says:

"At this stage (W) hit me. He hit me one in the left jaw with the back of his hand. I lifted my arm to my face to protect myself and he punched me in the ribs. It was then that the pregnancy came in my mind again. (M) was shouting

---

*The poster described a girl between 5'2" & 5'4", aged between 20 & 25, Carole was 5'7" and aged 17. The poster described a slim man, with prominent cheek bones, 5'10"–6ft. Armstrong, whom the police said it resembled, was chubby-faced and 5'7".

at me that I was a murdering bitch and how did it feel to
murder people. And (L) was just sitting there. (W) then said
that if (L) left the room, I would be splattered all round it.
(L) said nothing. This was the worst part of it. (L) keeping
silent. I guessed he was in charge and I didn't know what he
was thinking. Then a tall man with a moustache and balding
came in."

(Assistant Chief Constable Christopher Rowe was a tall
man with a moustache.)

"He said: Carole, I have just seen the others and they were
positive you were there.

"I said: 'Look, sir, I wasn't.' He muttered something and
then went out with (L). Then (W) hit me again in the face.
I just sat there. (M) then said:

'You think you are a hard little bitch, don't you?'

I didn't answer.

"(L) returned after about 5 to 10 minutes and said:

"Look, we need the truth and we will get it in the end."

"Then I got some fish and chips but I only picked at it.
This was served in the same interview room. I was shaking
and scared of (W) and my jaw was hurting."

The next question and answer as officially recorded began
with one of the officers saying: "Were you there?" and Carole
replying: "Yes, I was. I was smashed out of my head on
barbs, I don't know what happened. I was out of my head."

Carole reading this record five months later commented to
her solicitor:

"While I had been eating the meal I was scared and
worried. I did not know if they would start hitting me again.
The drugs were beginning to wear off and I said yes I was
at Guildford. I said this partly out of panic and also out of
the feeling that to agree with what was wanted would stop
them getting at me. Throughout my meal they sat quiet, just
watching me eat. It was a frightening feeling. Not knowing
what would happen next.

"The questions started again. I was in tears, and shaking
like a leaf. Their attitude changed in that they no longer
shouted but their tone of voice seemed more menacing while
they questioned me. I cannot recall if any of them left the

room at all. (M) gave me a purple tissue to dry my eyes".
Then the questions started again.

"Honestly, all I can tell you is I was there."

"Who suggested coming to Guildford?"

"Paddy just said we would go out."

"Did you know what was going to be done?"

"I had an idea."

As in the interview with Conlon, the official record of that
with Carole gives the impression that the police are hoping
to bring into a single focus two separate pictures of a car
journey, one muzzy and drug confused and another an
expedition to Guildford to plant bombs.

"What do you call Barbs?"

"Downers, Tuinol."

"How did you get here?"

"We got into a car and went out."

"Who drove?"

"A bloke with fuzzy hair. There was someone else in the
car, I don't remember who."

"Do you remember a parcel? Was there anything in the
car?"

"I can't remember if there was anything or not."

"Did you get out of the car in Guildford?"

"I was in no state to get out of the car."

(Here there was another contradiction with what
Armstrong had been saying in another room.)

"When you were left in the car how many of them were
there?"

"There were four of us in the car."

"Do you know where you went?"

"No. I nearly fell asleep."

At one point she was suddenly asked:

"Do you know Conlon's Auntie Annie?"

"No, may have heard the name." (She had just heard it.)

"What does Tuinol do to you?"

"It's like drink, you fool about and your head goes funny."

"When did you last have some?"

"Yesterday."

She was shown a sketch of the Guildford pubs and asked

questions such as "Was there music there?" to which she replied:

"Yes, I think there was."

She herself then asked, as if trying to be helpful:

"Was there high wooden beams and supports in this pub with a sort of partition?"

At one point she had said she was not sure that the pub was in Guildford at all. She thought it might have been Paddy Milligan's in Kilburn.

Later there was a passage in which she managed to identify a woman who made bombs with "a woman I have seen in the cells at Guildford". Later still she was to be saying she knew her as "Anne", but, though before long she was indeed to know her well, she had in fact never heard of her until this day when the police, having first shown her Anne's photograph, had then shown Anne to her in person in her cell. They asked Carole if this was the woman who had made bombs. She had obligingly replied, "Yes."

After spending more than four and a half hours the first day being interviewed in this fashion, Carole made a statement in the afternoon. It did not mention Guildford but rather, as both Gerard Conlon and Paddy Armstrong had already done, described a hazy and confused drive which stopped at a pub.

"On the day of Saturday, the 5th of October, Paddy came to 14, Algernon Road, Kilburn, where I was completely smashed on downers, and he asked me if I wanted to go for a drive. I agreed as I thought the fresh air would do me good."

There was talk of passing a field with horses in it, of a fly-over, a can of Pepsi and going to the lavatory, but no mention of a bomb. The statement even contained the phrase: "I did not see a parcel of any sort." She was shown a sketch-plan of the interior of the Horse and Groom and even marked herself and Paddy as sitting at the wrong table in the alcove, a distance away from the position at which the bomb was known to have exploded. She did slightly better the next day and added considerable detail the day after. Altogether Carole Richardson was interviewed for over twenty hours, excluding breaks, on four successive days, and made four statements altogether.

At the end of the first day she had become, in the terminology of the police record, "hysterical and in need of medical attention". A doctor, Kasimir Makos of Weybridge, was brought in to see her, and to him she made two additional comments. The first was that everything that she had been saying to the police was "a pack of lies". The second was that she had assisted her boy-friend "not knowingly" in planting a bomb in the Guildford pub. Doctor Makos afterwards testified that she had made these comments when she had completely calmed down and was in full mental control of herself.

On subsequent days her story, inasmuch as it could be said to gain coherence, did so only spasmodically and often at some variance with the facts as the police were seeking to perceive them. For instance, although by her second statement there was definitely a bomb in the car (a cream-coloured Ford, she thought, driven by someone she had never seen before called "Dodger") and a man in a black leather jacket sitting in front had turned round to her and Paddy in the back and said it was going to blow up some bastard British soldiers, this car took an odd direction out of London if it was trying to get to Guildford, namely "towards Hendon along the North Circular Road". However, when they stopped, Carole said she thought they were in Guildford and in a café there they met up with John MacGuiness. This time when she and Paddy and the black-jacketed passenger went into the pub she got the position in the alcove right.

In her third statement, on the following day, Carole changed her description of the driver. She had categorically denied that he was Paul Colman, now he was not "Dodger" either, but a six-foot-tall blond with an "athletic body" who spoke in a Belfast accent. She added that Brian Anderson from Rondu Road had been in the café at Guildford and that the woman whom she had seen in the cells had also been with the bombing party at Guildford. In her fourth and last statement Carole reversed this information and said that they had not been there.

All in all, her succession of statements provided a disappointing result for anyone seriously trying to build up a clear picture of what had happened at Guildford. They provided only one positive result of real use to the police. This was the categorical information that Paddy Armstrong had been on the bombing expedition, and that, aware or not of what he and his companions were up to, Carole Richardson had been there too. In ratification of these specific points a significant detail emerged in her fourth statement. This was to the effect that she had gone to the bar in the Guildford pub and bought Paddy a Pernod. As the police knew, one of the last memories of the wife of the manager of the the Horse and Groom, serving behind the bar just before the bomb exploded, was, as she had told the police soon afterwards, of someone ordering a Pernod.

Carole told her solicitor some weeks later that the statements themselves were dictated to her from a summary of her answers or were dictated to one police officer by another who had been questioning her. "He would ask me detailed questions and I would answer 'Yes' or 'No' . . . I was giving these answers in the hope they would leave me alone. So I could get a solicitor and prove I wasn't in Guildford. I knew I wasn't there but I knew I wouldn't convince them. I was trying to pull myself together. I didn't realise what I was really saying. I was more worried about where I was and what would happen." (The police denied any dictation.)

As to the people described, such as "Dodger" and the blond with the athletic body, she said:

"I was trying to think of people I didn't know. I thought of people I had seen in the past week and tried not to describe them. I didn't want any of my friends to be arrested. Not after what they did to Lisa." As for some of the small incidental details, she said these had been culled from her own genuine experience elsewhere. For instance, when at one point she said she had hit her head on a weighing-machine at the top of the stairs, she was thinking of a weighing-machine in a public toilet in Willesden Lane; when she spoke of the Coke or Pepsi she had had she was thinking of the Coke or Pepsi she used to have when coming back from the Lyceum dance-hall. "We used to buy the Coke from a tobacconist almost opposite the toilet in Willesden Lane."

One genuine concern informed a part of her answers. She knew Paddy Armstrong's criminal record and, although she did not in her heart believe that he was capable of putting a bomb in a pub, she could not be absolutely certain that he had not been involved. She was honest enough to admit this gnawing doubt in part of her answers to the police and indeed, when she later talked to her solicitor, to admit to its presence in her mind in the first days of her arrest.

She had been asked by the police:

"Could Paddy have been involved with the I.R.A.?"

She had replied:

"I suspected he might have been."

She told her solicitor: "I said this because by now, after what I'd been told by Harlesden and Guildford police, I suspected Paddy."

It was to be some weeks before she herself became convinced that he had not been in any way involved. Indeed, her first letters to Paddy, written while on remand, expressed the doubt equally honestly to him.

In the meantime she herself had no qualms about submitting herself to the searching test of an identification parade. On the morning of Friday, December 13 she appeared in the Club Room at Guildford police station in a line of eight other women whose ages ranged from 16 to 22. She was allowed to choose her own position among them, which she did, and was told that she could change her position after each witness, which in fact she never bothered to do. She remained in the same position throughout. Eight people who had been in the Horse and Groom early on the evening of October 5 viewed the parade.

The first witness came in at 11.50. It was Mr Burns, the father of Carol Burns who had held her birthday celebration in the fatal alcove that night. He had been so badly injured that he had been unable to be interviewed by the police until the middle of November. It was he who had nodded so enthusiastically when shown the artist's impression of that "courting couple", of which Carole, in the police view, composed the female half.

He walked slowly down the line.

"I'm sorry, I can't be sure."

Mrs. Burns came next.

"I can't recognise any of them."

Carol Burns, their daughter, passed down the line. She shook her head.

Two of the Scots girls who had been in the alcove that night followed. One of them, Julie Spooner, stopped in front of Carole.

"No," she said.

The other, Jean Kettles, spent two minutes examining the parade.

"No," she said.

The last two were the paratroopers Cook and Lynskey, who had eventually supplied the police with the most detailed accounts of "the courting couple".

All this time Carole had remained in the same position. Cook passed down the line.

"I can't remember."

Lynskey was more categorical:

"I can't see her there."

After this experience the police called no identification parades of any of the other accused, despite all the hard work two months earlier to secure reliable witnesses from the alcove of the Horse and Groom.

At the end of the month Carole had another opportunity to tell someone other than Dr. Makos that what she had been telling the police was a pack of lies. Officers from Surrey came to see her on the afternoon of December 31 in Brixton Prison where she was being held on remand. After the routine caution she said to them:

"I won't answer any questions, before we start."

"Have you any more to say?"

"My solicitor told me not to say anything. I wasn't in Guildford. I've forty witnesses to prove it and I don't know half of them."

That at least was the police account of the meeting. Carole's own account was rather more graphic. She said that, when told that they wanted to ask her more questions about Guildford, she replied:

"You know I weren't in Guildford and I was forced to make those statements."

"Are you saying that you were hit by me?"

"No, but you bloody well know who did."

She says that at this point she looked straight at another of the police officers present.

"Why didn't you tell us you weren't in Guildford at the time?"

"I know I weren't in fucking Guildford and you wouldn't believe me when I told you. I've got about forty witnesses who can prove it and I don't know half of them."

11
"I don't believe in brilliant detectives"

From the statements of Paul Hill, Gerard Conlon, Paddy Armstrong and Carole Richardson, the Surrey Constabulary now had their scenario for the Guildford bombing. It is understandable that, for all the shortcomings in some of these statements, after three months of relentless hard work they should have felt a temptation to rest on what they felt to be their laurels. That they had been unable to obtain from any of the other people implicated by these statements and thus arrested for murder (Anderson, MacGuiness, Colman and Anne Maguire) any confessions to make that scenario more convincing seems to have troubled them no more than the many contradictions and apparent absurdities contained in the statements themselves.

These were of course numerous and remarkable, even in their final version. Hill had said that the expedition had started from London around midday and had been back in London by 5.45 p.m.; Armstrong and Richardson had said it started about 3 p.m.; Conlon had said it started about 6 p.m. Hill had said that Armstrong had driven one of the two cars and Paul Colman the other; Armstrong had talked of a car in which Colman was the driver and he himself a passenger.

Hill had put Armstrong and Richardson in separate cars; Armstrong had said he travelled with her. Richardson agreed with Armstrong about this, but had first named the driver of their car as not Colman but "Dodger" and had then described a different man altogether, a blond with an athletic body. She had specifically said that Paul Colman had not been a driver. Conlon, who had specifically said that Colman had been a driver, put himself in the back of the car sitting between Hill and Armstrong. Armstrong had him in the front. The cars themselves had conflicting descriptions: a grey Ford Capri and with it a light-coloured Ford Anglia (Armstrong); a lemon-coloured or XL Granada and a dark two-door Morris 1100, or partnering the latter in one of his later versions, a dark-colour four-door saloon (Hill).

Accounts of the actual operation at Guildford varied just as startlingly. In Hill's version, Conlon and Anne Maguire had planted the bomb in the Horse and Groom; Carole Richardson and Paul Colman had planted the bomb in the Seven Stars. Conlon said that he had gone into the Horse and Groom with Carole. Armstrong said that it was he who had gone into the Horse and Groom with Carole. Carole agreed with this but said that they had also been accompanied in the Horse and Groom by the mysterious black-jacketed passenger from the car. Brian Anderson and John MacGuiness appeared in some versions to have taken part in the expedition, and in others received no mention, though in these there were unnamed persons with whom they could be identified.

There were two possible explanations of such contradictions which it was in theory logical for the police to adopt. In the first place, memories of what by every account had been a confused expedition, with two of the participants at least high on drugs, could be expected to have been less than perfect. Alternatively, the confusion introduced into the accounts could have been deliberate. The contradictions could have been all part of a skilfully conducted exercise in counter-interrogation technique with which the four had all carefully armed themselves beforehand in the course of their training as I.R.A. terrorists. A motive for putting it into operation could easily be found in the need to protect other members of the expedition who had not yet been identified or arrested.

Whether the personalities of Hill, Conlon, Armstrong and Richardson – particularly the last, an English girl who had only been in Ireland once in her life, to spend a weekend in Dublin with nuns – were really compatible with the ability to perform in this way, and whether the apparent spontaneity and lack of sophistication in their early responses to questioning were capable of being feigned by the sort of people they were, were not considerations with which the police were by tradition or temperament inclined to deal. They could rest reasonably content in the knowledge that they had four separate individual confessions of participation in the Guildford bombings which in themselves could be sufficient evidence with which to secure convictions. By tradition and temperament they were inclined to accept as true the peripheral details with which such confessions were accompanied, including the incrimination of people like Anne Maguire, John MacGuiness, Brian Anderson and Paul Colman. The more convincingly they could make these details stand up, the more likely they would be to secure convictions for the central four. But failure to do so did not undermine the basic theme. The Surrey police could now in fact congratulate themselves on the sort of achievement to which they had so industriously aspired over the past two months. And congratulate themselves they now did, to the accompaniment of applause from the general public.

In interviews with the Press that month the Assistant Chief Constable of Surrey, Christopher Rowe, revealed that they had had an "amazing number of letters of goodwill" from the public since the arrest of the suspects. He was able to talk as if the matter was now virtually concluded. He disregarded the fact that the case, if it had been cracked, had been cracked by the arrest of Paul Hill and his subsequent revelations, and that the commendably hard work in which the police had been engaged for the previous two months had in fact contributed little to what he now saw as success. (The Richardson identification parade had made this plain.) Rowe found himself able to talk as if he was, for once, not too embarrassed to take credit where credit was due.

"You have certain basic principles you work on. Like any enquiry it's 99% bloody hard work and 1% luck. As far as we are concerned it's a routine enquiry – it's been a big one – it's been time-consuming."

And he added:

"I don't believe in brilliant detectives."

They had, he said, taken 3,000 statements altogether in the immediate enquiry after the bombings, and as a result of these there had been 2,800 further enquiries. He had had 150 officers in the initial enquiry and even more engaged in what he called "the security operation of recent weeks". The arrests were presented as the fitting climax to a most commendable effort.

"I suppose the longest we worked without going to bed was when we did the arrests. About 50 of the team went up to London and we worked from 8 a.m. on Friday to 11 a.m. on Sunday and had a couple of hours' sleep. Then we were back again until midnight on Saturday [November 30th]." His only regret, he said, was that this had made him miss the Rugby match at Twickenham.

For the Metropolitan police Bomb Squad the arrests, particularly those of the Maguire household, were also a matter of self-congratulation. The Guildford confessions had been a sort of windfall. The apparent connection of Anne Maguire with the Guildford pub bombings enabled them to see 43, Third Avenue as at least a link with that I.R.A. bomb factory whose whereabouts had so tantalisingly eluded them. And this chance was especially welcome since the initial hope aroused by Hill's revelations of the bomb factory first in Brixton and then at Rondu Road had been disappointed. The fact that no body of explosives or bomb-making equipment was found at 43, Third Avenue either, though disappointing in itself, did little to mar a partial sense of achievement. The Surrey police had after all already found a connection between the Maguire household and the I.R.A., through the alleged presence of Anne Maguire at the Guildford pub bombings. Revelations of traces of nitroglycerine on the hands of many in the household seemed to clinch the argument that some of those involved with the long-sought bomb factory had at last been run to earth.

The value of the explosive charges to the Surrey police, who hoped to get Anne Maguire to confess to the Guildford murders while they held her for seven days under the Prevention of Terrorism Act was that they placed a threat over her in terms of her family. That threat could act as an inducement to her to confess. Should she confess, and these charges become unnecessary for that purpose, they could always be dropped on the grounds that an inexperienced 18–year-old laboratory assistant named Wyndham had been allocated to the tests (as he had been) which tests therefore, it might be said, were not wholly reliable. The explosive charges brought against her in the following week on the basis of her gloves was a useful fall-back position should she still delay confession and the magistrates not agree to her continued remand.

Hill and Conlon had already been charged with murder and formally remanded in custody by Guildford magistrates. The same official procedure was now applied in that following week to Patrick Armstrong, Carole Richardson, Anne Maguire, Brian Anderson, John MacGuiness, and Paul Colman. Anne collapsed in hysterics in the courtroom. Paddy Maguire, Giuseppe Conlon, Pat O'Neill and Sean Smyth were formally charged with the possession of explosives. All those arrested at 43, Third Avenue and at 15, Rondu Road continued to assert their innocence and Gerard Conlon himself got a first chance to retract his confession when he was seen by Detective Chief Inspector David Munday and Detective Superintendent Peter Imbert of the Scotland Yard Bomb Squad, in Winchester Prison on December 13.

The interview began with a small example of the sort of police interview technique which bewilders prisoners. Conlon said he was not going to answer any questions, but that he was "not bothered about this charge".

"I've got a good defence," he said. "There are two people, a bloke and a girl, who will say I was with them when the bombs went off."

Imbert asked:

"Which bombs?"

"The Guildford bombs, of course. That's all I've been involved in."

"Do I take that as an admission?"

"What do you mean?"

"You say that is the only one you are involved in."

"No – the only one the police have involved me in."

"That was a slip of the tongue, then?"

"No. I meant what I said. I've been involved in the Guildford bombs but I have a good defence."

"It sounds to me as if you slipped up then when you said you were involved in the Guildford bombings."

"What I meant was, I am not involved but the police have involved me by charging me. You are trying to trick me, aren't you?"

"No. I want to ask you some questions, but not about the Guildford bombings. You have already been charged with those."

"Yes, and I'll get out of it. What others? I have not been involved in any bombings at all, so there's no point in asking me any questions . . ."

But Conlon then said something which seemed to worry Munday:

"I'll tell you something. It's something when you bring my Dad in here – he is a sick man – for possessing explosives. He is going to say you rubbed explosives on his hands and that's how he got it on his hands."

"When did he say that?"

"That's my business. That's what he's going to say so there's nothing you can do about it. I only admitted it because I had to."

"What do you mean?"

"I'm not saying any more. You'll find out."

"What about your father saying explosives were rubbed on his hands?"

"I've told you. You'll find out. I have nothing else to say without my solicitor."

The interview thus had to be aborted.

Five days earlier Gerard Conlon had written his first letter home from prison. He was then not aware that his father had been arrested on December 3, and the letter was addressed to him as well as to his mother.

". . . It feels as if it's ages since I last saw the family but I know when this is all over I'll be home again where I belong . . . I hope that Dad is keeping well and I hope he has backed a few winners. Tell him I miss and love him very much and hope to see him soon as I miss and love you and all the family and Granny as well . . . Before I go to bed every night I kneel down and say my prayers and ask God to watch over the family and me and keep all of us safe and ask Him also to let the truth come out in the case and everything will be all right. I never knew how much I missed the family till they took me away that Saturday morning and I thought it was just another raid but look at the way it has all turned out, but we also know it will be all right in the end, you'll see . . . If any girls call and ask for me just tell them I'm on holiday and will take them out for a good night or two or three when I come back again and ask if I am still the best looking fellow in the Falls . . . God bless and look after you. NOT GUILTY. FROM YOUR LOVING SON GERRY CONLON.

This was the first of what was to be a remarkably affectionate, sensitive and often lively series of letters to his family, always maintaining his innocence, written over a period of more than eleven years.

The day before he had his interchange with Detective Superintendent Imbert and Dective Chief Inspector David Munday he was writing to his mother again. By this time he knew what had happened to his father. He had seen him in Court that morning when they were all remanded together. He hoped that his mother would send him a transistor for Christmas and that his father would be out on bail before then. The letter ended with two drawn hearts with the words "Merry Christmas" in them, and his next letter, written on December 23 before going to Court for further remand on the following day, when he again hoped to see his father, contained the words:

"Mum, I am sorry I have caused you so much trouble but

it was not my fault as I did not do anything like they said I did. I also know that as long as you believe me that is all that counts. Also God knows the truth as well as you and I do." The rest of the letter was written in capitals: "MUM A VERY MERRY CHRISTMAS AND HAPPY NEW YEAR HOPE TO BE BACK HOME WITH THE FAMILY FOR NEXT CHRISTMAS GOOD LUCK AND GOD BLESS, GERRY."

On the last day of the old year he wrote again from Winchester Prison:

"At Court yesterday Annie Maguire was asking how you are and if you have been to see me yet and I told her you have not been over yet but you will come over as soon as you can . . . So Mum say a prayer for her as she is also not guilty like me and the rest of the people in here. Paddy Maguire and Sean Smyth and Pat O'Neill were all asking for you and everybody back home . . . Everything is looking a bit better in my case so with a lot of luck I could be out very soon and be back home again and everything will be like it was . . . FROM YOUR LOVING SON THE BEST LOOKING BLOKE IN WINCHESTER NO PROBLEM X=X=X GERRY THE KING HA HA."

On the second day of the New Year he wrote to his two young sisters:

"Well kids . . . I hope the two of use are not giving my mother any trouble but are giving her a helping hand instead. If use are not, I will knock the pair of use as soon as I get back home understand . . . Bridie and Anne I hope use are praying for me and Dad but don't worry as we know we will get out soon, as it is a frameup and we are both not guilty of what they say . . . "

It is of course reasonable to say that Conlon knew quite well that his letters were being read by the prison authorities and that, if guilty, this could have seemed to him a useful device for trying to create an impression of innocence. However, a certain unaffected spontaneity which runs through all his letters, coupled with the fact that long after he had been convicted and had his appeal rejected he continued these assertions of innocence, might suggest to any but a purely legal mind that such assertions were genuine.

The same criteria applied to others who were on remand at this time.

Anne Maguire's first letter was addressed to her children and a Mrs. Kearney, who was looking after them. Knowing that she herself was held on a murder charge she was still able to think of the arrests of the others from her house as something that should blow over quite easily. She was confidently expecting Paddy to be out on bail very soon. "I have not stopped thinking of you," she wrote to the children, "and it breaks my heart to know you are also suffering this pain and we all know that I am the innocent person and has been accused of this terrible crime. My loving boys I want you to be brave as I am trying to do, for please God soon I will be able to prove my innocence. Promise me to go to Church and Holy Com, every Sunday. Pray hard to God to listen to children's prayers. Patrick my Son, be brave be good and love Anne-Marie as I did. Say your prayers with her and for your Mum and Dad . . . Please God Dad will be with you, love him be good to him for I know he loves you and me more than anybody or anything in the world. Aunt Teasy [Mrs. Kearney] Anne-Marie wanted a cot for her dolls for Christmas. Vincent will get it for her . . . Tell my family . . . to keep praying hard, that God will help me prove I am innocent..If you get to see Paddy give him my love and tell him to pray for me. I hope he gets home for Christmas . . ."

But Christmas came and no-one got bail. Anne was further charged with possessing explosives. Her brother-in-law Hugh McCaffery came over from Belfast to see her and the others. The interview took place of course under the eyes of warders. This is his description of what happened.

"She rushed straight over to me. She put her arms around me and cried. I could feel the tears in my own eyes. I had to get her to sit down and talk. Time was short. There was a lot to find out. She said she was innocent of the charges; she could not hurt anyone. I believed her for I know her."

Previously, under interrogation, Anne had searched her mind for a recollection of what she had been doing on the

night of October 5, the night on which, according to the
police charge, she had been murdering at Guildford. At first
she told her interrogators that she thought she had been at
Chipperfield's Circus at Shepherds Bush with Anne-Marie
that day. But when it was pointed out to her that Chipperfield's Circus had not opened there until October 21 she had
had to think again. Now she remembered that October 5,
being two days before Anne-Marie's birthday, had itself been
the birthday of the son of a neighbour, Sally Irvine. She had
discovered this accidentally by calling in on her that evening
– just about the time when she was supposed to have been
at Guildford. She now told this to Hugh McCaffery. Next
day McCaffery saw Paddy Maguire, Pat O'Neill and Sean
Smyth in Winchester Prison. Both Sean Smyth and Pat
O'Neill told him they were not worried because they were
not guilty of anything. "The whole thing," said Sean Smyth,
"was a frame-up." Paddy joked about coming in for a holiday.

On January 16, 1975 Anne wrote to Hugh and to her sister
in Belfast:

". . . I still think I'm dreaming. I just can't believe these
things can happen to innocent people. All I have ever done
is work hard and keep to myself. Paddy was the same, bothered no one, always on his own. He is heartbroken, but tries
to keep it back from me, but I can see it in his eyes and when
he is talking. I see him every Monday [in Court] for a few
minutes . . . He wrote and told me I had given him 17 years
of care and love and he didn't deserve it, but he will make it
up to me." There then follows a shy allusion which only the
most cynical prison censor could suspect of being an attempt
to mislead: "So as Kate [Anne's other sister] said, she will
keep her baby clothes and send them to me next year, please
God."

A little later comes a passage: "I only wish I were having
a baby, instead of this misfortune that has come to us."

On January 20 she wrote to Mrs Kearney who was looking
after the children. She herself saw them every week when she
came up with the others in Court to be remanded.

"They are looking well, but just like myself they feel hurt
because we are not involved in anything and Paddy and I

always condemned the I.R.A. for their killing off innocent people and here we are involved through no fault of our own. Teresa it's got to be proved we are innocent. I don't know about Gerard Conlon what he has done or his pals with him, but I know Paddy Sean and Pat and myself are not guilty of this terrible crime. I pray so hard that it will be over soon, for it's killing me being away from the kids and they're hurt too, for they know their Mum and Dad are Innocent. I don't know what this cross is for but its a heavy one . . ."

In her weekly appearances in Court the press more than once reported her as collapsing, sobbing and having to be helped to a chair.

On January 27 Anne wrote again to the McCafferys to congratulate them on the birth of a baby son: ". . . Mary I feel a bit better in myself, and I also get a Mass every Thursday morning to Our Lady, and Blessed Martin, but I know I'm innocent and leave it up to God . . . Vincent seems to have grown into a man since this happened, instead of a boy of 16. I don't know what I would do without him. He keeps a smile when he comes to see me, but I can see the worry in his face, for they all know I'm in here for doing nothing. Mary you said you'd got a house in the country for the holiday. I don't think we will be back to Belfast after this happened, as I feel inside me that whoever done the bombing are back in Belfast, and walking free, while we are here blamed for their dirty work . . . Tell Dad . . . to stop worrying about us, for they can't find the innocent guilty . . . I have to be brave. Its the longest rest I've had since I got married and settled in London, but I do miss my routine of work and the kids, Paddy, Sean and the house, but I know if God sees me through, I wont work as hard, and will make life for living, not killing myself working hard. What do you say?"

It is in fact difficult to see how prison authorities could have read such letters without themselves beginning to consider whether Anne Maguire might not be innocent.

Carole Richardson too had been writing letters while on remand. Between December 19, 1974 and Easter in April 1975 she wrote 37 times to Paddy Armstrong. In these letters she did not so much bother to protest innocence as assume that it would not be long before she was freed again. After the sociable life of the squats, she was finding prison existence intolerable.

'It's funny how you miss people when you're used to being with them all the time . . . I'll really be glad when this is all over. I'm really fed up with no one to talk to and nothing to do except smoke and write."

She too had been thinking hard about what she could have been doing on the night of October 5. The diary which she had been so sure would have told her had apparently been burned by one of her squat-mates at Kenilworth Road in a panic after he heard of her arrest. He was afraid it would contain details which might incriminate people in drug offences and other petty crime. But, with the help of Lisa Astin and an acquaintance of theirs from the twilit world in which they had been living, a young man from Newcastle called Frank Johnson, she remembered that it had been on the night of October 5, 1974 that they had all three attended a pop concert at the South London Polytechnic at the Elephant and Castle. Frank Johnson had been a friend of the group playing there and had taken some pains to reconstruct the memory of that evening. So that when Carole wrote to Paddy Armstrong on Christmas Day, saying she hoped he was keeping in good spirits and had had a nice Christmas ("the food here was loverly and plenty of it"), she told him that her solicitor had said that even if the pop group were in America he would "bloody well go over there" and get in touch with them wherever they were. "Keep your head togever," she ended. "All my love, Carole." Kisses followed.

Her next letter written on January 7, 1975 in fact told Paddy that Frank Johnson, who had read of her arrest in the paper, had gone to the police "and told them where I was so I hope that's cleared it up for now anyway I hope".

Her spirits remained quite high for a time, even dealing with the awkward fact that some of her former friends had been prepared to think her guilty. "Do you remember Patsy? She lives round the corner from Linstead Street. You should have seen the letter I got from her. What a telling of to put it mildly. She really thought I might have been there. Her brother was the only one who stuck up for me, and me and Jimmy weren't exactly the best of friends either. It's funny it takes something like this to learn who your real friends are . . . Belfast Frank [another acquaintance] Lisa and Geordie Frank [Frank Johnson] were the only ones who believe I wasn't there even before it crossed their minds the concert was on the 5th. I didn't remember myself for about a week. I couldn't tell where I was without my diary and I couldn't have that. Anyway alls well that ends well I suppose."

She was seeing Paddy Armstrong regularly once a week at the remand appearances in Court. Much of her concern was still for him:

"Why don't you get rid of that beard? It looks bloody awful. Its a pity Jimmy took the electric razor with him. I'll get Lisa to bring you in some clothes all right so make an application for them will you? Then there won't be any trouble at the gate when she arrives all right."

There were signs, however, in this letter that she was beginning to lose heart. "I am really fed up and I think I've got flu or something coming. I really feel sick at times." But her letter ended with kisses for him after "All my love, Carole" followed by the anarchic slogan: "Bob Hope for President!"

Her own doubts about Paddy Armstrong's innocence were still as yet unresolved and still troubled her. In her next letter on orange paper, posted from Brixton on January 21, she wrote to him:

"I really wish you would pull yourself together and name the people who were with you on the 5th. They wouldn't stop at putting you in it. In fact someone did. How did they have your full name and everything else if someone didn't talk? In Harlesden I thought it was a bit of a joke until they showed me what was written underneath. I nearly broke down. It's only hitting me now just how bloody serious this is and you had better realise it pretty soon. Who are you afraid of? What can they do to you whoever and whatever they are? . . . In Guildford they said I was probably at Woolwich as well. Dear Paddy, what have you got me involved in? I wouldn't believe them at first until they said you said I was there, which I don't believe now at least I hope you didn't say it. Tell Andy

and John [Brian Anderson and John MacGuiness, whose
names she had given in her statement] I'm sorry but the
police said they said I was there and there was nothing else
I could do and all I do is hope and pray that you will have
the sense to tell the truth in court and the same with Paul
Hill and whoever was there, that is if you and Paul were,
and nothing either of you have said or done made me think
otherwise. I wouldn't mind but as far as I can remember I
have never seen Paul Hill before in my life, how many times
have I seen Gerry? Once maybe twice. How could you get
involved in anything like this? You were always fairly quiet.
Oh Paddy, it's cracking me up, locked up nearly 20 hours a
day. I am used to being out all the time, never having to
worry about a thing. I keep crying for no reason at all. I'll
go mad if this doesn't end soon. I can't sleep at night and
have dreams, bad ones most of the time, I feel like killing
myself at times.''

The letter ended with an injunction for him to keep his
chin up "and please do tell all you can before I crack up".
Once again the slogan "Bob Hope for President" appeared
at the bottom.

Recriminations about who had got who into trouble were
still flying about the squat world.

"Tell Paul [Paul Colman]," she wrote about the same time,
"Maggie [Carass] had better watch her big mouth or my fist
will fill it. She's telling everyone you and me said that Paul
was there, that's why he's being held. She better not be in
Kilburn when I get out, so tell Paul to tell her to get out of
England if she's got any sense because if I get hold of her she
won't have a bloody head left and then I'll be up for something I did bloody well do.''

An obscure reference then follows to some business
connected with a woman in Chichele Road, Cricklewood,
which, it is hinted, though unlawful in itself, might provide
an alibi. "I'm not sure of her name but I expect the police
could find out about her. Have a good think because I don't
intend doing time for something I didn't even know about or
anyone else whoever it is. So let me know before I start the
ball rolling, because I'm sorry Paddy, but I'll talk.''

Love for him underlay much of what she wrote.

"I meant what I told Lisa to tell you because I don't blame you and nothing changes it because I do love you. But what good am I to you in here? I see you for 5 minutes in court once a week and that's it. Have a good think because you are helping me, but you are helping yourself in the long run you know, and people don't have to know it was you if you keep quiet about it but for God's sake think. Lisa won't think much of you if you put me in it and I doubt if anyone else will because they know in their hearts where I was that night but still it's up to you." Once again the letter ends with "All my love, Carole" and kisses, while at the bottom, before the slogan "Bob Hope for President", comes the injunction, "Have a shave".

Carole's love for Paddy Armstrong, tinged with nostalgia and apprehension, received poignant expression in a letter recalling their hitch-hiking tour and shaped instinctively in the form of a poem. This ran:

Thoughts of you bring tears to my eye
As when I think of you in the past
I think of the freedom and the good times
With not a care in the world
Just the two of us alone Alive for each other
The miles we walked up and down hills
Passing through little villages
Looking in shop windows and the marvels they held
Never thinking we would be apart for more than
A day or two at the most
Each other's company was all we needed then
We were happy and nothing else mattered
But not
I hope and pray it's a mistake
I don't know if you were there
I hope and pray you weren't but if you were there
it's only one thing I can say why did you do it?
There must be a reason but what is it?

If only you'd explain. But now all I do is hope and pray that we'll be together again soon.

This time after she had sent "all my love, Carole" two hearts were drawn, made out of kisses, in one of which was the word PIG and in the middle of the other the words I LOVE YOU.

Once again it is difficult to think that prison authorities reading such letters could seriously believe them to be part of a cunningly-devised scheme to mislead them and disguise the truth.

There were in any case some signs that part of the police case was beginning to crumble. On the same day as Anne Maguire had written to the McCaffereys congratulating them on the birth of their son, January 27, there came news that could be interpreted as encouraging. John MacGuiness and Paul Colman, together with Sean Mullin from 15 Rondu Road, who had been charged with conspiracy to cause explosions simply because he lived at that alleged bomb factory, were given bail on their own recognisances of £1,000 each. Although they still had to report to the police every day there seemed some hope that the truth was at last beginning to be recognised. There was no bail for anyone else. But Carole's spirits began to rise. She wrote to Paddy Armstrong:

"I'm really glad Paul and John get bail but I'll feel even better when we get it if we do. That is poor Paul I really feel sorry for him. I wouldn't mind if we knew him in October but we didn't and I don't know why I've been dragged in or how they got my Mum's address but still board and lodgings a change. Anyway I'll be glad when its all over and I can go home. I am trying to decide what to do first, go to the stables, or go for a drink. I miss horses and beer but I expect the pub will come first . . . How is everyone coping with the situation? They all seemed a bit brighter in court today. Even Andy and he looked really down the last few weeks. When you get out you can have a go at beating your work record. All I hope is I get bail. If I do I'm getting out of London and going to work in the country somewhere miles from humans, only animals and fields all around me. It will be great, I hope . . . I think I'll become a hermit when I get out, then I can't be accused of anything because I won't see anybody. Does that makes sense? Anyway have a shave, keep your chin up and look after yourself. Love, Carole XXX."

On February 1, 1975 she was at last able to resolve her doubts about Paddy Armstrong's involvement:

"Dearest Paddy, I've just seen Lisa and she told me what happened, of course I believe you weren't there. The way the police put it, it made me think I was there. But when it's all over we'll show them . . . Lisa will be up again next Wednesday. I told her not to worry about me but to get to see you whenever she could. She won't take my advice I know, but I wish you all the luck in the world, because I didn't think you would have done such a thing and I'm really glad now I know for sure."

Optimism began to infect her, but there was still one thing she could not understand.

"Paddy, just answer me one question. Why did you make a statement against me? I don't think you did now, and the way everything is going we'll be making statements to the press fairly soon. It'll be good to walk down the road with you again though. Maybe we can go hitch-hiking again. I still want to see the palm trees in Wales, if there are any that is."

She really was beginning to feel that it was all over bar the shouting.

"It's done you some good though, you've lost weight and that can't be bad. All you need is *a shave* (hint hint). You could do with a haircut as well . . . For the last time have a blooming shave. All my love, Carole."

On the last page was a postcript:

"Just say this to yourself every now and again. 'Sacred Heart of Jesus, I place my trust in You' and believe it."

On February 3 came more good news. MacGuiness, Anderson and Colman were all finally cleared in the magistrates' court of the murder charge and Mullin was cleared of conspiracy. All were set free.

This aroused in Anne and the others from the house on Third Avenue both hope and cause for concern. If, after all, it was now accepted that neither MacGuiness, Colman nor Anderson had been at Guildford at all, then not only was there just as much reason to realise that Anne Maguire had not been there either, but substantial parts of the statements which had ultimately led to the arrests of the Maguire household were at last being accepted as untrue. On the other hand, all this could lead to an attempt to make the case against those still held tighter than ever. It emerged that neither Smyth nor O'Neill who had been hoping for bail on account of their very temporary presence at Third Avenue on the day in question, nor Giuseppe Conlon, who had been hoping for bail on the grounds of ill-health, were to have it granted. Nor, still, was Anne Maguire. She tried to keep her spirits up.

On February 10 she again wrote to the MacCafferys:

"... Inside me something keeps telling me not to worry, for when you're innocent and tell the truth, how can these people punishment you, but the hardest cross is being away from my kids and them to suffer for nothing, and them, God help them, to know their Mum and Dad are as innocent as themselves ... "

On February 24 the murder charge against her at last had to be dropped because, as had been the case with Anderson, Colman and MacGuiness, there was no other evidence against her than what the police had obtained from Hill and Conlon. But it had already been made clear to Anne in private that if the police had to drop the murder charge they had "got her on the gloves" – those plastic gloves which according to the test at the Government laboratory at Woolwich revealed traces of nitroglycerine. She was still refused bail and, with what some would see as an act of vindictiveness, on the very day on which the murder charge had to be dropped, the police charged her sons Vincent and Patrick for unlawfully handling explosives on the strength of the swab tests made three months before. They at least however were given bail.

Anne wrote to Hugh and Mary McCafferey on March 20:

"Well, what do you think of them not giving bail? They are trying to break me one way or another. It's heartbreaking being here four months doing nothing. Even the boys are taken it hard, but they don't show it. At court on Thursday they were laughing and joking, but I could see our Sean's face when they said [to him] no bail." She was worried that the Long Kesh wallets were going to count against her and was anxious that Hugh should come over for the trial to explain that even British soldiers bought them. "The two kids are still on bail, God help them, Hugh, they never done any wrong, never had any trouble from them and the law plants this on us all. I feel sorry for Vincent just started his apprentice, and it all could be wasted because of lies. Hugh, I also say the Rosary every morning and night. Sometimes I think my mind is going to go, when I look at Anne-Marie. I ask myself, is there a God to let this happen to innocent people? . . . Anne-Marie said, 'Mum, I wont make my first Communion until you come home in May.' That was one day I was always looking forward to her being the only girl. Hugh, they have got to believe us we are innocent people, and not mixed with those people who do these bombings. I know, Mary, and the kids and yourself are praying hard and you are doing your best for us."

Just after Easter she wrote to them again, more cheerfully because she was now hoping to get bail at last in May. ". . . I'll start knitting baby clothes, MAD! Paddy said Pat O'Neill is keeping our Sean going to get the operation done, so as they will have no more kids, Pat is getting it done as Helen has been told that she will be in danger if she has any more kids." Sean's reply to Pat was, she reported, one to make everyone laugh. She was looking forward to being able to be at Anne-Marie's first Communion, when she got bail in May and ended the letter with a postscript:

"Make a drop of punch, brandy water, give it to the baby and he will sleep like a top HA! He will get up next morning singing 'Seven Drunken Nights'. Thanks for the relic I got it."

In May at last she was granted bail, and could return to her family in Third Avenue. Paddy's "holiday" continued. But even that now could be seen as a sort of convalescence from which in the end they both might benefit, because the worst seemed over. She knew it would not be an easy time for her and the boys as they waited through the months before the trial but that trial's outcome was one which none of them now seriously doubted.

Carole meanwhile, pleased as she was by the release of

MacGuiness, Anderson, Colman and Mullin, had her own problems to worry about. After commenting that in Court, on the day the four were cleared, Paddy had looked better than for ages, she complained that he still had not had a shave. But she was also endeavouring to come to terms with what had happened to her.

"I'm still trying to think what I put in my statement and nothing enters my head at all. I must have been mad, but as you know I hate pain and it got them off my back. But when it gets to court the truth will come out and then what!" She added: ". . . I really miss you. God, I'll be glad when this is over but then I'll have another worry on my hands, won't I? Lucky old Sean, Paul, John and Andy. Well at least they can have a pint in the pub – that's probably where they are now . . . "

After the usual "All my love, Carole. XXX" she concluded with, "And remember you're innocent" and below that, to the left of the page, there was a bracket: "God Bless the Innocent and May the Guilty be Brought to Justice."

This became a catchphrase for her, to be continually repeated at the end of almost every letter. Curiously she had something to say in favour of British Justice in one letter. Paddy Armstrong had apparently made some disparaging remark about it in court. She wanted to correct him: "What you said about British justice. It's Guildford C.I.D. that haven't got their heads screwed the right way around, not British justice. That doesn't come into it until the trial." Her mood was volatile. "God," she wrote one day, "I feel ill. Why the Hell did they put these charges on me they must know by now I wasn't there it's really getting on my nerves."

But even when depressed there was often a certain optimism at work: "I keep thinking I'm going to die, silly really but it's not a nice thought. I wonder what it would be like to die because I believe in reincarnation. I wonder what I'll be in my next life. Maybe I'll be the daughter or son of a rich rancher in Texas with plenty of horses. Or maybe I'll be a fly buzzing around and annoying people. I don't know which I prefer because I like buzzing and I like horses. Maybe he'll own a poppy field in Texas so that I can have the best of both. I'm not mad I'll assure you of that so don't think I am or else."

And it was on the next day, Valentine's Day, that she wrote: "I feel so miserable and fed up and just sick of life, oh well, I can always think of Texas and poppy fields."

There were two constant themes in all her letters. She loved Paddy, and she was wrestling with the frustration of knowing that she was innocent, hardly yet able to believe that the judicial system in which she was enmeshed could not be forced by the logic of truth to release her again.

"I want to know what they have against me other than statements which don't stand for much seeing as everyone is denying them as far as I know, well you and Gerry are I don't know about bloody Hill. He's so sure of himself it's blooming stupid . . . I am gonna be a godmother in September, blooming Patsy would pick on me. I just hope I'm out by the christening if not I'll be dead. The thought of what this is all about is really bad, but when it ends I'm going to get a job in some stable in the country and you are not going back to Belfast, that's the worst place to go. You'll be found innocent of this but if there's any trouble round the Divis Flats you'll be one of the first to be picked up as we'll all be watched for a good few years when this is all over." She was actually looking forward to the committal proceedings and what she thought would be the discomfiture of the police. "Because no court is gonna believe what those lying sons of bitches have said. But who cares let them say what they like I know we all know the truth, well I do anyway know the truth that is."

On March 22 she wrote to him:

"Dearest Paddy, Not long to go till freedom now, I hope. It'll be great to get out again straight to the pub for a drink, a luverly Scotch and lemonade. I haven't had one for ages . . . There's a rumour going round about June 2nd for the trial. Maybe I'll be out for my birthday . . . " And she was going to write to Sir Robert Mark, the Commissioner of Metropolitan Police, about the case if she could get permission from the Governor, ". . . because some of the lies they have come out with are utterly ridiculous, I don't know if any of what they

163

said you said was lies or not but I know what they said I said was a load of bullshit not all of it but some of it . . . "

One reason for Carole's confidence was the apparent firming-up of her alibi. Unknown to her there had developed around this a small interesting sub-plot to the history of the Guildford bombing.

12
Strange Interlude

Frank Johnson, the young man from Newcastle who had taken Carole and Lisa Astin to the South Bank Polytechnic pop concert on October 5, had himself, for much of 1974, been a part of that individualistic drifting London sub-culture in which the two girls were at home. He had already served a prison sentence for drug offences when he hitch-hiked to London early in 1974. Living in a friend's flat in West Hampstead he worked for a time as a petrol pump attendant and car cleaner in Golders Green. He then drifted to Ireland where, after attending a friend's wedding in Dublin, he spent two months on a farm in Co. Donegal, came back to his old job at the Golders Green petrol station, and then took a job as a machine minder's assistant at a printing works in Colindale. He had lived in a squat in Brixton before returning home to Newcastle early in November. It had been from Brixton that he had travelled to the Elephant and Castle to meet Carole and Lisa for the pop concert on October 5. He had got to know them drinking in the Memphis Belle in Kilburn, where incidently he had also met Paddy Armstrong who at that time had a part-time job collecting glasses for the pub.

On December 11, eight days after Carole's arrest, he came back to London to collect some belongings he had left behind there, and calling in at one of the squats met Lisa, who told him for the first time of Carole's arrest. He was amazed at the news but did not immediately connect the date of the Guildford bombings for which she had been arrested with the date of their visit to the pop concert. Lisa's view at the time of this conversation was that although she thought that Paddy might have been involved she did not think Carole could possibly have been.

It was on his way back to Newcastle on the bus that Frank Johnson thought about the pop concert. He recalled that a Newcastle group "Jack the Lad", had been playing at it and on getting home he rang up a member of the group, William Mitchell, who confirmed that it was indeed on that evening that they had been playing at the South Bank Polytechnic. Johnson then consulted a number of friends as to what to do next and they all advised him to go to a solicitor. After first drawing up on paper as detailed an account of the evening of October 5 as he could recall, he went on December 17 to a solicitor who, however, made clear he was unwilling to take on business associated with a charge of terrorism. He advised Johnson to contact Guildford Magistrates' Court, which he did. He was told by them that none of the solicitors involved wished to have their names publicly released. In view of his police record for drug offences Johnson had a certain disinclination to present himself at a police station but thinking that he had a responsibility to Carole, he went to the Newcastle police on December 19. He told them that a girl who he believed had been charged with murder at Guildford on the evening of October 5 had in fact been with him then at the pop concert.

This was to turn into an all-important alibi for Carole Richardson. The prosecution was to dispute it as having been deliberately devised previously. There are two points to be made about it. Firstly, Carole at this stage, while hoping to prove an alibi for herself and trusting that the diary which had in fact been burned would supply it, had not put forward the South Bank Polytechnic concert as an alibi because she had not yet connected it with the relevant date. It is difficult not to think that if the alibi had indeed been previously devised it would have been ready to hand immediately – unless, that is, the police were crediting such people with the super-subtlety of not wishing to present an alibi that seemed immediately convincing. Secondly, Frank Johnson at this point knew absolutely nothing of the details of the case against Carole. Details in the account he was about to present, including times, had no particular significance so far as he was concerned; his only concern was to register that she had in fact spent the evening of that day with him.

The Newcastle police listened to Johnson, took his telephone number and said they would ring him back later, which they did. The police officer to whom he had spoken telephoned at 5 o'clock that evening and then came to collect him and drive him to the police station. There he was kept in a room for some time, held in what struck him as rather pointless general conversation. Then the door opened and Detective Chief Inspector Longhurst, Detective Constable Wise, and Woman Police Constable Mills, all of the Surrey Constabulary, walked in. Johnson thought they looked like something out of a movie about Chicago. He afterwards described their expression as being like that of people whom "the boss had sent to collect money that you owe him". He repeated to them what he had to say about the evening of October 5 and was eventually taken to the Charge Room where he was told:

"Are you sure you were with Carole that night, because if so, we've got no option but to charge you with murder."

He says he got the impression that if only he would say that he had not after all been with Carole that night there would be no more problems for him. But, unaware perhaps of the full complexity of the case in which he was about to become entangled, he replied:

"That's fine. You're going to charge me with murder then."

They told him that he would have to be kept in a cell overnight while they made further enquiries. This was not as great a shock to him as it would have been to some people, possibly because in the somewhat picaresque nature of his lifestyle an odd bed anywhere was often part of the normal pattern of events. Blankets and a mattress were provided, and he was even given a comic to read. He did not spend a bad night, secure in his knowledge of his own truthfulness and thinking only that some sort of mistake had been made which he hoped would be ironed out with apologies in time for Christmas. Next morning he had to wait a long time in his cell without being quite sure what he was waiting for, but as he was to say later: "I wasn't taking it that serious." That afternoon he made an official police statement.

He said he had arranged to meet Carole and Lisa at the Charlie Chaplin pub at the Elephant and Castle at about 6.30 p.m. on Saturday, October 5. He had arrived at the pub from his squat at Brixton between 6 and 6.10 p.m. and they had arrived about a quarter of an hour later. Their intention was to see a member of the group who was a friend of Johnson's and get the girls in for nothing. They had eventually found four of the group at the Polytechnic and had gone to have a drink with them in a pub. At about 9 p.m. they had left the pub so that the band could get their instruments tuned and had all gone into the Polytechnic together. They had left about 10.45 p.m. and after some fish and chips had parted company about 11.10 p.m.

This, then, was his statement of December 20, 1974. The Surrey police who took it had seemed quite friendly. The only thing which he had not particularly liked about the whole business had been the way in which he had been told to stand in the corridor and have his photograph taken. He left, thinking only that he would shortly be hearing that Carole had been released.

After Christmas, however, it began to dawn on him that he was not hearing any such thing. He began to develop a certain anxiety for himself, even to suspect at times that he was being followed. It became clear at least that he would very likely have to appear in Court as a witness and, considering that as a witness he would cut a more impressive figure if he were in employment, he got himself a job. The job was in an abattoir where he was to work with pigs' and sheep's guts, squeezing out the unwanted contents such as worms and undigested grass through his fingers and placing them in barrels of salt to be cured for sausage skins. On only the second day in this job he came out in the evening to find a police car waiting outside. He was asked by one of the officers to get in and come with them. Asking if he were under arrest and getting no reply, he said he wanted to see a solicitor, but was told somewhat sinisterly that he could not and that no one now knew his whereabouts or where he was going to. On arrival at the police station he asked if he could wash his hands. One of the officers agreed and left the room, but as he was about to go to the sink to turn on the tap another officer came in and asked him:

"Where do you think you're going? You're trying to wash the nitroglycerine from under your fingernails."

This was not a joke. The officer's demeanour was even intimidating. Frank Johnson was not allowed to wash his hands for the next two days. He was then told that some people were flying up from London to talk to him.

"It's up to you. You can satisfy them here and now, or you'll go back with them. You'd better provide them with what they want or things aren't going to be too nice." He is not quite sure whether it was at this point or after the Surrey police had arrived that he was told it could be arranged for something unpleasant to happen to his mother, an invalid in a wheel-chair.

The reason for bringing him in soon became apparent. Detective Chief Inspector Longhurst and Detective Sergeant Wise had come for him. When they found that he had still not changed his story they told him that he would have to accompany them to Guildford. They saw him put into the same cell as before for the night. This time the blankets were taken out, but he had often slept rough out of doors and, curling into the foetal position, found this no particular hardship. Next morning he was driven to the airport, then handcuffed and taken by Longhurst and Wise on the early morning plane down to London. On arrival he was put into a police car, his handcuffs linked to a hook on the floor of the car, and driven to Guildford where he was shown the pubs that had been bombed. It was even suggested that they might take him to the hospital to see the injured who were still there. For the first time he began to feel confused and to ask himself the question: "Do they really think I was there?" When interrogation started the next day the implication was that the police had no alternative but to press the charge of murder against him unless he was sensible enough to alter his account of what had happened on the night of October 5.

He was now formally arrested under the Prevention of Terrorism Act which enabled him to be questioned for seven days without being brought to Court. He says that the pressure put on him became so disorientating that he cannot now remember how many days exactly he was held there but it was not more than three.

The first day was spent trying to convince him that the police knew exactly what had happened that evening and that if he thought that he was right about what had occurred he was in fact wrong: they would persuade him to acknowledge this. Their concentration now was not so much on the point that he must himself have been a party to the murders at Guildford but that he had got the times of the meeting with the two girls at the Elephant and Castle wrong. They wanted to make clear to him that it had been 7.45 at the earliest when he had met Carole and Lisa, whereas he had said in his previous statement that it had been at about half-past six. The difference was crucial because interviews with surviving witnesses of the Horse and Groom had made clear that the "courting couple" were last seen there about 7 p.m. Even if the police were right about the timing an almost superhuman effort would have been required for Carole to get by car from Guildford to the Elephant and Castle in three quarters of an hour, but if Frank Johnson were right it would have been impossible.

Johnson today describes the atmosphere on the first day of the interview as psychologically curious. If, he says, he had been a member of some organisation knowingly pitting his wits against the interrogation skills of the police it would have been easier, but he found it disconcerting to have such an attitude from people whom he was regarding as ordinary human beings. It was on the second day that their attitude began to seem intimidating.

One of his interviewers, clicking his fingers, carefully took Frank Johnson's spectacles off his face and placed them on the table, saying that they would be safe there and would not get broken; he might have to pay for them if they got broken. "Not a direct threat," says Johnson. "A sideways threat. It was all done very gradually . . . Yes, physical violence did start but it's the continual intensive pressure of one sort or another on at you all the time and the fact that they get through to you that nobody knows you're there and you can be there as long as they want you to be. You feel they'll keep at it until you go into a mental hospital because your brain can't take it."

Johnson says he was made to stand against a wall. One interrogator continued to sit at the table to write down answers. Another stood close in front of Johnson, "eyeball to eyeball with me but just slightly to one side". He told him to look at the man asking the questions.

"The first question, I got the wrong answer. I just caught out of the corner of my eye this fist coming towards me."

He ducked and it caught him on the side of the face. He remembers some conversation between two interrogators about the unwisdom of marking him. He was told to take a step forward away from the wall and the next question which he answered wrong was followed by a blow on the side of the neck which, he says, left it stiff for a couple of months afterwards.

"I didn't see that coming at all."

It knocked him to the ground. He was brought to his feet. There was nothing particularly horrific. "Soon I was just swinging around the room between the two of them." He was banged against the wall, banged against a locker, threatened with being shut up in the locker and being thrown out of the window when the "lollipop" man on duty on the pedestrian crossing outside had gone home. He says he didn't really take this seriously, "but when there are so many things happening throughout the day you're never really sure what to believe and what not to believe."

Just before 6 o'clock on January 22 he signed another statement. This began:

"I would like to say that some of the things I said in my last statement are not true."

He now said that when he left his Brixton squat on the evening of October 5 it had been dark and the street lights had been on. (This would have put the time of his arrival at the Elephant and Castle at 7 p.m. or later.) The statement continued: "I don't remember exactly how long I waited in the pub for Lisa and Carole to arrive but it could have been as long as forty minutes." This would have meant that Carole arrived at the pub no earlier than 7.45. The statement concluded: "In the previous statement I had fixed the times earlier because I didn't believe that Carole had done such a thing and I wanted to help her. I am sorry for all the inconvenience I caused to all the people concerned."

The new statement ran to about 350 words, a curiously truncated version of two days' intensive questioning. But it secured his release which by that time was his main concern. He said to his interrogators simply, "If you want a statement on those lines, write it out and I'll sign it." His mental reservation was that he would have to try and get the matter sorted out in court.

They asked him if he wanted to read the statement through. He told them he did not but that they ought to read it through themselves and check to see that it contained what they wanted. It would not, he said, make any difference whether he read it or not because what he knew to be the truth had been put into his earlier statement. The police thus had no difficulty in getting him to sign a rider saying that he had in fact read the statement through. An additional rider ran:

"I would like to add that I have no complaints about my treatment in Guildford police station on Wednesday 22nd January 1975."

On leaving the police station one of the officers who had been present at the interviews but who, Johnson thought, had been plainly embarrassed by some of what had gone on gave him 50 pence for a meal on the way home. ("That would be about £3 now," Johnson adds fairly.)

A few months later, before the trial of the Guildford Four, Christopher Rowe the Assistant Chief Constable of Surrey was awarded the Queen's Medal in the Royal Birthday Honours. "He will always," wrote the *Surrey Daily Advertiser*, "be remembered as the man who led investigations into the Guildford pub bombings of 1974." He himself commented modestly that "the award was in recognition of all the work put into the pub bombings – not just his part".

It was almost as if the matter was already settled. But technically there still had to be the traditional style contest between the Crown and Carole Richardson, Patrick Armstrong, Gerard Conlon and Paul Hill.

Through the confessions of Conlon and Hill, one other person would figure with some prominence in that contest, although she herself was not on trial for the offences with which they were charged: Anne Maguire of 43, Third Avenue, Harlesden. And through her, six other people's lives would be affected by the course of that trial, however much the niceties of English law might maintain otherwise. The local Guildford newspaper, the *Surrey Daily Advertiser*, recognised this straightforwardly enough from the start. "Ten Weeks for Bomb Trial?" it headlined its front page article announcing the opening of the trial of Richardson, Armstrong, Conlon and Hill for September 16, 1975. Local security, it reported Christopher Rowe as saying, had had to be stepped-up somewhat as a result of a recent bomb attack on a pub at Caterham in Surrey (a virtual carbon copy, oddly, of the Guildford bombing.) The newspaper continued:

"The murder trial will be followed by the trial of seven other persons accused of explosives offences.

"Mr William (Sean) Smyth (36), Mr Patrick Maguire (41), Mrs Anne Maguire (39), Mr Patrick O'Neill (34) and two boys aged 16 and 13, all of 43, Third Avenue, London W.10, are accused of having in their possession or control in the Greater London area on or about December 3rd, 1974, nitro-glycerine, an explosive substance, in circumstances to give rise to the suspicion that it was not in their possession or control for a lawful object."

PART II

Arguments

13
The Trial of the Guildford Four

At first it was difficult even to find any local solicitor in Guildford to take on the defence of Hill, Conlon, Armstrong and Richardson. The man who to his own credit decided that such a situation did no credit to the law and finally took on Armstrong was told by the policeman who saw him shake hands with his new client: "You'll want to wash your hands now, won't you?" It was almost with a feeling of guilt among themselves that he and the three solicitors who were eventually found to represent the others, rather sheepishly confessed to each other when they met just before the committal proceedings that they actually thought their clients innocent.

Carole Richardson's optimism that the prosecution case would seem so flimsy, once another account of the confessions was known, that the defendants would not even be committed for trial, proved of course, unjustified. Far too much care and prestige had been invested in the case by the prosecution for it to be easily dismissed out of hand. One detail of the committal proceedings indeed revealed just how thoroughly it was being pursued. Carole Richardson's application to join the WRAC in April 1974 was adduced as evidence of her intention to carry out a reconnaissance for the bombing, since part of the training would have been in Guildford. This evidence was heard seriously.

When the trial proper began in September 1975 the atmosphere was tense. Armstrong's solicitor admits that, as he went into the Old Bailey and submitted to the inevitably rigorous security measures which prevailed, he himself felt on the defensive against an unspoken reproach for representing such people as those on trial. They were at a correspondingly greater disadvantage.

The rightly dignified and even awesome setting in which a trial takes place can hardly help acting to the disadvantage of the lowly defendant. In an atmosphere alien to the world in which he feels at home it is almost impossible for him not to become *over*-awed, aware of his role as "accused" rather than of his status as a "defendant" with, as is technically the case, equal or even greater rights than the prosecution. Certainly his own representatives are an integral part of the dignified proceedings but this in itself can make it hard for those in the dock, who have often arrived there handcuffed, not to feel that even the men representing them are part of the other side.

On the morning of Tuesday, September 16, of the four people brought into court to face charges of murder at the Horse and Groom on October 5, two – Hill and Armstrong – were facing further charges of murder for the bombing of the King's Arms at Woolwich on November 7. All had been in prison for over nine months. The three men spoke with strong Belfast accents. Armstrong's was so heavy that his solicitor could hardly understand a word he said when he first met him. This further emphasised an identity alien to the court, while Carole Richardson was in a psychological condition so precarious that her counsel would not take the risk of letting her go into the witness box where she could be cross-examined on oath.

Just after dawn on the day of the trial sniffer dogs had been through the law courts and as the jurors arrived armed police were on duty in the building with marksmen placed at strategic points on roof-tops. If the accused were what they were accused of being, an IRA attempt to rescue them was not beyond the bounds of reasonable possibility. As if to substantiate such a possibility Paul Hill at the opening of the trial refused to plead, in the IRA tradition, and called out to the judge, "Your justice stinks!" This did nothing to help him. On the fourth day the proceedings had to be held up for half an hour at the start because he had failed to arrive in court. He eventually appeared with one eye bruised, swollen and black, which appeared to the *Guardian* correspondent to get worse in the course of the morning. No public explanation of the cause of his injuries was ever given.

When, against this psychological background, the judge in the course of his summing-up appealed to the jury to decide whose word they were going to take about whether or not the defendants' confessions had been partially obtained by police brutality, it must have been, in the nature of things, difficult for that jury to divest themselves of an inclination to believe the police. And since the only evidence on which the defendants could be convicted was the credibility or otherwise of these statements the decision was of vital importance.

The police, dressed in their uniforms, accustomed to the requirements of performance in court, gave their evidence calmly and collectedly. Even when the allegations of improper treatment were put by the defendants' counsel with their own appropriate decorum the denials had a convincingly authentic ring.

Lord Wigoder, QC for Gerard Conlon, accused Detective Chief Superintendent Wally Simmons of threatening his client repeatedly, and of extending the threat to his family in the Lower Falls area of Belfast.

"No, my Lord," replied Simmons calmly.

". . . You banged on the desk and put on an act of a wild man saying you would kill him if you came round the desk."

"Certainly not, my Lord."

Mr John Leonard QC, for Armstrong, asked Detective Sergeant John Donaldson if his client had not been hit once by Assistant Chief Constable Christopher Rowe and once by Simmons and then pushed in the chest by Rowe.

"No," was Donaldson's reply.

"He was told about the scene at the Horse and Groom –

people with no arms and legs, etc. – and told the same thing will happen to you?"

"Certainly not, sir."

Detective Inspector Blake was accused by Counsel for both Conlon and Hill, Mr Arthur Mildon QC, of using violence towards them. Blake had, said Mr Mildon, knocked Hill down in one of the last interviews, pinned him to the floor, sitting astride him with a knee in each shoulder and shaking his head by the hair.

Blake strongly denied this, at which there was an outburst from Hill in the dock.

Blake said:

"I never used violence to him at all."

Equally accused by Lord Wigoder of violence to his client, Blake equally strongly denied it. In answer to allegations that he had taken off his jacket, rolled up his shirt sleeves and set about Conlon, pulled his hair, made him strip and squeezed his testicles, Blake denied that he had even seen Conlon that day. Asked to explain how Conlon was able to describe a tattoo with a dagger and some sort of writing on his arm, he said that Godalming Police Station where Conlon had been held was centrally heated and sometimes when he was working in his office he did take off his coat and roll up his sleeves to be more comfortable. He added that apart from passing a remark to Conlon at one of his court appearances he had never spoken to him. This was not of course in itself a complete answer to the allegations that he had struck him but the Detective Inspector's equanimity under cross-examination was impressive.

When Detective Sergeant Richard Jermey equally resolutely denied that any physical or mental threats had been made to Conlon, Conlon too shouted in protest from the dock that the man was a liar. He became so outraged that he had to be restrained by officials. Detective Sergeant Jermey remained convincingly impassive.

When Mr Eric Myers QC, counsel for Carole Richardson, suggested to Chief Inspector Alan Longhurst that at one of the interviews with his client he had make a remark about "mad Irishmen" he agreed. But when counsel suggested that

Carole had begun to smile at this and that Woman Police Constable Mills hit her with the back of her hand he denied the suggestion. Equally when counsel suggested that as he, Longhurst, continued to question her Detective Constable Martin Wise had hit and punched her, Longhurst replied:

"No, certainly not."

Standing up as competently as they did to learned counsel the police witnesses inevitably made an even better impression when compared with the somewhat bedraggled figures in the dock with their strong Belfast, or, in the case of Carole Richardson, Cockney accents. The Judge, Mr Justice Donaldson*, it is true, scrupulously warned the jury against making *ad hoc* judgments of this sort:

"Do not," he said to them in his summing-up, "do not forget that when people come forward and enter the witness box and take the oath, they all start equal. There are no classes of witnesses. You have had police officers coming here in uniform, police officers out of uniform, people who are not police officers . . . They all start equal . . . "

He then however reminded them that they did not all end so, and that the difference depended on how their evidence was judged and on how they appeared to stand up under cross-examination. But this second part of his advice largely undermined the first. For, of course, judgment on the quality of a person's evidence, and of his or her stand under cross-examination, is not easy to separate from judgment of their quality as a class of person. Armstrong's "I never done no bombs at all" inevitably contrasted unfavourably with the "Certainly not, my Lord" of police officers responding to the allegations made against them.

The traditionally impeccable summing-up such as Mr Justice Donaldson meted out to the jury is full of such examples of fairness turning on itself in a manner that might be dubbed hypocrisy were not the intellectual honesty of British judges so traditionally taken for granted. Thus almost the opening words designed to soothe a jury facing the daunting task of having to reach a verdict on a matter of such conse-

*Now Sir John Donaldson, Master of the Rolls.

quence told them that it was the Judge's business to interpret the law for them, "but when it comes to the facts, then that is entirely a matter for you".

The sentences that followed form something of a masterpiece of convolution. Mr Justice Donaldson immediately qualified the above statement by continuing: "The purpose of the summing-up is to tell you what the law is you have to apply *and to try and give you some assistance as to the facts.** But when I say 'give you assistance as to the facts' do not misunderstand me. I know that there is a popular view that juries get some assistance from the judge as to what the proper verdict is, but that is quite wrong ... Of course ... it would be contrary to human nature if I had not my own private view about the matter, but you are not concerned with that at all. If you think you can detect what my view is, ignore it." His view was to be detectable enough by the end of the trial. The jury did not ignore it. Since in fact his summing-up both constitutes a resumé of all that went on and contains pointers to why the jury reached their verdict it is useful to pay it some attention.

In technical legal terms it could not be faulted. Scrupulously it outlined the rights of the accused and the obligations of the prosecution. In doing so it placed on the prosecution a burden which was particularly relevant to this trial.

"The accused," said Mr Justice Donaldson, "under English law has the right to be found not guilty *if there is any doubt about it at all.*"

Jurors might well have asked themselves at this point if the course of the trial really had been such that there was *no doubt at all* about the guilt of the four in the dock. Could, for instance, anyone who had read the police accounts of interviews with the accused after their arrests and compared their subsequent statements really feel that these four were without doubt the people who had planted the bombs at Guildford?

In the trial nothing effectively new had been brought forward in the way of evidence against the accused. Rather, the reverse had been the case. Alibis had been put forward

*Author's italics.

on behalf of all of them with varying degrees of conviction. That for Hill – that he had been with his girl friend at Southampton at the time the bombs were planted – was weakened by a number of apparent contradictions, for some of which he himself was responsible. Armstrong's was unconvincing because, though detailed, it referred to another Saturday night altogether than that for which it was produced. Conlon's was equally so because the man who he said could substantiate it, one Patrick Carey, had returned to Ireland and did not re-emerge. Carole Richardson's alibi, that she had been at the Elephant and Castle pop concert, was by far the most compelling.

Both Frank Johnson and Lisa Astin had appeared in court to confirm it. Lisa had even produced details of how she had spent the whole afternoon of Saturday, October 5 with Carole, visiting between 4 and 5 p.m. a friend Maura Kelly, who worked at an ABC bakery at Primrose Hill, before going back to Algernon Road to change for the concert. Maura Kelly was 16 at the time. Her mother had taken her back to the Republic of Ireland by the time of the trial and did not give her permission to attend it, wishing to have nothing to do with its terrorist overtones. Lisa arrived late at the court, necessitating its adjournment for twenty minutes.

Frank Johnson's second statement to the Guildford police in which he had agreed to place the time of the two girls' arrival at the Elephant and Castle later than he had first stated made the latter end of Carole's alibi precarious. He did disclose in some detail how, he said, this second statement had been obtained from him, referring to the blow on the neck from a police officer and the threat made to his mother in her wheel-chair. But he admitted that it was the psychological rather than the physical pressure on him which had told. After a morning of questioning he said he had completely broken down. His previous convictions for drug offences, and consequent imprisonment, were before the court and he also admitted in all honesty that although he was opposed to violence he had pro-Republican Irish sympathies and had been a member of the Newcastle branch of the Anti-Internment League. He had had an Anti-Internment handkerchief on him when he was arrested by the police. When asked why he had not complained to the National Council of Civil Liberties about his treatment at the hands of the police he had replied equally honestly: "I was too frightened to complain." Anyway, he added, he thought they were just doing their job. He is even today a man whose calm dissociation from the manner in which conventional society conducts its business confers on him an appropriate lack of rancour. Mr Justice Donaldson addressed him:

"You never complained about police treatment, you say, because you did not think the police were doing anything but their duty?"

"I did not think I was being believed."

"I suggest to you that you do complain when you leave this court. Do you want this investigated?"

"I prefer to forget about it."

No inquiry was ever made into Johnson's allegations.

On the other hand Mr Justice Donaldson very properly drew the jury's attention to two matters concerning the alibis of all the accused. He said that, if you do have an alibi which you wish to prove, the type of witness whom you call to prove it is no responsibility of yours.

"It is certainly right that you should not hold it against any of the accused if they have been obliged to call some people in support of their alibi who, you may think, lead lives of which you would not wholly approve . . . "

But then, with his customary judicial fairness, he gave the pronouncement a double edge:

"When they do come into the witness box their evidence has to be weighed like the evidence of any other witness. If it carries conviction, well and good. If it does not carry conviction weigh it accordingly."

A fuller factual analysis of whether Lisa Astin could have been telling the truth, or whether or not the police had really persuaded Frank Johnson to change his evidence against his will and what their reasons might have been, could have served the cause of justice better. But none was forthcoming. The judge's only attempt to do something of the sort occurred when, reciting the evidence which Johnson had given, he reminded the jury that he "was the gentleman who . . . said, somewhat generously, you may think, that despite the pressure by the police he had no complaint against them because they had no hatred in their eyes". One of the most telling phrases in the judicial armoury is the innocuous "you may think".

On the subject of alibis in general Mr Justice Donaldson properly reminded the jury:

"It is not for the accused to prove that they were elsewhere, it is for the prosecution to satisfy you that they were at Guildford . . . "

This could hardly be said too often in this case because the prosecution had nothing but the accused's own contradictory and now retracted statements to support the contention that they had been there. Moreover, those witnesses from the Horse and Groom who had seen the "courting couple" had positively failed to identify Carole Richardson as being there. But something more positive could have been added in favour of the accused's alibis.

It was an essential part of the Crown case, adroitly elaborated by Sir Michael Havers, that the contradictions and anomalies in the statements were part of a skilled, sophisticated technique of counter-interrogation, designed to confuse and mislead the police about the true nature of the way in which the bombing operation had been carried out. But, with the conceivable exception of Hill, the background of the accused and their demeanour since arrest hardly suggested that they were shrewd, sophisticated professionals of the type the IRA would employ in the first place, even if individually capable of being trained in such techniques. What seemed to strengthen this argument was the probability that if they had been such people they would have had a convincing alibi ready to hand. Sophisticated professionals would not have both failed to produce any alibi at all when first arrested and then so clumsily have groped around to find one. Mr Justice Donaldson did not make this point.

The argument applies particularly to Carole Richardson whose alibi once evolved had more than a seeming plausibility, since there were other witnesses besides Astin and

Johnson and even a photograph of her taken at the pop concert to prove she was there. On this alibi appropriately Mr Justice Donaldson did dwell, although hardly to Carole's advantage.

He said that the time during which the Crown had to prove that she had been at Guildford was between opening time for the pubs there, which he put at 5.45, and the time at which the bomb in the Horse and Groom went off, which he put (inaccurately) at 8.30. (The time was in fact 8.50, though this error was of no consequence.) Even accepting Frank Johnson's later adjustment of the time at which he met the girls, and adding to it the confirmatory evidence of a member of the "Jack the Lad" group who had seen him with Carole and Lisa at the door of the South London Polytechnic at about 7.45, the passage of time for which Carole had to account, in order to disprove the Crown's case, was between 5.45 and 7.45. But the Crown had in a way made things more difficult for itself by saying that Carole was likely to have been one half of the "courting couple"; the soldiers Cook and Lynskey had seen them in the Horse and Groom a few minutes before 7 p.m. For the case against her to hold, therefore, she would have had to have left the Horse and Groom, got into a car and driven off, sufficiently calmly to avoid arousing suspicion, to arrive at the South London Polytechnic in time to meet Astin and Johnson and present herself at the door with them, by 7.45 p.m. – a total period of less than fifty minutes altogether.

Unless Johnson and Astin had themselves been party to the plot (and except at the very beginning of police contacts with them, as part of interrogation technique, the police had never pretended they were or pursued any such charge) a minute or so at least would have been taken up by Carole's meeting with them either on the pavement or in a pub before arriving at the door. So that the drive from Guildford to the South London Polytechnic, allowing, say, only a minute each end for what the Judge described as "the times necessary to get in and out of a motor car", would have had to be completed in forty-eight minutes.

Arguments

Mr Justice Donaldson approached this problem with a certain populist touch:

"You may be surprised," he said to the jury, "I do not know whether any of you drive that road, what a relatively short time it appears to take."

A solicitor's clerk, he said, observing the 1975 speed limits which were slightly lower than those prevailing in 1974 had driven the distance in one hour and four minutes. A police car, observing the 1974 speed limits, had done it in fifty-two minutes. A police car observing no speed limits at all had done it in forty-eight minutes.

He reminded the jury of a point Counsel had made to the effect that anybody who had just planted a bomb would have been extraordinarily stupid to drive back to London breaking all speed limits. He did not remind them that, according to the Crown, Carole Richardson was said to be an extraordinarily clever terrorist. He simply added: "Whether you think in those circumstances you would follow the speed limits or whether you think it would be better to put distance between you and Guildford is a matter for you to consider." And there he left it.

To refer back – as he however did not at this stage – to his earlier dictum: could it really be said that there was no doubt at all in these circumstances that Carole Richardson could have been at Guildford?

There was another area of his summing-up in which an important lack of comment could be said to have acted in the jury's minds to the disadvantage of the accused. This was in the area which, as he rightly emphasised from the start, was absolutely central to the whole case against the accused: that of their own self-convicting statements. There was the same problem, he said, running through the case in relation to all the accused:

"Are these original statements made to the police in substance true? Are they true so that you can be sure they are true and that each of these four committed the offences with which they are charged, or do you accept the evidence which three of them have given in the witness box and Carole Richardson's statement from the dock that those statements were totally false and they had nothing to do with these bombings?"

He went over great tracts of these statements very faithfully in each individual case. What he did not do was draw attention to the considerable number of instances in each case in which the statements had been shown to be nonsense. For instance the statements of Hill and Conlon from which he quoted at length had specifically led to the arrests of Brian Anderson, John MacGuiness, Paul Colman and Anne Maguire for murder as having been present at Guildford too. The statements had appeared to be sufficiently substantiated by the further statements of Armstrong and Richardson for such charges not to be dropped against these people for over a month later in the first three cases, for over two months later in the case of Anne Maguire. Yet here was Mr Justice Donaldson reciting passages that referred to these people without any explanation of who they were or why, if these parts of the statements were true, such people had not been tried for murder after all. Again, if these passages were not true, why should credence necessarily be given to any of the other passages? Contradictions about the make of car used or indeed the drivers concerned were equally blandly passed over. Earlier Mr Justice Donaldson had said specifically of Armstrong's statements:

"He says that they are almost entirely untrue and that the only true parts are his personal particulars and the account you will find of his hitch-hiking activities . . . You must not at any stage in your deliberations, either in respect of Patrick Armstrong or the other accused, lose sight of the fact that what you are trying to decide is whether their confessions are false . . . Because if you think that these confessions even might be false, so that you are left in doubt about the matter and are not sure, then, of course, he is entitled to be acquitted."

The Crown, he reminded the jury, based their case on the theory that these confessions "were much too detailed, far too detailed for them possibly to be false". But was the Crown to be allowed to say that only those elements were true which it suited them not to find false? Such questions were not placed before the jury by the Judge.

The unspoken reasoning behind his silence may have been that there seemed no need to repeat the Crown's belief that what was false in the statements was the result of a sophisticated attempt to protect other people who had in reality accompanied the accused. There was one significant objection however to this argument. If the four accused had been genuinely involved, if the introduction of the other names had been a blind, why should they have introduced one name which, according to continuing Crown belief, had been actively involved in the operation and was cited in the trial as showing Conlon how to make IRA bombs: that of Anne Maguire? Would they have really given the name of someone who was genuinely involved in their organisation in order to protect their organisation? Or, alternatively, was she perhaps as innocent of the charges against her as Anderson, MacGuiness and Colman had been proved to be? It certainly would not have suited the Crown to suggest this: they were at that moment holding Anne Maguire on bail on a charge of unlawfully handling explosives. Indeed Sir Michael Havers in quoting from Conlon's "not false" statement had given a graphic description of her "with a long black tube, some sand and a watch face" showing him how to make a bomb. This could not be used as evidence against her because it was hearsay, but Havers was nevertheless using such hearsay to substantiate the truth of Conlon's statement. Could the oblique and unresolved doubts and questions which surrounded these statements really be said to leave the jury "in no doubt at all" that the statements were true?

The fundamental test of the validity of the statements lay, as Donaldson J* rightly stated more than once, in the question of whether the accused's allegations of police brutality were to be believed. To this he gave a great deal of attention.

---

*It is a conventional courtesy when using the surnames of High Court Judges without title to follow them with the initial J.

He faithfully repeated to the jury the allegations which Armstrong had made:

"I said I knew nothing. I was struck in the face by Mr Rowe with his fist under my right eye. He called me a fucking lying bastard ... I said that I knew nothing. Then Mr Simmons said: 'Let's try the other side.' He hit me on the other side, the left hand side of my face with his hand just above the lip ... I answered these questions because I was frightened of the police. Atwell came in in the course of the taking of the statement. All the officers came into the room and were supposed to be telling him something about me. Atwell said: 'If these officers hear anything about you, they will come in here and throw you out of the window and put it down as suicide.' I was crying and shaking. I started to make the statement. Being hit and thrown against the wall had affected my mind. . . . I was compelled by fear and force to make the statements and the statements were taken by question and answer. The questions were put in such a form as to suggest an answer, to which I assented . . . "

Donaldson J had two main comments to make about all this. In the first place he thought the jury might ask themselves why Armstrong had not complained of such treatment when he was interviewed by senior officers of the Metropolitan Police bomb squad about the Woolwich bombings. There was a reply to this which the learned Judge had to acknowledge when Armstrong's Counsel pointed it out. Quite apart from a man like Armstrong being psychologically disinclined to differentiate between one policeman and another in the circumstances, that interview with the Metropolitan police had taken place in Guildford police station and it was in the care of the Guildford police that he knew he was to remain. A complementary question the jury might also have been invited to ask themselves was why, if Armstrong was making this all up, he had not made up accusations of violence against the Metropolitan police officers too.

The other consideration was the basic one from which in the respectable environment of a law court police witnesses can always expect credit to the disadvantage of less respectable accused. Once again the Judge reminded the jury of the names of those against whom Armstrong's allegations of improper treatment had been made: Assistant Chief Constable Rowe, Detective Chief Inspector Style, Detective Sergeant Donaldson and Detective Constable Atwell.

"You have seen," he said, "these officers in the witness box and you may like to ask yourselves whether this evidence could be true. If it could be true, then you might like to ask yourselves whether, if you can visualise those officers offering him violence, it would be sufficient violence to make him confess to murder."

And he added with his usual fairness:

"You may not like the man, you may not like his way of life, but that is nothing to do with it. He is entitled to be acquitted if you have real doubts. But if, of course, you have no real doubts, then it is your duty to convict."

Paul Hill was a special case as far as the allegations of violence were concerned. Of the six statements he had made only the last was, he alleged, preceded by police brutality, a statement incidentally which gave a graphic description of Anne Maguire going into the Horse and Groom with Gerard Conlon to blow it up, whereas the Crown was saying it had been Armstrong and Richardson. Donaldson J made no reference to this anomaly, which had become just one more example of the Crown discounting all information in the statements except that which suited its purpose to accept as truth. In one police officer's frank words: most of the statements could be regarded as "fairy tales . . . a mixture of fact and fiction". But on the specific issue of the alleged violence to Hill Donaldson J presented his previous formula:

". . . It is said that before the last statement Detective Inspector Blake sat on Hill and clouted him off a chair. You will have to make up your minds, having seen Detective Inspector Blake and having heard Mr Hill in the witness box, whether there is any truth in that allegation."

What had induced Hill so readily to make his other five statements remained something of an enigma even to his own Counsel who apart from putting forward Hill's explanation that he wanted to protect his girl-friend Gina simply had to present him as a compulsive talker. But a fact which might have made both this tendency and Hill's own explanation more plausible could not in fairness to him be revealed in court. This was a paradoxical state of affairs since it could have worked to his advantage. The fact was that before he made any statement at all about Guildford he had admitted a part in the Ulster murder of Brian Shaw to officers of the RUC while Guildford officers waited close by: he might have reckoned that he had very little to lose if, to protect Gina Clarke, he admitted to a second murder charge. An additional fear of difficulties with the IRA if he served his sentence in Ulster, which may or may not have been present in his mind, was also understandably not referred to by anyone.

In the case of both Conlon and Richardson, Mr Justice Donaldson returned with diligence to the central problem of the statements. Virtually the only evidence on which the accused could be convicted was their own evidence that they had been involved in the Guildford bombings.* Yet if those statements had been obtained from them by improper means they were invalid and they could only be found not guilty. The Judge rightly never let the jury shirk this point.

He recapitulated Conlon's own evidence to the effect that Detective Superintendent Wally Simmons had threatened to have his mother shot in an "accident"; that his first statement giving the truth about his innocence of the Guildford bombing had been torn up; that Jermey had pressed painfully below his ears with his fingers and that Blake had squeezed his private parts. "I then wrote the statement," Conlon had concluded from the witness box, "with a lot of help from the police. They dictated what to write down."

Again Donaldson J drew attention to the persuasive impression made by the police. "You will consider," he said to the jury, "having seen those officers and having heard Mr Conlon's evidence, whether he was subject to those threats, whether he was subject to the ill treatment and if he was, or could have been, whether it had any effect on his making that

---

*Hill and Armstrong of course were also charged with the Woolwich bombings on the strength of their confessions.

statement, or could have had any effect, because in the end what you have to decide is whether this admission is true."

In Carole's case too he had to tackle the same point central to the whole indictment, but in her case he had understandably reminded the jury that the allegations were made not on oath but in a statement from the dock. It was her perfect right to choose to do this, he said. He reminded the jury that she should not be criticised for so exercising her choice, adding however: "Whether you think it [her statement] carries the same weight as it might have done if it had been tested by cross-examination is a matter entirely for you." And then just in case that remark might have influenced a juror he made it clear that he was bending over backwards to be fair: "But I repeat, because it is so important, that she is not to be criticised for not giving evidence on oath, and her decision not to do so does not point to her being guilty of any of these charges."

Faithfully he recounted Carole's account of events:

" ' . . . Mrs Steer [WPC Mills] hit me on the jaw with the back of her hand and hurt me. I was again accused of being at Guildford and denied the accusation. Wise then hit me on the left jaw. I lifted my arm to my face to protect myself and then he punched me in the ribs . . . the answers and statements which the police have given in evidence against me are not true. The statements which I wrote were virtually dictated to me and I wrote down what they said and suggested to me. When I wrote out my statement I did not know what to write. Longhurst asked me questions and made suggestions and would indicate that I should write down what he said. I was forced to go along with what was happening because I was terrified of them and of what further treatment I would get if I continued to deny my involvement. . .' "

Donaldson J reminded the jury that all the officers concerned denied on oath that there was any truth in these allegations which had been made "of course . . . not on oath".

He did make one more positive assay in favour of the police, citing something which one of the officers accused by Carole, Detective Constable Wise, had said in the witness box. Wise had recounted a conversation, officially reported to the authorities, which took place between himself and Carole in Brixton prison long after the statements had been taken, on December 31. At one point, he said, he had asked her: "Why did you admit it?" She had replied: "Because you hit me and called me a liar and a murderer." He had countered: "No one hit you."

Of this interchange Donaldson J commented with judicial humour that although it might have been unwise ("extraordinarily unlike his name") for Wise to have asked: "Why did you admit it?", the significant thing was that he had reported the complaint.

"Members of the jury," he asked, almost as if he himself were prosecuting counsel, "would the complaint have been reported if Detective Constable Wise had been the sort of man that Carole Richardson says he was?"

At this point however Carole's counsel had the presence of mind to intervene. He pointed out that there had been two prison officers present at this conversation and Detective Constable Wise had therefore had virtually no alternative but to report it.

"Members of the jury," Donaldson J then said, "you will of course take into account the possibility that if Mr Wise was the sort of man which he necessarily would have been if Carole Richardson's evidence is right, faced with the prison officers, who would give evidence of the complaint, he might, as Mr. Myers has rightly pointed out, have come to the conclusion that he had no choice but to report it. That is a very fair comment and has to be read with the other comment."

His inclination towards the other comment – his own – was understandable.

His inclination – it could hardly help becoming apparent throughout – was to give the benefit of such doubt as there might be to the word of the police on what he constantly reiterated was the central issue of the trial. For all his early injunction to the jury to disregard his own view, this was bound to influence them in the end. The gentle weight of such inferences was to prove more crushing than at least one specific error which he made to Carole's disadvantage. For, going over the timing of her alibi once again, he said that she had said in her dock statement that she arrived at the Elephant and Castle at 7.25 to 7.30 p.m. whereas in fact he had earlier quoted her as saying that she arrived there "around 7 p.m." But no one picked him up on this. The alibi was in any case valueless if the confession statement could be taken as genuine.

On the general question of the validity of confessions obtained by the police, however, there had emerged, it so happened, over the weekend preceding his summing-up, details of a quite different case with features nevertheless of some relevance to the Guildford Trial. For the Court of Appeal had just set aside a conviction for murder based on statements to the police by accused people which it was now satisfied had been false confessions; the three young men concerned had been given an absolute discharge.* Donaldson J very properly drew the jury's attention to this event ("you will no doubt take full account of the possibility that the statements of the accused in *this* case were false"). But in doing so he also said it appeared that two of the three originally so convicted had been "congenitally retarded". (In fact this was true of only one of the accused in the Confait case.)

A still more relevant affair which could have been brought to the jury's attention was never mentioned by anyone. It was more relevant because it concerned the Surrey police themselves and in the very period in which they had managed to obtain the Guildford confessions.

On the night of December 14, 1974 a man named Roy Thomas Malloyon of 115, Foxburrow Avenue, Guildford was arrested at 11.45 p.m for damaging the shop window of World Wide Carpets, Madrid Road, Guildford. He was put in a cell and asked every fifteen minutes if he was prepared to make a statement. He protested his innocence throughout. He was, he said later with some reticence, "frightened by the circumstances which prevailed". He was told that two friends had made statements against him and on that basis he became afraid that he would not be released until the statement was

---

*The Confait case, so known after the name of the victim.

made. After nearly five hours of this, at 4.45 a.m on December 15, 1974 he admitted his guilt and was released.

He came up in court at the end of February 1975. The occasion was one of some embarrassment to the Surrey Constabulary. Inspector Graham Robinson had to tell the magistrates that, though the charge had been made against Malloyon on the basis of the statement he had made, he now had to ask the magistrates to dismiss it. "Another man," he said, "will be dealt with for that matter and brought before the court."

Dismissing the charge, the Chairman of the Magistrates said that allegations had been made against the police which should be investigated.

Mr Justice Donaldson had told the jury at the start of the Guildford bombing trial that the four accused had "the right to be found not guilty if there is any doubt about it at all". If, by the end, they were able, as they apparently were, to feel certain that there was no doubt at all then it is possible that knowledge of what had happened to Mr. Malloyon would not have given them additional pause. Allegations against the Surrey police of "sexual assaults, hair-pulling and kicking in the ribs" in Guildford police station in another case reported on the same day as the Guildford bombing trial opened might also perhaps have left them untroubled, although these troubled the Judge in that case "extremely".

By a unanimous verdict after one and a half days' deliberation the jury found Paul Hill, Gerard Conlon, Patrick Armstrong and Carole Richardson guilty of murder at Guildford on October 5, 1974, and Paul Hill and Patrick Armstrong guilty of murder at Woolwich on November 7, 1974.

Mr Justice Donaldson clearly concurred in the justice of the verdicts. He seemed at times almost carried away by his own arguments, saying incidentally that the four had claimed that the Horse and Groom was a military target – whereas in fact they had spent the trial saying they had never been there at all.

"The English language is rich in words," he said, "but no single word can describe your crime."

He sentenced Carole Richardson to be detained at Her

Majesty's Pleasure for murder (because she was under 18 at the time of the bombing), and also to life imprisonment for conspiring to cause explosions (a charge not subject to the same age condition as to sentence).

She broke down and buried her face in her hands.

Sentencing the three men to life imprisonment, Donaldson J informed them that there was no question of their being released on licence after twelve to fifteen years, and since the Home Secretary was obliged to consult the trial judge before granting licence "it must be doubtful whether any question of release will arise during the life-time of the trial judge". (Donaldson J was then aged 54.) He specifically recommended that Conlon should serve not less than 30 years. To Hill he said:

"In my view your crime is such that life must mean life. If as an act of mercy you are ever to be released it can only be on the grounds of extreme age or infirmity."

The three were described as "impassive" as they listened to this.

"On behalf of the public," Donaldson J expressed his appreciation of the skill with which the police had undertaken their task. The *Surrey Daily Advertiser* which was the only newspaper to report the trial fully throughout, often headlining boldly the allegations against the police, now made amends. Describing those convicted as the "warped dregs of humanity" for whom "the quality of mercy is strained to the limit in attempting to feel anything but loathing and revulsion", it assured the police of "our boundless admiration and gratitude for the vigorous and determined way they handled the case. Our confidence in them is increased, not diminished."

The morning after the trial a bomb exploded in London under the car of Hugh Fraser, M.P., killing a distinguished cancer surgeon who was his neighbour. The Assistant Chief Constable of Surrey, Christopher Rowe, admitted handsomely that they had not yet "got the lot". Bombs continued to explode in and around London for the rest of the autumn. On the night of December 8, 1975 shots were fired from a car at Scott's restaurant in Mount Street, W.1., which had already been bombed once before. A police chase followed and four Irishmen were eventually surrounded in a flat in Balcombe Street, N.W.1. where they held the occupants hostage for six days before surrendering. They had been caught red-handed. In the course of the interrogation which followed they admitted freely to having been part of an I.R.A. Active Service Unit which had been responsible for over a year's bombing and shooting incidents in and around London. One of them declared that the two people who had recently been convicted of the Woolwich pub bombings had had absolutely nothing to do with that operation. Another admitted to having taken part in it himself. Detective Chief Superintendent Peter Imbert of the Metropolitan Police Bomb Squad, who had questioned Hill and Conlon, was the man who talked the Balcombe Street gang into surrender and heard their admissions. The reference to Woolwich was reported to the Director of Public Prosecutions but not further investigated. By the time the Balcombe Street men were eventually brought to trial in 1977, three had admitted to taking part in the Woolwich bombing and one of these to having taken part in the Guildford bombing too. He said that none of the four people convicted for either bombing had had anything to do with them and that he had never heard of any of these four before their arrest. None of the Balcombe Street men was ever indicted for either bombing.

Meanwhile the date was set for the trial of the Maguire Seven. Prosecuting for the Crown would be Sir Michael Havers who had already described Anne Maguire publicly in graphic detail as a bomb-maker and had secured convictions on the basis of statements which so described her. The Judge would be Mr Justice Donaldson who had heard her so described and who had handed out four life sentences in the firm belief that those statements were in substance not false.

14
The Trial of the Maguire Seven

The trial of the Maguire Seven started on January 27 1976. It was to last six and a half weeks but to attract little attention in the Press. This was partly because there were other domestic news items seemingly of greater interest before the courts, such as the connection between Norman Scott, former friend of Jeremy Thorpe, and the Liberal Party, and whether or not a book called *Inside Linda Lovelace* was pornography. A contributory factor to neglect of the Maguire trial may also have been that so much of it was concerned with difficult scientific evidence about the tests made on the hand swabs and on Anne's plastic gloves.

From the start of the trial, the pretence that the matter before the court was unconnected with anything else which might have been held against Anne Maguire was immaculately established. According to Havers there was no connection whatever between this trial and that for the Guildford and Woolwich bombings. Any diligent reader of newspapers would have known that this was untrue at least inasmuch as he and Mr. Justice Donaldson officiated at both, and Havers had got Conlon convicted on a statement which described Anne Maguire as a bomb-maker. There was, Donaldson J acknowledged to the jury, a connection between this trial and the arrest of Gerard Conlon because, but for that arrest, Giuseppe Conlon, his father, would never have come to England and been in the dock, nor would there have been what the prosecution saw as the consequent panic at 43, Third Avenue to dispose of nitroglycerine. But Donaldson J, supporting the fiction that there was no connection between the *trials*, insisted that it was only this alleged panic which made the arrest relevant and that the name of the person arrested had no significance in itself. The only reason it cropped up, he said, was that it could not be dissociated from that of Giuseppe Conlon, the father.

"This relationship," he told the jury, ". . . Does not help you at all to your decision as to whether these people are guilty or not guilty . . . "

And he added without irony: ". . . Having warned you of that I hope the position will be clear."

The positions of both prosecution and defence were clear enough. Both took the same starting point: the results of the tests made by the Government Laboratory at Woolwich on the hand swabs and the gloves. But whereas Sir Michael Havers maintained that the traces were what remained after "the gathering of the clans" had worked "all hands to the pump" to get rid of the nitroglycerine, the defence said that whatever the traces were they were not nitroglycerine. In boldly stating this theme Quentin Edwards, Q.C. for Anne Maguire, committed himself to what was to prove for the defence a self-imprisoning assertion.

"There are," he said, "potentially millions of substances which would have the same chemical reaction to the tests carried out on behalf of the prosecution, and it must raise a very grave question about the reliability of that test if it stands alone . . . "

The test did not in fact stand quite alone in the prosecution's argument. There were some minor pieces of ancillary evidence. One was the fact that Giuseppe Conlon had not given the correct reason for his visit to Britain to the immigration officer at Heysham but had said that he had to come to pick up a lorry in Surrey. This was treated fairly as a "fringe matter" by the judge, who suggested that Giuseppe Conlon might reasonably have wanted to provide an innocuous explanation for his visit in order to conceal the embarrassing truth of his son's arrest. Guiseppe denied having said this. Incidental evidence to which the police had at first attached significance, such as black tape found in the house, the rubber bullet, the Long Kesh wallets and Patrick's home-made woollen mittens, were not pressed by the prosecution. But two other pieces of ancillary evidence were given serious attention by the judge.

One was the conversation between Paddy Maguire and the local housing officer in October when Paddy, after his row with Anne and somewhat the worse for drink, had threatened that the house could be "blown up".* The other was the evidence about the object Vincent had found under Sean Smyth's bed in the play-room when looking for cards which had dropped on the floor. Inasmuch as the prosecution had no evidence of any nitroglycerine in the house and neighbourhood other than what was allegedly found on hands and the gloves, this could be made to assume some importance. Vincent, during his police interrogation had heard his younger brother Patrick crying next door. Searching desperately for some explanation of the results of the swab tests on his own hands, he had referred to this object as ". . . a candle thing . . . like a candle, about eight inches long and smooth like a sort of wax. I could get my fingers right round it . . . "

Dr. T. S. Hayes, a Scientific Officer at the Government Research Laboratory at Woolwich, was called to the witness box by the prosecution. Woolwich was already under attack by the defence about the reliability of its tests. Hayes said:

"It does not suggest a candle. I have seen things which fit this description better. There are sticks of gelignite with white wax wrappers eight inches long and one inch in diameter . . ."

Vincent in the witness box said that he knew perfectly well at the time that it was a stick of chalk, such as Patrick indeed in his police interrogation had said he had got from his gym master. (A photograph of such a thick stick of chalk was

*See page 80.

shown in court.) Vincent said he could not remember whether he had described it to the police as an off-white stick or a candle but emphasised that he had been experiencing some violence from the police at the time. ("Harvey ran at me with his forearm against my throat up against the wall. He twisted my head. He hit me in the stomach. It hurt and I cried. There was no other violence. I decided to tell the story about the candle when I heard Patrick scream . . . ")

To this allegation of violence Donaldson J applied his mind in much the same style as he had applied it to allegations of police violence at the Guildford trial, though because here there were no "confessions" in the Guildford sense such allegations were not germane to the question of guilt or innocence in the same way.

"Do you think," he asked the jury, "that he was beaten up? You have seen the police officers. It was put to them and they denied using any violence towards Vincent at all . . . You no doubt will consider whether, if he really was beaten up like that, he would not have complained to somebody at the time . . . Again you may consider why young Patrick never complained at any time, why he had no marks of bruises so far as is known, and if it is untrue, why is he lying? Why is Vincent lying? Is young Patrick simply supporting Vincent in a lie? And what about Vincent? Is he lying because he regrets now having told the truth about this stick of gelignite?" [But he had not said it was a stick of gelignite.] "Well, it is a matter for you . . . "

What should also have been a matter for them but which Donaldson J cannot be blamed for not drawing to their attention, because the defence never adduced it in evidence, was what Vincent says happened when he was returned home to Third Avenue from Guildford police station at the end of that first week in December 1974. He had, he says, shown the candle-like object to the police who drove him there. Having survived all intervening searches by sniffer dogs and police it was indeed seen by them to be just a thick stick of chalk. No material evidence of this "stick of gelignite" was ever presented in court.

But, even given the weight which Donaldson J allowed it in

his summing-up, this ancillary evidence of the "candle", was of very secondary significance compared with the central evidence on which the contest between the Crown and the Maguires was fought, namely the result of the tests made on the swabs and nail scrapings from the hands of Paddy, Vincent and young Patrick Maguire, Sean Smyth and Pat O'Neill, and on Anne Maguire's plastic gloves. As Donaldson J was to tell the jury: ". . . it did seem to me that if you were not satisfied with the scientific evidence, then that was really the end of this case and you could not possibly convict."

The test said to have been applied to the hand swabs and the nail scrapings and the gloves at Woolwich was known as the Thin Layer Chromatography (TLC) Test. In this the substance to be tested is first dissolved in a powerful solvent such as ether, and a drop of this solution is applied to one end of a specially coated absorbent plate where it is allowed to dry. A spot of a known substance (in this case nitro-glycerine) is applied alongside it. The plate is then stood upright, sample end downwards, in a dish of working solvent. This solvent is drawn up the absorbent plate like water up a sheet of blotting paper. As it rises it carries with it the known and unknown substances and their final positions are revealed in a coloured spot by spraying a developer onto the plate (Griess's reagent). The performance of the tested substance in terms of colour and their final positions on a scale between 0 and 1 is compared with that of the known substance.

An all-important piece of information about this test, provided in court by Douglas Higgs, the Woolwich Chief Scientific Officer, but seemingly not fully recognised as all-important by the defence lawyers or the Judge, concerned the precision of the positions which could be reached on the scale. They were not exact. Higgs said that in the tests made at Woolwich final positions within plus or minus 0.03 of each other were regarded as the same. Each separate position thus covered 0.06 of the scale between 0 and 1, giving only just over 16 possible positions altogether.*

It was the prosecution's contention that if, in terms of

*1 divided by 0.06.

colour, rate of climb and arrival at one of these sixteen positions, a tested substance behaved identically with that against which it was tested then the substances were identical. But because the positions were not exact this was not scientific proof without doubt. The test results of the substances had only been shown to be within six per cent of each other. The matter was never put in these explicit terms to the jury.

The TLC test, in other words, was a negative test only – an excellent one, but negative. It could appear to show conclusively that two substances were not the same by sending them to different compartments on the scale. If it sent them to the same compartments it showed only that they might be the same. Scientifically a confirmatory test was required to make sure that they were.* But even as a negative test an additional factor cast some scientific doubt upon the TLC test. For the use of different solvents was capable of bringing about different results. The solvent used by the Government Laboratory at Woolwich was toluene, for which superior discriminatory properties were claimed. But the defence at the trial was to report that in other solvents nitro-glycerine could not be distinguished from tobacco.

The way in which the jury assessed the evidence of the TLC tests was to be decisive, because both prosecution and defence built their opposing cases almost entirely on it. It could have been argued, though it never was, that the issue of whether or not the TLC tests provided an accurate analysis of the swabs and nail scrapings was not necessarily relevant to the guilt or innocence of the defendants. In fact, if the prosecution's view of the test's accuracy is accepted it becomes easier to concentrate on the only real issue: whether or not the hands and gloves of the defendants could have had nitroglycerine of them at the time of their arrest. It was however evidence about the accuracy of the TLC tests that was allowed to dominate the trial and become paramount on the all-important legal question of doubt.

---

*This is today recognised by the Home Office. A Home Office letter dated April 21, 1986 states: ". . . it would now be standard practice to establish the presence of nitroglycerine through confirmatory tests . . . "

Mr Justice Donaldson outlined the vital role of doubt in a case like this early in his summing-up:

"If you have any reasonable doubt," he said, "not a fanciful doubt, but a real doubt about the matter . . . you must bring in a verdict of not guilty. The Crown bring the charges; they must prove them so that you are sure. When I say 'sure' I mean sure in the same sense as you would use the word about really important matters of everyday life . . . "

A little later he concentrated doubt specifically on the area of the scientific evidence:

". . . Unless you are satisfied by the scientific evidence that nitroglycerine was present on those people's hands, or as the case may be, on the gloves, it would be quite unsafe to convict any of them; in other words if you are in real doubt as to whether the material analysed was nitroglycerine or Substance X that must be the end of the case because you must be in doubt about whether any of them had anything to do with nitroglycerine at all . . . "

Unequivocal as this was, it also contained a misleading implication that if only doubts about the quality of the scientific evidence could be resolved it would be safe to convict. It was the phrase "in other words" that was misleading: it treated the two questions – whether the accused had had nitroglycerine on their hands, and whether the material analysed was nitroglycerine – as if they were the same. They were not necessarily so. Donaldson J was merely reflecting the way in which the trial had come to revolve around the assumption that they were. Since the area of doubt as a whole was thus allowed to become virtually indistinguishable from doubt about the quality of the scientific evidence, it becomes necessary, in trying to discover what happened to doubts in jurors' minds, to devote to the scientific evidence the same sort of attention as the trial did. For the eventual apparent resolution of the scientific doubts was to serve as the resolution of all doubts.

The tests had been carried out more than a year before they were discussed in court. That the results were what the Woolwich Laboratory said they were could of course no longer be verified, for the original specimens no longer existed.

Normally there could hardly have seemed reasonable grounds to query the results of such a respectable institution but there were two features of the tests in this case which gave the defence an opportunity to raise this sort of doubt. The first was that some tests had been conducted by a relatively inexperienced young laboratory assistant named Wyndham. Wyndham's work had however been carried out under the supervision of superior officers in the Laboratory. One test, on Anne's gloves had been duplicated by Dr. Hayes and found to be identical in result with Wyndham's. The final responsibility in any case was that of the Chief Scientific Officer, Douglas Higgs, who was ready to accept it. He was present in court throughout Wyndham's evidence and cross-examination to lend him support.

A more demonstrable query could be raised about the reliability of the Woolwich results on another score. One of the results recorded was, as even Donaldson J had to concede, "certainly a very odd result". It was that registered from the hands of Paddy Maguire. On the dry swab of his hands he had been found to be positive; but on the ether swab, designed to detect traces of nitroglycerine under the skin, he was found to be negative. Now, nitroglycerine has a very rapid rate of absorption by the skin and since some time had elapsed between Paddy's arrest and the swabbing of his hands it was virtually impossible that it should have been on his skin but not beneath it. The only possible explanation could be either that the swabbing or the test itself had been faultily conducted, or that the swabs had become contaminated with nitroglycerine independently of his hands, or that he had somehow acquired nitroglycerine on his skin in Harrow Road police station. Gerry Conlon had after all told Detective Chief Superintendent Imbert and Detective Chief Inspector Munday, somewhat to the latter's alarm, that his father Giuseppe was saying that nitroglycerine had been rubbed on his hands.

The possibility indeed that the Maguire Seven might conceivably have been "framed" by the police, convinced that they had got the right people but unable otherwise to prove it, was virtually unthinkable in the climate of that court. Certainly it was never for a moment suggested by the defence. Mr Justice Donaldson in his summing-up merely put forward as explanation of the freak Paddy Maguire result the theory that Detective Sergeant Vickery might have done the swabbing badly, either using too much ether and thus washing away all traces of nitro-glycerine below the skin or simply not swabbing in the right place. No such anomalies were in any case registered in any of the other tests. But when, in summarising the general possibilities which might explain the presence of any nitroglycerine at all on any of the hands, Donaldson J confined these possibilities to four – guilty handling, innocent handling, innocent accidental contamination for some and no nitroglycerine at all but some other substance which reacted identically on the TLC test – he was being inaccurate. He was not misleading the jury but he was failing to lead them in a direction from which another look at the possible truth was available. For there was always this other possibility, less unthinkable perhaps in the second half of the 1980s than in the mid–70's, that the swabs as tested at Woolwich were not true evidence of the state of the hands and the plastic gloves when the Maguire Seven were arrested.

Such a drastic consideration, if even taken into account by the defence and discarded because of the tactical disadvantages of pursuing it in the climate of the court, possibly seemed unnecessary given the confidence with which they felt they could demonstrate weakness in the scientific evidence as it was.

For they had secured as witness for the defence the very man who when working at the Government Laboratory at Woolwich, from which he had now retired, had invented the Thin Layer Chromatography Test. His name was John Yallop. It was Yallop who drew the court's attention to the anomaly of the two tests made on Paddy Maguire. But he went much further. He stated categorically in court that he no longer thought a single TLC test was a satisfactory basis on which to form a conclusion that nitroglycerine had been present. A confirmatory test was necessary. When specifically asked if he thought a sniffer test was a confirmatory test he said: "Yes, certainly." Asked if he thought that the sniffer test, as in fact carried out at the Maguire household on the evening of the arrests, constituted a confirmatory test, he said it had been a reasonable condition under which to expect a positive response and the fact that it gave a negative one was in his view a pointer to the fact that no nitroglycerine had been present. Asked about the substance which appeared to have contaminated the six accused's hands and Anne Maguire's gloves and whether he thought it was or was not nitroglycerine he replied categorically:

"Taking into consideration all the things which I have said, in my view it was not nitroglycerine."

It was this latter point which led Yallop into the main body of his evidence on which, virtually to the exclusion of every other consideration, the defence was to rely. This was his belief that on a single TLC test some other substance was capable of giving the same reading as nitroglycerine. In the course of the trial in which the jury had to spend many hours listening to complex scientific technicalities this other substance became known as "Substance X".

Curiously, and somewhat to the embarrassment of the prosecution, one of their witnesses, a scientific officer from Woolwich named Elliott, who had conducted some of the tests, seemed to go some way to support Yallop. He was asked by Counsel for Sean Smyth:

". . . It must follow, must it not, that there is a possibility that the substance that you found might not be nitroglycerine? That is right, is it not?"

"Put like that, yes."

"Therefore, what I am suggesting is that what your opinion boils down to in relation to that test is that on the balance of probabilities Exhibit 10 indicates nitroglycerine on the person tested. At any rate you have agreed that so far."

"Yes."

"The second part is, one cannot be sure because there is a possibility that there was no nitroglycerine, or if you prefer, that there was something other than nitroglycerine?"

"Yes."

But the prosecution's main opposition to Yallop was more formidable: the Scientific Officer then in charge at Woolwich,

Douglas Higgs. Higgs was as categorical in his way as Yallop had been, saying that under the TLC test, when conducted in the most suitable working solvent, toluene, the reaction of nitroglycerine was unique.

"I seek to establish," he said, "that the TLC test is infallible and I believe it to be. I think we have now reached the point at which we have tested enough by TLC to exclude other substances."

He said that "in a purely scientific sense" the chances of "a rogue elephant" turning up were one in ten thousand. "In the real world they are millions to one."

This was a by no means scientific statement. The odds "in a purely scientific sense" were neither one in ten thousand, nor millions to one, but just over 16 to 1. Presumably what Higgs meant was his own personal estimate of the 16 to 1 chance coming off – a view worth noting, given his experience, but hardly scientific. To invest this personal view with the authority of scientific truth was likely to have a misleading psychological effect on the jury. And when Mr Justice Donaldson, repeating the "millions to one" in his summing-up, added that of course Higgs had not meant it exactly, the inference was still that the chances of the TLC test being wrong were not far off that figure.

This was a typical example of the way in which the jury were "blinded with science" and led into thinking that science was the only area in which doubt about the case needed to be made sure. Much of it certainly had an effective ring in favour of the prosecution. For instance, Yallop's attempt to find the innocuous "Substance X" could with some plausibility be made to seem a failure. He had with great industry tested the substances to be found in a number of everyday products in domestic use including those in the Maguire household. He had used the same solvent as had the Woolwich Laboratory, toluene. Neither Boots 1001, Dabitoff, Johnson's air freshener, nor Winfield's freshener arrived at anywhere near the same point on the TLC scale as nitroglycerine, though some turned the same colour, pink. Using different solvents he did however find that Players No. 6

tobacco and Benson and Hedges gave identical results to nitroglycerine.

Mr Justice Donaldson virtually dismissed results obtained with solvents other than toluene.

"We are not," he said, "strictly interested in other eluents [solvents], because the Crown here used toluene for the accused and the whole burden of the inquiry we have been making is, 'Is there a Substance X which is not nitroglycerine which could give these results in toluene?'"

But toluene was only being taken as the criterion because the Crown had used it. This was close to saying that because the Crown had used toluene, only toluene could be looked-to for the right answer. Even if its discriminatory properties were conceded as superior, Yallop's test in another solvent at least marginally increased the area of doubt. Above all what was significant about Yallop's experiments was not that he had failed to find a Substance X in toluene, but that he had raised doubts about the validity of a single unconfirmed test and sustained the possibility that Substance X might exist. He had kept scientific doubts alive. Donaldson J seemed concerned to set all such doubts at rest in jurors' minds. In what reads almost like a parody of a traditional judge's remarks he thus addressed them:

". . . Players No. 6 and the Benson and Hedges – there, ether was used for the solvent and 0704/2/R111. I regret to say I forget what they are; they are alcohols of one sort or another, possibly the ethyl-alcohol and prophyl-alcohol. It means nothing to me and may mean nothing to you. They are not toluene and they produce this confusion. So there it is . . ."

They only produced confusion inasmuch as they contradicted the Crown's evidence. Yet somehow this was used to diminish their credibility.

However, doubts in jurors' minds about the possible existence of Substance X were subjected to further effective bombardment in court by a whole series of tests which the prosecution had conducted themselves. Donaldson J recapitulated them to further effect in his summing-up. Specialist police officers in the Home Counties, he reminded the jury, had been commissioned to take swabs from the hands of a number of people at random in their areas. More than 900 had been swabbed altogether. These swabs, when tested in toluene, from the hands of ordinary people in the Home Counties going about their everyday business, failed to produce a single result identical with nitroglycerine. Certainly there was no detailed evidence of the manner in which such swabs had been taken, but out of a sample of this size it was reasonable to suppose that there had been a fair number of swabs correctly taken from smokers and other people handling a wide range of domestic products such as were in everyday use in the Maguire and other households.

On the other hand there was something scientifically suspicious about the results of these tests, to which the jury were not referred at all. Nitroglycerine is a chemical constituent of a wide range of medicines used for apparent heart pain. Some can be bought even without prescription. For others, doctors issue over 800,000 prescriptions a year.* A single tablet contains enough active nitroglycerine to register positively on a whole series of TLC tests. (A claim for the TLC test made at the trial was that it was capable of registering a quantity of nitroglycerine equivalent to one millionth of a lump of sugar.) The chances of nitroglycerine showing up on a random sample of the adult population may therefore be reckoned at about 100–1 against. And yet here were 900 adults taken at random without a single one registering positive to nitroglycerine.

For the jury it was impressive to hear that simple fact on its own account. Donaldson in his summing-up never reminded them of the use of nitroglycerine in medicine. He did not need to do so in the context of the Maguire household itself, for there was no suggestion that anyone in it had been taking heart medicine. But a reminder of the extent to which nitroglycerine was in use as medicine among the general public would certainly have allowed a question mark to arise over the validity of these 900 tests. Without such a reminder the results could not help seeming impressive. It was one

*809,000 in 1984.

more example of the jury being impressed scientifically by evidence that was not scientifically sound.

The psychological impact of these more than 900 tests was reinforced by evidence of a still further series of prosecution tests carried out on people at Woolwich itself, and at another Government establishment at Waltham Abbey, and, in a separate type of experiment altogether, by the young Woolwich assistant Wyndham. In these he tested 175 chemicals which were actually part of the nitro group and found that not one of them produced the same result as nitroglycerine.

Again, none of this was quite as convincing scientifically as it sounded. None of it met the fundamental scientific objection to the TLC test that, without a further test, the suggested identity of a substance with nitroglycerine could not be confirmed. Nonetheless, Substance X itself had, by the time Mr Justice Donaldson came to his summing-up, been made to seem little more than a very theoretical and even unlikely possibility. Even the most conscientious juror could be forgiven for beginning to abandon reasonable doubt on the scientific score, that is to say on the main score on which the accused were being defended. Which was why a sudden development on the very morning when Donaldson J was about to start summing-up was so dramatic and potentially disturbing.

For much of the trial Yallop had had a recollection of some document which indicated doubt about the uniqueness of a single TLC test in toluene for nitroglycerine. Only after all the evidence had been heard did he manage to find it.

The evidence in question was provided by a communication from Elliott of the Government Laboratory at Woolwich sent to Yallop in the summer of 1974 and informing him that another explosive, Pentaerythritol Tetranitrate (PETN), gave on the TLC test in toluene, an identical result to nitroglycerine in colour, rate of climb and final position reached on the scale. Only the rate of development of colour (not a detail considered definitive) was slightly different. From the point of view of the trial two significant deductions could be drawn from this.

In the first place it questioned to some extent the reliability as a witness of Higgs, the Chief Scientific Officer at Woolwich, who, it turned out, could have had known all along that there was another substance which registered identically with nitroglycerine on the TLC test in toluene but had said nothing about it. Secondly, whether the substance was an explosive or not, the proven existence of *any* substance which registered identically with nitroglycerine undermined the entire principle on which the prosecution case was based. Either the TLC test was a unique test for nitroglycerine or it was not. There was in fact a Substance X, and whether or not it was an explosive was irrelevant to the argument of principle. If there was an explosive Substance X when the prosecution had said there was none at all, why not a non-explosive one too? At the very least a new area of doubt now entered the prosecution's scientific evidence, just when it had seemed to become convincing.

Once again Mr Justice Donaldson did his best to minimise the area of doubt.

The unexpected appearance of the PETN document obviously presented him and the court with a difficulty. All the evidence had been heard and the closing speeches for prosecution and defence completed. Much of the morning of Monday, March 1, 1974 was spent at the Old Bailey discussing the situation in the absence of the jury. The new evidence was accepted as Exhibit 60.

When the jury sat again in the afternoon Mr Justice Donaldson's only references to it for that day came when he was outlining the defence proposition of "Substance X". He referred to it as a matter "of importance" which they had had "to clear out of the way". All he did to clear it out of the way for the jury was to say, as follows:

"But it now being the case that there is no suggestion by either the prosecution or the defence that PETN was in fact the substance which was found on the swabs or gloves, you can ignore that part. Substance X, if it exists at all, is not PETN."

A little later when outlining the Crown case that no substance behaved in the same way on a TLC test in toluene as nitroglycerine he added:

"I have to qualify that to-day of course by saying no substance other than PETN, where the colour comes at a slightly different rate, but you may think that PETN can really be put out of your minds for the purposes of this case."

Since the defence had no opportunity to argue before the jury the significance of the PETN in destroying the principle of the prosecution's scientific case, all they could do was to bring the point up before the judge the following day, in a break in his summing-up and in the jury's absence. After some discussion Donaldson J again made it clear that he thought the matter was of no relevance, but conceded:

"I will certainly try and draw the jury's attention again to Exhibit 60 and do it convincingly notwithstanding the fact that I think it has absolutely nothing to do with this case."

There was further intervention by counsel.

Donaldson J went on:

"The point, as I understand it, is this. Everybody, for some reason, is very keen that I should draw the jury's attention to this great problem about PETN which arose in June 1974 before these swabs were ever taken. PETN is an explosive substance. Nobody suggests that it was present in this case."

To which Counsel for Anne Maguire replied:

"Perhaps the real importance is not in relation to the facts of this case but it does undermine the Crown theory that the position of nitroglycerine in toluene is unique."

"All right," said Mr Justice Donaldson.

So how would he "convincingly" put this real point to the jury?

When they re-assembled he told them that during the gap he found he had admitted certain matters "on the scientific section".

"The first matter," he said, "is that from Exhibit 60 you will see that in June 1974 it was known that there was a problem in dealing with the TLC test in distinguishing between nitroglycerine and PETN which of course is another explosive. Whether that is a fact which you will take into account in your deliberations, whether it assists you or whether you think it has any relevance to this particular problem, is a matter for you and you will no doubt bear in mind that there is no suggestion by anybody that PETN was present anywhere where any of the accused were at the relevant time."

That was all. That was the only encouragement the jury received to consider what, out of their hearing, defence counsel had referred to as this point "of considerable importance" which "does undermine the Crown theory that the position of nitroglycerine in toluene is unique".

The whole argument between prosecution and defence on the scientific issue had depended on whether or not the TLC test could give a unique test for nitroglycerine. Crown evidence had maintained that it did. Defence evidence maintained that it did not. What was now revealed as having been known all along about PETN was that TLC did not give a unique test for nitroglycerine. Yet, in spite of Mr Justice Donaldson's assurance to defence counsel that this point would be made to the jury, all they heard of it on their return was that there had been this "problem" in distinguishing between PETN and nitroglycerine on the TLC test. Far from being used as a point for the defence, the whole matter was dealt with by the Judge almost as a coup de grâce to any doubt over the prosecution's scientific evidence.

On this score alone it becomes difficult to see how subsequently the Court of Appeal, in refusing the Maguire Seven the right to appeal against the verdict delivered in Donaldson J's court, can have done so, as they did, on the gounds that there had been neither non-direction nor misdirection in his summing-up or that his summing-up was in any way unbalanced.

To the man on the traditional Clapham omnibus who had read Mr Justice Donaldson's summing-up this would have seemed a curious conclusion, explicable perhaps only by a sense of traditional brotherhood among judges.

The question of whether or not the swabs and nail scrapings contained nitroglycerine had been allowed to become synonymous with the question of whether or not the Maguire Seven had had nitroglycerine on their hands. They were not the same questions. Donaldson J had confirmed an impression that they were. Now, by dispelling the doubt that had at the last moment re-attached itself to the question of whether nitroglycerine had been on the swabs, he had appeared still further to dispel doubt from the question of whether nitroglycerine had been on the hands and gloves. The jury could think more confidently than ever that they only had to resolve doubt over the first question to dismiss it over the second.

Mr Justice Donaldson's non-direction therefore, on other issues which might have led to some consideration of whether the scientific issue was really as all-conclusive as it appeared to be, became decisive. For instance, early in his summing-up he had actually said to the jury on the question of the unlawful possession or control of explosives:

"... when we are talking about possession or control of an explosive substance we are not talking about traces of it on the hands of any of the accused, if there are traces on their hands, we are talking about *the bulk from which the prosecution say those traces came*."*

But what they talked about for most of the trial was "traces of it on the hands of the accused". The only exception had been Vincent's "stick of chalk" found under the bed which under police interrogation he had described as a candle and which, a Crown witness had said, sounded from this description like a stick of gelignite. No material evidence whatever was produced at the trial that any "bulk from which the prosecution say those traces came" had been found. Indeed, there was positive evidence that it had not been found. The police had searched not only the house with sniffers on the day of the arrest but the neighbourhood and the local canal on subsequent days. They had found neither nitroglycerine nor any trace of bomb-making equipment such as detonators or timing mechanism. Yet Donaldson J never followed-up his important reference to the "bulk", of whose existence the jury must be certain before they could convict. He only returned to the subject once to deal with it in a manner that hardly carried conviction, though curiously conveying an impression that it did. He cited a comment made by Yallop for the defence to the effect that if the accused had been, as the

*Author's italics.

prosecution were maintaining, remarkably careless about the state of their hands they had been at the same time remarkably careful with the material they had been handling. Given, Yallop said, their various movements on the afternoon of the 3rd it was difficult to see how they could have had the time to be so careful.

"One possible thought that may occur to you," said Donaldson J, "is that the material was not in the house but somewhere else, we just don't know where. Obviously it is a thing which you will discuss. No detonator was his next point. Well, we do know that if there ever was any explosive there it had gone by the time the police arrived. Might you not perhaps think, members of the jury, that if somebody was concealing explosives they might take the trouble to conceal the detonators too? It would be a bit silly to leave the detonators behind, so was not Mr. Yallop perhaps searching round rather desperately if that really was a point which bothered him? And the same applies to timing devices. Would one really expect if there ever was any nitroglycerine, would you expect that the timing devices would be left behind? Surely not. So you may think that those last points don't amount to very much."

Thus was the absence of any incriminating "bulk" subtly turned into a possible basis for incrimination.

Mr Justice Donaldson had several times made his explicit point about the need for the jury to overcome all reasonable doubt before they could convict. He had shown himself ready enough to assist them in the dispelling of such doubts where criticism was made of the Crown's scientific evidence. Yet possible doubt in the jury's mind about whether or not there can have been a bulk of nitroglycerine at all, given the absence of any evidence to that effect, either in the house or surrounding neighbourhood, was a matter to which he gave no further attention, other than in the incident of Vincent's "candle".

On the second day of his summing-up he again went over all the possibilities of what might have happened. He again omitted the possibility that the contamination might have come onto all their hands and the glove, or onto the swabs and nail scrapings, after the arrests. Much later he did bring up, in the context of innocent contamination, the possibility that because of a failure by Detective Sergeant Vickery properly to wash his hands after swabbing Giuseppe Conlon, whatever had been on Conlon's hands could have been transferred to the other three males swabbed in Harrow Road police station. But because a control sample of the swab used in each case had been retained and found uncontaminated this could very reasonably be dismissed. The thought that any of the material might have been deliberately contaminated, or contaminated through some gross error either at the police stations or while being held at Scotland Yard, was introduced once only at the very end of the summing-up and then only to be registered as unthinkable. Donaldson J was talking about Anne Maguire's plastic gloves after the Bomb Squad had taken them from the house.

"Quite rightly," he said, "the course of those gloves, where they went, who looked after them, has been very fully explored. They were taken off to Scotland Yard and put in the Exhibits room. You have heard from various Exhibits officers. They said that people would not be allowed to take them out unless they were authorised. All right, supposing somebody was authorised, where would they have got nitroglycerine on their hands and so contaminated them? It is a matter for you, members of the jury, but you may think it is somewhat unlikely, to say the least of it, that those gloves became contaminated in police custody. If you take that view then you are back at the earliest stage: how did those gloves become contaminated?"

Once again, failure to make anything of possible doubt on this score, as on the score of the absent "bulk", is particularly unfortunate if the Crown's view of the validity of the TLC test is accepted. If what was analysed was indeed nitroglycerine then doubt settles firmly in one area only; whether, given the movements of the Maguire Seven on December 3 and the absence of any nitroglycerine or bomb-making equipment in the house and neighbourhood, they could possibly have been handling nitroglycerine at all. And looking at the movements of all the accused there was much to sustain that doubt.

That area of doubt is today most powerfully reinforced by something which by definition was not available to the jury at that time: the consistent demeanour with which all the accused have continued to assert their total innocence over a period of twelve years through their long imprisonment and since. But completely discounting this, and discounting too knowledge of certain police practices in drugs cases disclosed in recent years, that doubt would have been likely to loom large had not the question of the reliability of the TLC test been allowed to overshadow it.

Of course there were also unspoken background considerations at work. On the delicate ground of the connection between this case and the Guildford bombing Donaldson J moved warily. The Crown, he said, did not "allege that any of these accused had any connection with the Guildford pub bombing". Yet the Crown in the same person of Sir Michael Havers had actually obtained a conviction for the Guildford bombing by alleging just that.

When outlining other aspects of evidence, Donaldson J seldom failed to go out of his way – as he was quite entitled to do – to ascribe a "strange", if not sinister, interpretation to the defendants' actions. Thus, of Paddy Maguire's reactions to receipt of the telegram on the afternoon of December 2, he said the jury might "think them very natural, you may think them very strange" – though, beyond the fact that Paddy was on his own admission reacting under the influence of a number of Guinnesses and that his matrimonial relations were uneasy at the time, it is difficult to see why they should have been thought strange at all.

An example of the way in which Donaldson J seemed prepared to look for quite incidental points in order to place a sinister interpretation on the accused's behaviour occurred in a discussion of how long the four men were in the pub before the police called for them on the evening of December 3. Paddy said they had only had time for a fairly quick pint, while the police said they were seen going to the pub at 7.45 and that they did not move in on them until 8.45 to 9. But

what possible significance could it have if Paddy was wrong
about the times at this point? The police had had both the
house and the men under observation. It was not easy to see
what relevance the difference in timings could have had. Yet
Donaldson in his summing-up was keen to say to the jury:

"Can those two things stand together? There is something
wrong there somewhere, is there not?"

Another trivial conflict of evidence which Donaldson J
seemed anxious to make significant concerned the time at
which Paddy had telephoned Belfast on the evening of
December 2. (Vincent had said 4.30 to 5.30; Paddy: 7.30 to
8.) This difference again could have no particular relevance
to anything except possibly the reliability of Paddy when
rather drunk. Yet Donaldson J was anxious to draw attention
to it. He concluded his summary of this point:

"There is a conflict of evidence which you will no doubt
wish to consider and decide whether it helps you in the
conclusions which you have to reach."

He made the most of Vincent and the "candle", and,
dismissing in this context Vincent's allegations about police
brutality, he passed on to the same subject where Sean Smyth
was concerned.

Although Smyth had made no admission whatever under
what he claimed had been the Surrey police brutality towards
him and therefore can hardly have introduced the claim into
his evidence with any hope of advantage, Donaldson J
managed to turn it to his disadvantage with the jury. Smyth
had said on oath such things as:

"He told me that they had forensic tests which showed that
there was nitroglycerine on my hands. I said that I had no
explanation, that there must be a mistake. I was called a liar
and the side of my face was slapped. I was told that I had
to answer the questions right. They sat me near a window. I
was asked how I got nitroglycerine on my hands. I said it
must be oil. I was asked if I had a bad heart. I said no and
Hughes bashed me in the ribs. I kept on saying it was diesel
oil. I said I had never handled explosives. I was picked up
and lifted to the window and they said they would throw me
out . . . "

Smyth had gone on:

". . . I was subjected to five or six assaults. Hughes smacked me about the face. Hughes pushed me in the ribs every time I did not answer a question. Mr. Simmons hit me very hard on the face. Hughes and Simmons hit me very hard on the cheeks. I had no marks of injury or bruises . . . "

On all this Mr Justice Donaldson's comment was as follows:

"Well now, members of the jury, it is very odd, is it not, Mr. Smyth's attitude? He does not say that anything he said to the police was untrue or that they have got it wrong . . . yet he makes these very serious complaints about the police. There is nothing odd about it if you think he is right, but is he right? You have seen the officers . . . Simmons has denied it, the other officers have denied it. Are they the sort of officers that you think would behave in this fashion? Are they the sort of officers that you think would lie about it? You have got to make up your minds about that because, as I say, it is very odd, this story of attacks. It cannot be entirely disregarded. If they did it they did, but did they do it? Is it that he merely has some feeling against the police in general or is he attempting in a rather stupid, muddled sort of way to discredit the police, feeling that he has some cause to discredit them. Those are matters that are supremely matters for a jury. You may decide to put it one one side, you may decide that it gives some sort of pointer to other evidence although, of course, by itself it does not prove anything at all."

The whole tone of Mr Justice Donaldson's summing-up is best summarised in the final words he addressed to the jury. "If you have a real doubt," he said, "on any of the accused then each is entitled to be acquitted, but if, members of the jury, having considered all these matters, you are sure, then it is your duty, your duty in accordance with the oath that you have taken, to bring in a verdict of guilty."

A juror could have been forgiven for interpreting this to mean that it was primarily his duty to bring in a verdict of guilty.

The jury retired at 3.04 p.m. on Tuesday March 2, and went back to their hotel at 5.30 p.m. They deliberated all next day from 9.30 a.m. to 5.30 p.m. and resumed deliberations the next morning at 10 a.m. At 12.23 p.m. on Thursday, March 4 they returned to the court room and delivered their verdicts. Unanimously they found Anne Maguire, Paddy Maguire, Vincent Maguire, Giuseppe Conlon, Sean Smyth and Pat O'Neill guilty. They found young Patrick Maguire guilty by a majority of 11 to 1.

Anne, who had impressed the *Guardian* correspondent by "the outwardly simple, homespun manner" in which she had given her evidence, screamed:

"I am innocent, you bastards. No, no, no."

She had to be carried from the dock shoulder-high by prison staff.

"The fact," said Mr Justice Donaldson "that these offences were committed for terrorist purposes gives the unique character to this case and must and will be reflected in the severity of the sentencing which it is the duty of the courts to pass."

He sentenced Anne and Paddy Maguire to 14 years' imprisonment, Giuseppe Conlon, Sean Smyth and Pat O'Neill to 12 years' imprisonment, Vincent Maguire to 5 years' imprisonment and young Patrick to 4 years in youth custody.

Before the proceedings terminated he addressed Sir Michael Havers:

"Sir Michael, I would like to congratulate Detective Chief Inspector Munday and all those who worked with him in his team on this investigation, which was very well conducted."

Havers said:

"I am very grateful . . . "

Peter Mathews, the Chief Constable of Surrey, allowed himself a small share of the general acclaim.

"We are delighted with the verdicts," he said. "These are the people we were after . . . We have cut off a major pipeline to the terrorists. We are only sorry we did not find the bombs."

A fortnight later the Bomb Squad discovered two I.R.A. bomb factories in Brixton and Clapham. These were, said the police spokesman, "typical of the type of accommodation known to be favoured by I.R.A. terrorists, that is, short-let, furnished rooms or flatlets in areas where such accommodation is common and where there is a substantial local Irish content among the residents".

Only 16–year-old John Maguire and his 9–year-old sister Anne Marie were left in the house at 43, Third Avenue, Harlesden.

PART III

Conclusion

15

Appeals:
How the Guildford Bombing
Was Done

The law had done its work. Paul Hill, Gerard Conlon, Patrick Armstrong and Carole Richardson – that is to say, a fringe I.R.A. collaborator who had fled from Belfast and a former schoolmate of his, with whom he had been working in London as a labourer, together with another Belfast man and a young English girl living in Kilburn squats – had been sentenced to life imprisonment for that crime of which the Chief Constable of Surrey had said, "it was not the work of a scatterbrain". Anne and Paddy Maguire and their two sons, their brother-in-law Giuseppe Conlon, who had come to the house on the afternoon of December 3, 1974, Anne's brother Sean Smyth who had come back from work half an hour before the police had come to watch that evening, and Patrick O'Neill who had called there on a visit less than half an hour before the police came, had all been sentenced to many years of imprisonment for handling nitroglycerine unlawfully for the purposes of terrorism. Sir Michael Havers, later to become Mrs. Thatcher's Attorney-General, and Mr. Justice Donaldson, later to be Master of the Rolls, had done what they saw as their duty. The Chief Constable of Surrey, Peter Matthews, later to be knighted, and his Assistant Chief

Constable, Christopher Rowe, already rewarded for his work over the bombing with the Queen's Medal and to-day cultivating his garden in Lincolnshire, enjoyed the acclaim of having got "the right people".

The people they had got were small people in comparison with themselves. In accordance with the conventions of society these people and their names now disappeared from public view. But the law of England prides itself on a claim that great and small are equal before it. It gives all a further chance to be heard before they finally disappear. All of the Maguire Seven applied for leave to appeal to the Court of Appeal. The hearing took place in 1977 and Lord Justice Roskill delivered the Court's judgment.

In outlining the case at the beginning of this judgment he referred to the Guildford public house bombings of October 5, 1974. He declared with legal rectitude: "There is no shred of evidence that any of these applicants was in any way involved in that matter." In recalling how specifically and in what detail Sir Michael Havers in the Guildford trial had cited Anne Maguire as involved in that matter, it is difficult not to wonder whether a trace of concern may possibly have crossed the mind of Sir Michael Havers as he listened to Lord Justice Roskill's pronouncement.

The rest of the judgment was in the same measured vein of apparent detachment, delivered with intellectual clarity after the court had listened attentively for days to the arguments of the appellants' counsel that Mr. Justice Donaldson's summing-up had been unbalanced and misleading or both. There is a sense in which a judge is himself being "tried" for his summing-up in the Court of Appeal. Lord Justice Roskill seemed almost to go out of his way to give Mr. Justice Donaldson the benefit of any doubt.

His judgment in fact reads more like an opportunity seized to reinforce the case against the Maguire Seven than a balanced hearing of the appellants' complaints. In the various specific areas where Donaldson J's own judgment might have seemed to someone on the Clapham omnibus to have been questionable, Roskill LJ came down firmly in its favour.* In one specific area he actually made much more of the case against the Maguires than Donaldson J had done.

It might have been said for instance that Donaldson J had strained a point over the discrepancy in timing between the police account and that of Paddy Maguire in the period the four men spent in the Royal Lancer after the police arrived at Third Avenue. There had been about half an hour's difference between the two sets of timing and Donaldson J had attached a strangely sinister interpretation to the discrepancy. ("There is something wrong there, is there not? It is a matter for you . . . ") The house was after all now under observation. The men had been seen leaving it, presumably without carrying anything suspicious or giving other cause for suspicion, or Detective Sergeants Elbourn and Hunter who had observed them would have reported it. The two Detective Sergeants had seen them enter the pub, before themselves returning to observe the house. The four men did not know they were under observation. If they had indeed had nitro-glycerine or other bomb-making equipment to dispose of which they were somehow managing totally to conceal, they would surely have been unlikely to go straight to a public house in order to dispose of it. The time during which Donaldson J seemed to suppose they were up to "something wrong" – a time which Paddy Maguire and the others maintained the police had assessed as inaccurately long – was the time which they said they had spent in the public house. There was no evidence from those who had been in the public house at that time that the men had left it again, or behaved strangely, as in the manner of people who had nitroglycerine of which they wished to dispose.

Lord Justice Roskill actually took pains to emphasise however the sinister interpretation which Donaldson J had suggested attached to the matter. He did so at two separate points in his judgment, and it is difficult when reading these

*It is a conventional courtesy analagous to that of following the surnames of High Court Judges with the letter J, when using them without title, to follow those of Appeal Court judges with the letters LJ.

two separate analyses of this incident not to feel that he was in some way trying to shore up a weakness in the Crown case. That there was such a weakness, quite apart from the weakness which the defence had unsuccessfully sought to demonstrate in the scientific evidence, was indisputable.

This weakness lay in the complete absence of any evidence of nitroglycerine or other bomb-making equipment to be found anywhere, either in the house or in the surrounding neighbourhood, other than in the purely verbal evidence of Vincent's "candle". The only firm existence of any nitro-glycerine at all alleged was on the swabs and nail scrapings made from the Maguire Seven's hands and Anne's plastic gloves. Assuming the Crown's scientific evidence to be valid and the swabs and scrapings correctly to indicate the presence of nitroglycerine, two of the pertinent questions to be asked were: where had the nitroglycerine of which the swabs and scrapings gave only traces gone to? And when could the Maguire Seven have got rid of it so totally, accepting, as Donaldson J had been prepared to do, their own account of the movements during the afternoon up to 7 p.m?

The only person who could, on a reasonable view, have disposed of it was the friend Sean Tully who had called to discuss the mysterious disappearance of Hugh Maguire early that evening. He had driven away in his car, but he had been seen to do so by Detective Sergeants Elbourn and Hunter. Subsequently arrested and swabbed (by the Surrey police), both his person and his car had given a negative result to the test for nitroglycerine. So how, short of using a balloon, could they have disposed of the incriminating material?

It was not a question which appears to have troubled Lord Justice Roskill. Without apparently wondering why the police reported nothing suspicious, or why the men, not knowing that they were being observed, did nothing suspicious but went straight into a public house, he commented blandly:

"Certainly so far as the four male applicants were concerned, and this includes Smyth and O'Neill, there would have been an opportunity extending over about half an hour to have handled explosives knowing perfectly well what they were doing, between the time when, on the police evidence, they left the house and the time when the police entered the public house."

It is difficult to see this as anything but an outlandish attempt to cover a gaping hole in the credibility of the Crown's case.

In relation to the same salient question of where the bulk of the nitroglycerine had gone to, Lord Justice Roskill was of even greater assistance to the summing-up elsewhere. Counsel had argued strongly before the Court of Appeal that the material absence of any explosives other than the traces found to have been on the swabs and scrapings after testing, was indeed a major weakness in the Crown's case.

"The judge dealt with this point early in his summing-up," said Roskill LJ, referrring to Donaldson J's statement that the jury needed to be satisfied as to the existence of 'the bulk'.

But the whole point was that Donaldson J had not "dealt" with the absence of the bulk at all. What he had done was to remind the jury that: ". . . by talking about possession or control of an explosive substance we are *not talking about traces of it on the hands of any of the accused, if there are traces on the hands, we are talking about the bulk from which the prosecution say that these traces came.*"

But he then said nothing about the prosecution's failure to prove that the bulk had existed.

Lord Justice Roskill now did exactly the same thing. He said:

"The judge's direction made it absolutely plain that before any of the applicants could be convicted not only had the presence of traces of nitroglycerine on the hands, under the nails or on the gloves *to be conclusively proved*, but that the jury had to be certain that the presence of nitroglycerine, if proved, was consistent with and only with each of the applicants' having knowingly handled and thus had in his or her possession *a quantity of nitroglycerine* – the corpus, to use counsel's phrase – from which those traces came."*

But he too said nothing about the failure of the Crown to show that "that quantity" had been there. Only the

*Author's italics.

Trial and Error

expedition to the pub under the eyes of the police was offered
as explanation.

Having thus said that he had disposed of an objection,
without actually disposing of it, Lord Justice Roskill then
concentrated, as indeed the trial itself had done, on the
scientific evidence, saying correctly that the case for the
Crown rested almost entirely upon that scientific evidence
"which, it was claimed, proved to the requisite degree of
certainty – that is, beyond any reasonable doubt – that what
was found could only be and therefore was nitroglycerine".

Here of course, Lord Justice Roskill was on much firmer
ground. The appellants' counsel had repeated all those
queries over the validity of the TLC which had been the
mainstay of their argument at the trial itself. The weakness
of the summing-up on this central issue had been not that it
had over-emphasised the strength of the Crown's case – which
was indeed considerable – but that, from the point of view of
fairness towards the defendants, Mr. Justice Donaldson had
not sufficiently emphasised to the jury the area of doubt that
could still reasonably be attached to it. The defence had
indeed made their own scientific evidence the mainstay of
their case. But its only really telling quality lay in the shadow
of doubt it did just manage to throw over the Crown's own
confidence. Donaldson J, in understandably stressing how
much more effective the Crown's scientific evidence seemed,
wholly failed to draw proper attention to this characteristic
arising from the defence's argument, and to the way in which
it added marginally to that much greater shadow of circumstantial doubt over the case as a whole. Roskill LJ again
compounded Donaldson J's lapse. No attention was drawn
to the fact that the doubts which could still be shown to
linger over the strong scientific case and which had at least
something to add to the required sum total of doubt in the
jurors' minds, had been virtually dismissed out of hand in
the summing-up.

It was in this respect particularly that Lord Justice Roskill's
treatment of the PETN issue was so unsatisfactory. There
had been a strange gap in Mr. Justice Donaldson's summing-
up on this issue. Having promised counsel, in the jury's

absence, that he would put to them "convincingly", when they returned, counsel's point that PETN undermined the whole Crown claim that the reaction of nitroglycerine on the TLC test in toluene was unique, he did nothing of the sort. When the jury returned he addressed himself to the subject in only two sentences. He said that there was a "problem" in distinguishing between nitroglycerine and PETN, which he pointed out was another explosive. He said that whether or not its being another explosive helped them to decide whether it had any relevance to "this particular problem" was a matter for them. That was all. He said nothing at all about PETN having undermined the Crown theory that nitroglycerine's reaction on the TLC test in toluene was unique.

Roskill LJ, where he could have drawn attention to this lapse, merely compounded it. He quoted the two sentences which Donaldson J had addressed to the jury on PETN after their return. This did not take him long. All he himself said was:

"It is true that in that passage the learned judge does not in terms refer to the point that had been made in the absence of the jury that Exhibit 60 [the Exhibit referring to PETN] was capable of casting some doubt on the so-called infallibility of the TLC test. He took the view, and we can understand his view, that since there was no question of PETN having been found, the contents of Exhibit 60 were really irrelevant and did not of themselves cast serious doubt upon the validity of the TLC test conducted with toluene by the Crown experts. But he left the point to the jury, whether or not they got any assistance from Exhibit 60, including whether or not they accepted the expert evidence from the Crown's witnesses."

In other words, Roskill LJ, having admitted that Donaldson J left something out – something which the defendants' counsel thought of extreme importance – left it out too. He did go on to say that the Court of Appeal had often said that, in summing up, a judge had no duty "to put every conceivable point that has been taken on behalf of the defence". But this particular point, as defence counsel saw it, was one of the greatest importance.

In fact Lord Justice Roskill's judgment throughout similarly compounded all Mr. Justice Donaldson's errors by saying that they were not errors. Counsel for one of the appellants before Roskill LJ and the Appeal Judges put his finger on the essential issue involved in the whole case, and one which Donaldson J had totally ignored. Counsel said that Donaldson J should have told the jury that they had to be convinced that the *circumstantial evidence* excluded any explanation other than that the nitroglycerine found at Woolwich showed beyond reasonable doubt that the Maguire Seven were guilty. Again Roskill LJ employed exactly the same device as he had done over PETN:

"It is true that in the present case the learned judge did not use the form of words of the absence of which counsel complained. But when one looks at the totality of the summing-up, we cannot see that any complaint can reasonably be made that he did not do so . . . "

Roskill LJ rightly isolated the scientific evidence as having been the central area of contest between defence and prosecution at the trial. But, like Donaldson J at the trial, he accepted almost without question that this was the only area in which the contest was to be fought. He encapsulated this point succinctly when he said:

"Once the jury accepted the evidence of the Crown witnesses, as they clearly did, as to the reliability of the TLC test, and as they were entitled to do, and disbelieved Mrs. Maguire, the jury were entitled to convict, even though the quantity found on the gloves was so small."

But Anne Maguire was maintaining not that the TLC test was unreliable but that she had no nitroglycerine on her gloves. The reliability of the TLC test was by no means the only point which a conscientious jury had to take into account.

On the central scientific issue itself – the reliability of the tests – Roskill LJ was pleased to praise Mr. Justice Donaldson's summing-up in the highest terms. "It seems to us to have been faultless," he said, speaking of its "clarity and succinctness". This is a fair assessment of this limited part of the summing-up. But praise obscured the fact that it was

Conclusion

limited. Appellant's counsel's point was that the summing-up was out of balance because Donaldson J spent too much time dealing with whether or not the presence of nitro-glycerine had been conclusively proved and too little time upon whether, even if the presence of nitroglycerine had been proved, the Crown had also proved beyond all reasonable doubt that each of the accused had knowingly handled the substance.

Roskill LJ looked at this under the heading of what counsel had called in argument "innocent contamination". He was quite categorical about this. "It would indeed have been the most astonishing coincidence," he said, "if . . . the expla-nation of the presence of what was found under those finger-nails was in every case due to wholly innocent contamination."

That depended on what was meant by "innocent contami-nation". As in the trial itself, the main assumption under this heading was that nitroglycerine must have been present somewhere in the house and that innocent contamination meant that one or other of the accused had become acciden-tally and innocently contaminated with what someone else had been unlawfully handling. It would indeed have been a coincidence if they had all been innocently contaminated in this manner because the presence of nitroglycerine in the house, as it were of its own accord, would have needed some explanation. Attention under this heading did in fact centre on whether one or other of them, particularly perhaps O'Neill, had innocently been contaminated from what one of the others had been unlawfully handling. At the appeal, counsel for both O'Neill and Smyth, both of whom had been in the house such a short time on the evening of December 3, suggested that the circumstances were such as to raise a "lurking doubt" on their behalf in this respect. With extra-ordinary blandness Roskill LJ dealt with such a possibility in the following manner: "Without going into further detail on this part of the case we need only say that no member of this Court was left with any lurking doubt in the case of O'Neill and having considered Mr. Cripps' seven points on behalf of

Smyth . . . no member of this court has any lurking doubt in this case either."

In other words he dealt with the lurking doubt by saying it did not exist.

Counsel for Anne Maguire, on the grounds that traces of nitroglycerine had been found not on her hands at all but only on the gloves taken from the house on the following day, raised the point that there was no proof that she had contaminated the gloves. After all a sniffer had been passed over the gloves on the evening of the arrest and had failed to detect any presence of nitroglycerine in the drawer from which the gloves were removed. Donaldson J in his summing-up had suggested that this might be because "inadequate gas" was coming off the gloves to operate the sniffer, omitting at this point to draw the jury's attention to evidence that the sniffer was in fact capable of reacting to a contaminated towel. All Roskill LJ had to say about this omission was what he had already said at a number of other points in his judgment, namely that the Court saw no reason why a judge in his summing-up should repeat every point which had previously been made. The judgment therefore ran:

". . . We see nothing wrong in the way the judge dealt with the sniffer matter."

The possibility that the gloves had become "innocently contaminated" in police custody had just been looked at as a sort of afterthought by Donaldson J. He said: "It is a matter for you, members of the jury, but you may think it is somewhat unlikely, to say the least of it, that those gloves became contaminated in police custody."

It was the only reference he made to such a possibility. Roskill LJ, fairly enough, also raised this question as a possible explanation of "innocent contamination" of the gloves:

". . . The gloves, might while in New Scotland Yard and at any time before the tests were done at Woolwich on the 9th of December, have been contaminated."

He covered this simply by saying that Donaldson J had "dealt fully" with this point among others brought forward in Anne Maguire's defence and added: "We see no force in any of these complaints."

But the only way in which Donaldson J had "dealt" with the point was by saying it was "somewhat unlikely".

It was the jury's acceptance of the reliability of the TLC test which Roskill LJ saw as providing the basic soundness for the convictions. But it should be repeated: acceptance of the TLC test meant no more that that the TLC test was reliable. It did not necessarily mean that what the TLC test tested had anything to do with Anne Maguire or the other accused. If there had been any circumstantial evidence at all other than the story of Vincent's "candle" to suggest that there could possibly have been nitroglycerine at 43 Third Avenue, it might be thought pedantic to point out such a technical gap in the logic. But in this case there was everything other than the results of the TLC tests to suggest that the seven had not been handling nitroglycerine. The question of whether the TLC test, reliable or not, reflected what had been the state of the defendants' hands and gloves at the time of their arrest, was much more than a pedantic one. Neither in Mr. Justice Donaldson's summing-up nor in Lord Justice Roskill's judgment is there any sign that this, perhaps the most fundamental question of all, was thought particularly relevant.

No mention was of course made of the real reason why the police had suspected that there might be nitroglycerine at 43 Third Avenue, Harlesden. For Donaldson J had properly warned the jury against prejudice in the light of the bombing campaign at the time. Roskill LJ now applauded him for the way in which he had done so:

". . . The learned judge could not have dealt with that aspect of the matter with more fairness than he did. He reminded the jury of the possible dangers of prejudice and urged them more than once in the strongest terms to exclude any possible prejudice from their minds. In our view the verdicts cannot possibly be assailed on that ground."

Was it humanly possible for Havers and Donaldson J who shared some responsibility for the convictions at the Guildford trial to exclude prejudice against Anne Maguire and her household? The matter was one which since it was assumed not to exist, did not need to be investigated and since Lord

Justice Roskill's judgment had had nothing but praise, or at the very least, totally sympathetic comprehension for Mr. Justice Donaldson throughout, its conclusion was inevitable:

"We have considered all these seven applications individually in detail with the utmost care . . . But at the end no member of this court sees any reason for disturbing any of these convictions either on the basis that any of them is unsafe or unsatisfactory or that the learned judge was guilty of any non-direction or misdirection or that his summing-up in any way was unbalanced. In the circumstances we think it right to deal with all the applications by refusing all the applicants leave to appeal against conviction."

(O'Neill's sentence was to be reduced from 12 years to 8 years.)

In the case of the Maguire Seven there had been no new evidence with which to argue again their innocence. It was very unlikely that there ever could be any. The swabs and scrapings on which they had been convicted had long disappeared and could never be looked at again or physically reassessed. The unlikelihood – though not the impossibility – of a substance X which could have given an identical result to nitroglycerine from the Maguires' hands had been convincingly demonstrated. Only if a police officer had come forward to testify that while in police custody the swabs and the gloves had in some way been improperly handled, or perhaps even if a Surrey police officer had come forward to say that there had been perjury by himself or one of his colleagues in the court, could a new angle to the case be found. As things were, there was nothing that could be done but go over the same ground over again, with the hope of persuading the Appeal Court that the judge had somehow not enabled the jury to assess it properly. Given the conventional regulation care with which Donaldson J had undoubtedly delivered his summing-up, the defence's failure in the Appeal Court was predictable. But, in the application by the Guildford Four to the Appeal Court for leave to appeal, things were very different. New evidence of a most dramatic kind had become available.

Conclusion

One of the I.R.A. men taken after the Balcombe Street siege, Joe O'Connell, had told Detective Chief Superintendent Peter Imbert that the people who had just been convicted of the Woolwich bombing (Hill and Armstrong) had in fact had nothing to do with it. Another, Edward Butler, had admitted taking part in the Woolwich bombing himself. In prison awaiting trial O'Connell had also waited to see if there would be any further investigation of the Woolwich bombing. There was none.

One day in the middle of 1976 the solicitor who represented Armstrong, Alastair Logan of Guildford, received an anonymous telephone call from someone who had been visiting another prisoner in Brixton. The caller suggested that if Logan wanted to know something which might help his client he should go and see the Balcombe Street people. Logan got in touch with the Irish Republican Member of Parliament for Tyrone and South Fermanagh, Frank Maguire, and asked him to contact O'Connell on his behalf next time he visited him in Brixton. Soon afterwards Logan received a letter from O'Connell officially asking him to come to Wandsworth. He was interested to know what Logan wanted. Logan went to see him in Wandsworth and told him that he had just received information that Butler had admitted to a part in the Woolwich bombing. He wondered if O'Connell could help him. O'Connell told Logan at once that the two convicted for Woolwich had had nothing to do with it, and that he was prepared to help him. He said, however, that before he went any further there was another I.R.A. man, now in custody elsewhere, who had also taken part in the bombing, and whose consent would have to obtained first if he, O'Connell, were to give any further details. This was Brendon Dowd, an I.R.A. man who had been arrested after a shooting incident in Lancashire in July 1975 and was now serving a life sentence.

Again using the M.P. Frank Maguire as an intermediary, Logan eventually went to see Dowd in Albany Prison, Newport, Isle of Wight on Tuesday, October 26, 1976. To minimise any danger of leading Dowd in his questioning, Logan took with him as principal interviewer a retired police inspector, James Still, and they were both accompanied by

an official court shorthand reporter in the firm of Tennyson
and Co, Covent Garden. Because the information which
Dowd gave at this and a subsequent interview was later to
be largely dismissed by the Appeal Court when used as new
evidence for the Guildford Four, on the grounds that he "had
not learned his lines properly", it is valuable to glimpse for
a moment the spontaneous quality of this, the first authentic
revelation of what had taken place not only at Woolwich but
at the bombing of the Horse and Groom and the Seven Stars
at Guildford on the evening of October 5, 1974. For Brendon
Dowd and Joe Connell had been present on both occasions.

Dowd at first found it difficult to recall the exact date of
the Guildford bombing. He thought it might have been
August 1974. Still told him it was October 5 and asked him
what his position in the operation had been and how it had
been arranged and with whom.

"I won't name names or persons, no."

"Unless the persons are in a position you know it would
do them no harm?"

"It is up to these people."

"You do understand from the letter you received from
Mr. Logan that we are interested in one particular person
[Armstrong]?"

"That particular person, and the others which were
convicted were not involved in that . . . They had no connection whatsoever. Perhaps one of them but that was a long
time ago." (A reference to Hill.) "As far as any of the persons
convicted for the Guildford and Woolwich, they had no
connection whatever with it."

"How can we show that?"

"I don't know how you can do it, really. The evidence was
– it was really only a statement, wasn't it?"

"Would you be prepared to tell us how it took place?"

"Yes."

"Would you do that then, starting with Guildford?"

"For a start – four of us. Four people, or five people. Four
people in a motorcar, and parked up the car not far – in a
car park not far from that particular pub, the Horse and
Groom."

Dowd drew a quick diagram on a sheet of paper to show where the car park was.

"Was it a stolen motorcar?"

"No, it wasn't, but I can't say who it came from."

"It belonged to one of the persons with you?"

"It was actually a hired motor."

"Can you say its make, or anything like that?"

"I wouldn't like to say. You'd probably be able to trace it back – the police could trace it back."

"Who drove, by the way?"

"I drove."

He described how they had with them two six-pound packets of gelignite carried in two brown satchels, and how they split up, two and two to each pub. (The role of the fifth person mentioned by Dowd was left unclear – possibly a look-out not in the car, possibly another passenger about whom Dowd was confused being unable to remember whether they had been four or five. As he was to say in the course of the interview, it all seemed, in the middle of 1976, after so many "operations" in which he had taken part, a long time ago.)

"So that means you split up?"

"Yes."

"That is to the Horse and Groom and the Seven Stars. Could you say to which one you went?"

"To the Horse and Groom."

"With a companion. Male or female?"

"I won't say. Just say 'companion', doesn't matter."

"May I enquire, were any of the persons concerned in what is known as the Balcome Street affair, any of the party, and if they were, would you consider it would be harmful to say so?"

"I don't think it would matter. I believe one of these already had decided to meet Mr. Logan."

"Yes, I think all four, but certainly I am sure of two."

"In general, I don't like – I prefer to leave it up to them if they wish to."

"Then you entered the bar. Is it possible to say who, if anyone, was what might be described as in charge of the operation?"

"I was in charge of the operation."

He was asked if the expedition had been planned from elsewhere or by anyone else, and said that it had not. Guildford had been picked in particular because the pubs were used by soldiers.

"Had you found that out beforehand?"

"Oh, yes."

"Who had done that?"

"Same group that done it."

"All or some of the four had made a sort of visit, several visits, perhaps?"

"No, just one, two. About two visits, I am not sure."

"Did that include anyone other than these four?"

"No, nobody."

"You can't recall what the weather was like in Guildford?"

"It was raining that evening. I think it was raining, I am not sure. I think it was showers. I would say I have been involved in so many bomb and gun battles and what-have-you, I can't distinguish them."

"And the time that you got there?"

"About 7 o'clock in the evening, it was, half-six, 7 o'clock."

"You got in. Are there any different bars? I've never been to the places so I haven't the slightest idea. Does it have a public bar and saloon, or just one main bar?"

"Just one bar . . . Had a drink and went and sat down."

"What sort of drink did you have?"

"Beer."

"Do you know the brew-type?"

'No. It was lager, anyway. Some sort of lager."

"What sort of seating arrangements have they got in there? Is it a sofa alongside the wall or tables?"

'It's a seat along the wall and then there are tables, and on the outside there are more seats, individual chairs."

"But you sat on the seat around the wall?"

"Yes."

"That is the outer wall?"

"Yes, on the gable end."

"I am not sure I understand what a gable end is."

"It wasn't the front wall or back wall; it was the end wall."

"And put the parcel down?"

"Yes."

"Where and how?"

"Just dropped it under the seats."

"Was there space under the seats?"

"Yes."

He described how the final connections to the bombs had been made in the car park.

"And for what time was it arranged?"

"It was arranged, I think, for 9 o'clock. I am not sure; I think it was."

"Do you remember the seat under which you placed the explosives? Do you remember what type it was, the colour or material?"

"Where it was, it was semi-dark. You wouldn't get any details on that. That particular part was very bad lighting . . . the place was so dark you wouldn't really know."

"Having left it there under the seat, did you have another drink?"

"Had about two or three drinks. And then we just left."

"Were the other two doing somewhat similar things?"

"Yes. They were down the other pub."

"Did you leave by pre-arranged time? Or all meet together or anything like that?"

"Just arranged to meet back at the motor."

"Do you by any chance know Mr. Armstrong?"

"No, never met him."

"Or anyone who has met him and spoke to you about him?"

"There is nobody. Even the people in London don't know him; even the Balcombe Street don't know him."

It had been important to get from Dowd some details about the interior of the Horse and Groom, to make sure that he had really been there. The problem for Logan had been from the start the likelihood that those who believed that Hill, Conlon, Armstrong and Richardson had been rightly convicted would represent the statements of Dowd and the I.R.A. men from Balcombe Street as being a concocted attempt to free other I.R.A. colleagues. In fact there was no precedent that the I.R.A. had ever tried to do this, but it is an organisation whose ingenuity should never be underestimated. Dowd's account of the interior of the Horse and Groom and of the weather on the night of October 5, 1974 had been accurate, but it might just have been possible for him to have studied the details available at the trial of the Guildford Four sufficiently well to be able to reply with this accuracy. The only newspaper from which he could in fact have got sufficient details with which to fill out such an account would have been the *Surrey Daily Advertiser*, but, if indeed this had been a carefully-planned pre-arranged scheme to secure the release of genuine I.R.A. members, the known thoroughness of the I.R.A. might well have kept him supplied with copies. This would have been difficult because in fact he was already under arrest at the time of the trial and an influx of copies of the *Surrey Daily Advertiser* into the jails in which he was being held would presumably have come to the attention of the authorities. But Logan's awareness of the danger that the admissions would be represented as a deliberate falsification made him meticulous in securing as many details from Dowd as possible. He got Dowd to draw a plan of the interior of the Horse and Groom, and then himself personally put a question, though Still had done all the interrogating so far.

"You mention tables. Can you remember the layout of the tables at all?"

"They run along the seats."

"Do you remember how many?"

"I didn't count them."

"Do you remember any other furniture in the pub? You know pubs always have a certain amount of equipment. Do you remember any specific equipment?"

"It's so long ago now, but I think there was a juke box along here." He indicated a point on his plan. "I am not sure ... I am not sure now, actually. I never bothered thinking about it ever."

But then Dowd said something of which he was sure, and which he could not possible have got from any published accounts of the trial.

Conclusion

"That afternoon there were two old guys with shopping bags."

"In the bar?"

"Yes."

"When you were there?"

"Yes. Just sitting beside me. Carrier bags – must have been waiting for a bus."

"Could you put circles where the two old guys were sitting?"

"Yes." He again indicated the point on his plan. "Had some large bags of groceries with them. I think they must have been waiting for a bus."

These were of course the two "old men" who had been referred to by a number of witnesses when the police first took statements from those who had been present in the Horse and Groom, in the days after the explosions.*

On one other point too Dowd gave accurate information about Guildford which had never been brought up at all at the trial. There had been no mention of car parks because in the statements which the police had obtained from the Guildford Four the parking of the cars allegedly involved, though varying from statement to statement, had been in the streets of Guildford itself. Dowd now described in careful detail the exact rather complicated location of the car park in which he and the others had left the car after priming their bombs there.

"Did you arrange a specific time to meet back at the motor?"

"Yes. Back at the motor at about 8 o'clock, I think it was. I think it was about 8 o'clock."

"What about the timing of the devices?"

"I think they were timed for 9 o'clock. When you are using . . . you can't really gauge . . . . It can be ten minutes one way or another."

"You used the hour hand?"

"Yes, you have to. I think that the police know that I was there. They didn't charge me, because if they had charged

*See pages 13, 15.

me, they would say 'Why did they charge the other people?'
They found in the flat in West London in Kensington . . .
[This referred to a flat in Waldemar Avenue which the police
had raided after Dowd's arrest.] They found in the flat in
West London in Kensington – all the details, same type of
equipment was in the flat as they got in Guildford, so they
must have known I was involved. I suppose they were
satisfied with what they got . . . They found a lot of material
like that – would have shown them it was I who done it, like,
you know. I think they know I done it, afterwards. They
couldn't very well charge me after charging other people."

It was of course in the interests of these "other people"
that Dowd was being questioned. Still asked him:

"Would you consider any of your companions unreliable?"

"No."

"To put it another way, if you had a companion you
thought might be unreliable, what would have happened?
Would you have carried on with the exercise?"

"No, I wouldn't have, no."

"You relied on your companions?"

"Definitely, yes."

"The accommodation you used prior to this was rented
accommodation, or did you join groups of squatters or something of that nature?"

"No, no. Rented."

"Would you have considered joining groups who take
possession?"

"No, no. They attract too much attention to themselves,
don't they? Wouldn't be very practical."

"If anyone was considered unreliable by virtue of being
either alcoholic, drug-taker, or some other form, perhaps
homosexual, would you have continued?"

"Definitely not."

"How would that be decided? Would it be your decision
too . . . ?"

"For to start with – we haven't people like that. These
people are hand-picked before they come over. I mean, you
just don't send over a group of people without checking them
out first."

"Hand-picked, by whom? By you, or the source from where they come?"

"The source. When they come over, I vet them again, don't I, just in case one slipped by."

"Is the source Ireland?"

"Oh, yes."

"Would you have had any means of knowing, and indeed, have you any means of knowing, whether a man like Armstrong was in fact like yourself engaged in this sort of undertaking?"

"No, I haven't, no. But he was definitely not involved with me, the group I was involved in."

"If he was involved in this sort of undertaking, would you have known about it?"

"I wouldn't, no."

If Dowd's purpose had indeed been to shield Armstrong from any accusation of involvement with the I.R.A., this was an odd answer. It would have been easy enough to answer "Yes." As it was, his answer "No" still left it possible that Armstrong might have been operating in an independent I.R.A. group.

"He could be operating independently, so to speak?"

"He definitely wasn't in Guildford, because he couldn't have been in Guildford, and the other people convicted with him couldn't have been there."

"But you have no means of knowing whether he was in another cell or group?"

"I know definitely the people convicted weren't responsible for Guildford, the people convicted of it."

He then went on to give an account of how he and three of those taken in Balcombe Street, had thrown a bomb into the pub in Woolwich. At the end of this day's interview Dowd was asked:

"Did you afterwards read about them at all to see what was the result of your attacks?"

"Yes, I probably did. I am sure I did."

"Would you have read about someone being arrested for them?"

"Yes, we did."

"If you had been at liberty, would you have taken any action about that?"

"No. Not under the circumstances. I couldn't."

"And the names of the persons you read as being arrested, as charged for these offences, were quite unknown to you?"

"Yes, absolutely."

Six days later Logan and Still went, again with the accredited court shorthand reporter, to interview the men from Balcombe Street who were being held in Brixton. On November 1, 1976 they obtained from Edward Butler and Henry Duggan very detailed and graphic accounts of the way in which the bomb had been thrown into the Kings Arms, Woolwich, on the night of November 7, 1974. The details accorded in every way with those which had been established, though many had not been given publicity, at the trial which led to convictions for it for Hill and Armstrong. Duggan was asked:

"Could these people who were charged have been another section of your organisation without your knowing it?"

"They could have been anything without my knowing it. I tell you from – it is very unlikely they would have been members of the organisation. I will put it this way. They wouldn't have been members of the organisation in London because if anybody else was doing things like that in London, we would have known. We would have been told about it if anybody was likely to do anything like that in London at that time."

"Did you squat in any houses?"

"No, I never squatted."

"Would you have considered getting free accommodation? By that I mean going to someone else's flat and taking it over?"

"No, no. It would have been ridiculous in our position at that time to do anything – to break any laws would have been ridiculous for us. No, we always rented accommodation."

(In considering this answer, it is instructive to remember some of the activity of Carole Richardson, Paddy Armstrong, Brian McLoughlin and Lisa Astin based in their squat in

Kilburn in the days before the Guildford and Woolwich bombings.)

"Were any of your colleagues, for want of a better name, heavy drinkers?"

"No, not heavy drinkers. An occasional drink."

"Would it have been anything that would have caused you alarm or did you frown upon heavy drinking?"

"Well, personally I do frown on heavy drinking, but, anyway from a security point of view of our position at that time, it would have been very, very foolish to have engaged in heavy drinking or draw attention to ourselves, frequenting pubs regularly. We never did anything like that."

"Any of your associates have anything to do with drugs?"

"Absolutely not."

"Why do you say that?"

"I say it for one reason: that the organisation of which I was a member frowned on anybody who had any connection with drugs, and definitely they wouldn't have been engaged in that activity if they had any connection with drugs."

"Supposing you had a suspicion that someone was taking drugs. What would you have done?"

"I'd have checked it out very quick. Then, again, I didn't have any doubts of any kind about O'Connell, Butler or Dowd."

"If a person was the sort of squatter cum drug-taker, cum mixing-in these odd people, all this would have been found out beforehand?"

"Definitely, yes. A person like that would never have got as far as the centre of London to carry out the activity."

He added that when interrogated by Neville and Imbert after the end of the Balcombe Street siege he had told them that he did not know Hill or Armstrong as members of the I.R.A. or indeed at all.

The next day, November 2, Logan and Still interviewed Joe O'Connell who had originally sent them to Dowd. O'Connell too told how about a week after the Balcombe Street arrests he had told Neville and Imbert that those recently convicted of the Woolwich bombing had had nothing to do with it. He had refused to say anything to them about Guildford – presumably because of the other I.R.A. people involved in that operation, none of whom had been members of the Balcombe Street four. Neither Butler nor Duggan had arrived in England until after the Guildford bombing; Docherty, the fourth man in Balcombe Street, was involved in neither operation. O'Connell however had been at Guildford with Dowd and the two "companions" – presumably women – about whom Dowd had refused to talk. Because of this O'Connell was at first worried about talking about Guildford at all.

"Are you worried about there being other people concerned in it that we do not know about, or one other person?"

"There is a few things that I will be mentioning in this statement that could lead to the arrest of some other people. This is something that I haven't thought about."

He was prepared to talk about Woolwich because all four people who had participated in that bombing (Dowd, Duggan, Butler and himself) were under arrest. He therefore proceeded to give full details of the Woolwich operation while promising to think about what he might or might not be able to say about Guildford during the lunch break.

At first after lunch O'Connell cold-bloodedly continued to give details of the Woolwich operation:

"We used bolts and nuts. Brendon had got them the day before, I think."

"Who made it?"

"We used – I am just saying that we used bolts and that. We had nuts beforehand . . . "

He described how they had been worried by the Gas Board driver sitting in the back of his truck in Francis Street just outside the Kings Arms, Woolwich.*

"We decided one should watch and the other two should go to the pub. I took the bomb with me. Harry and Eddy got out of the back. Eddy started staking the entrance to the lorry. He just stood beside the lorry where he could watch the man. Harry and myself went to the window of the pub. I was just in front of him. When I got to the window of the pub you can't see into the pub through that window. Actually,

*See page 50.

you have to lean up and look in because the bottom of the glass . . . I am not sure whether there was a curtain or frosted glass. I stood beside the window. I had the bomb in my hand. I lit it."

"How?"

"With the matchbox."

"You lit the fuse?"

"Yes . . . I just held it for a second to make sure it was alight then I threw it at the window. I threw it very hard. It smashed the glass and went well into the pub. We then turned and raced back towards the car, keeping well down. The bomb would have exploded just as we were getting just past the lounge of the pub . . . We then jumped into the car, the three of us. Brendan already had the car started. He just drove off. He didn't drive off with speed. He just drove off casually so that nobody would notice the screech of tyres or anything like that."

The car, he said, had been a stolen dark four-door Cortina, and, revealing another detail, he said he had worn a hat – a bush hat – while actually throwing the bomb as a sort of disguise. (A dark four-door Cortina which had been stolen from central London that night was found next day abandoned, with a bush hat in the back.) Still now asked O'Connell if he had thought more about Guildford and he said he had, and was prepared to talk about it. He said that he, Dowd and another man who was not in custody had gone down to Guildford on a reconnaissance about three weeks before the bombings took place. He said that they had originally reconnoitred the Star bar and the Horse and Groom, but finding no soldiers in the Star bar had found the Seven Stars and decided that they had been given wrong information and selected that instead as a target with the Horse and Groom. He now gave Still and Logan a detailed description of the interiors of both the Seven Stars and the Horse and Groom. Dowd and "the other man" went back for a second reconnaissance to decide exactly how the bombs should be planted in both pubs. They agreed to plant the bomb in the Horse and Groom under a seat and that in the Seven Stars in the disco under the table behind the door. O'Connell and

Dowd made the bombs — two six-pounders. He described in
some detail how the timing mechanism was made from a
pocket watch.

They had left for Guildford, O'Connell said, about 4 o'clock
and got down there at a quarter past 5. He too described the
multi-storey car park in which they had parked the car, a
hired one on this occasion. And there, as Dowd had said,
they primed the bombs, connecting up the detonator, the
watch and the battery. Then, as Dowd had said, they split
up. Dowd went to the Horse and Groom with one girl. O'Connell, with "the other man" who had gone with Dowd on the
second reconnaissance, went with the other girl to the Seven
Stars. The table under which it had been planned to plant
the bomb was occupied so they placed it under a seat near
the corner of the hallway instead. In both pubs the girls
carried the bombs in satchel-type shoulder bags and in both
pubs it was the girls who ordered the drinks. O'Connell said
they left the Seven Stars at a quarter past 6 but when they
got to the car park they saw that Brendon and the other girl
were not yet back so they went and stood around in a field
beside the car park for about 15 minutes before the others
returned. They got lost for a time driving out of Guildford
but eventually found the way to London and when they got
back there had a drink in the Durrell Arms in Fulham. He
and O'Connell heard the news of the explosions on the car
radio as they were driving the two girls home to North
London.

Logan and Still returned to Dowd on the Isle of Wight on
Monday, November 8 to cross-check again his own information with that given them by O'Connell. On almost all
points of detail, much of it quite desultorily elicited, and in
a manner quite unlike that of a pre-arranged fabricated story,
they confirmed each other. It was clear that there had indeed
been five people at Guildford (Dowd, O'Connell, "the other
man" and two girls) while only four (Dowd, O'Connell and
the two girls) had travelled in the car. In only one area was
there a difference: all Dowd's times were about one hour
ahead of O'Connell's. But, given that, as he said more than
once, it was all so long ago and he had taken part in so

Conclusion

many different I.R.A. activities of one sort or another, the divergence in memory between him and O'Connell was not one which would have, in the circumstances, probably struck the man on the Clapham omnibus as particularly significant. Indeed, if the timing had been accurately synchronised in the two versions it might have struck him as suggesting pre-arranged fabrication.

In any case the opportunity for Dowd and O'Connell to co-ordinate false accounts of the Guildford bombing had been limited. They had not met since the beginning of July 1975, well over a year before. Hill, Armstrong, Conlon and Richardson had not even been tried for the Guildford bombing when Dowd was taken into custody on July 10, 1975. Logan said: 'You have told us that Armstrong had nothing to do with Guildford or Woolwich.''

'I said none of the people had anything to do with it, none of them.''

Still then asked: "Is there any way you can tell us that you know that the girls who were lifted were not the two who accompanied you to Guildford?" (Still was referring to the fact that Anne Maguire had of course originally been arrested for murder at Guildford along with Carole Richardson.)

"There is no way I can do it."

"Other than unless you knew that your two girls were at liberty when the other two were arrested.''

"They had a good laugh about it when they read those other people were arrested.''

"The girls?"

"Yes."

"Do you know that because you were in their company?"

"Yes."

When, in custody, he had heard of the Guildford Four's conviction, his comment had been: "So much for British justice."

The Balcombe Street Four came up for trial in January 1977. O'Connell who, in addition to the 18 counts of indictment on which they were arraigned, had taken part in the Guildford and Woolwich bombings, and Butler and Duggan who in addition to the same 18 counts of the indictment had taken part in the Woolwich bombing, refused to plead on the grounds that, dishonestly, they had not been charged with the Guildford and Woolwich bombings as well.* In most newspapers, including *The Times*, it was reported that the defendants had refused to plead but their reason for not doing so was not given. Readers were left to assume that the conventional I.R.A. procedure of refusing to recognise the court had been followed.** Only the *Guardian* disclosed the embarrassing truth. Its reporter, not being a holder of an accredited police press card, had not felt it necessary to respond to police lobbying to keep silent on the subject. The trial itself, however, was unable wholly to avoid some of the awkward facts. This may have accounted for the curious attitude of the jury who, while finding the four guilty of most of the crimes on the indictment, refused to find them guilty of some others which had occurred during that first phase of their operations in which the Guildford and Woolwich bombings had taken place and to which they had admitted in statements to the police.

There was one particularly awkward fact which to some extent even troubled the judge at the trial. In July 1975, before the Guildford Four had been brought to trial, the Government Forensic Scientist, Douglas Higgs, had drawn up a paper correlating certain scientific features of the Guildford and Woolwich bombings with other bombings which had taken place after the arrests of the Guildford Four. (This paper was not available for the defence at the trial of the Guildford Four because it was never served on them.) At the Balcombe Street trial Higgs and another Government Forensic Scientist, Lidstone, produced statements to the effect that bombings of 1974 and 1975 were linked by certain

*In spite of the statements under interrogation to Neville and Imbert that those convicted of these crimes had had nothing to do with them, no further police investigation had taken place.
**This had indeed been the stance of Docherty the fourth Balcombe Street man, who had been at neither Guildford nor Woolwich.

scientific features to suggest that they were all part of the same person's or persons' activity. This time, however, Guildford and Woolwich had been left out of Higgs's list. When the attention of the court was drawn to this Higgs stated that they had been omitted on the instructions of the police who, he had assumed, were acting for the Director of Public Prosecutions.

At the end of the Balcombe Street trial O'Connell, acting consciously in the tradition of Irish Republicans throughout history, made a statement from the dock. Much of it attacked British Imperialism in terms so traditional as to be of little interest. But one section of his statement cannot be faulted.

"Four totally innocent people," he said, "Carole Richardson, Gerald Conlon, Paul Hill and Patrick Armstrong, are serving massive sentences, for which I and another man now sentenced had admitted our part. The Director of Public Prosecutions has been aware of these admissions but has chosen to do nothing . . . "

His words, again like those of so many Irish Republicans speaking from the dock in the past, seemed to go, for the time being, into a void. When the appeal of the Guildford Four was finally heard later, in 1977, and the new evidence of the Balcombe Street admissions as made to Logan and Still was produced, the appeal judges were little troubled.

John Yallop, the former Government Scientist who had appeared for the defence at the trial itself, now reappeared to emphasise his agreement with the views of Higgs and Lidstone to the effect that scientific features of the Guildford and Woolwich bombings linked them to others known to have been carried out by the Balcombe Street unit, to suggest that they were all the work of the same persons. His views were referred to early in Lord Justice Roskill's judgment as "certain allegedly scientific evidence of a Mr. Yallop". The phrase set the tone of veiled dismissiveness which underlay the whole of Roskill L J's judgment, for all its technically unbiased approach.

For instance, it was correctly stated at once that the Crown's case was based overwhelmingly on the confessions. It was also stated in one sentence that "there was no evidence whatever against [the defendants] of identification." This might have been supposed to be a most powerful cause for lurking doubt about convictions based only on confessions which were themselves retracted in court. But the lack of identification was never mentioned in the judgment again.

The new evidence of the Balcombe Street unit's admissions was of course the primary consideration of the judgment. This too was urbanely dismissed, though in considerable detail and after the better part of eleven days' serious consideration.

The facts were carefully articulated – among them an original denial by Dowd to the police on his arrest that he had taken part in the Woolwich bombing and a similar early alleged denial by O'Connell of the same involvement. Lord Justice Roskill pointed out that before, during and after the visits of Frank Maguire and Logan and the admissions which followed from these, the Balcombe Street men had had the opportunity of associating together. He did not point out that there had been no opportunity since July 1975, before the conviction of the Guildford Four, for the Balcombe Street men and in particular O'Connell to associate with Dowd, since Dowd was arrested before the Guildford trial took place. Nevertheless their accounts as given to Logan and Still largely confirmed each other.

What had been argued by counsel for the appellants was that the new evidence made the original verdicts unsafe and unsatisfactory and that these should be quashed and a retrial take place. But the court made clear that to it only one aspect of the new evidence was relevant, namely that part in which O'Connell, Dowd, Duggan and Butler said that none of the appellants had been involved in the Guildford and Woolwich bombings. The fact that the Crown was prepared to accept as probably true the presence of Dowd and O'Connell at Guildford did not mean that the appellants had not been there too.

Such dissection of the new evidence was a fair one to make but in making it the court was being very selective as to what it accepted of Dowd and O'Connell's evidence.

What was being assessed, in other words, was whether or not Dowd and O'Connell and the others had concocted their version of the story in order to get their "comrades" in the I.R.A. released. It was indeed a helpful dissection for the Crown to make on its own account. For the very confusion and often self-contradictory nature of the confessions of the Four in relation to the Guildford bombings, with their references to Anne Maguire, Brian Anderson, John MacGuiness and Paul Colman, all later seen to be false, left an embarrassing quartet and a whole carload on the Guildford expedition which needed to be filled up. The Crown, which had previously selected those parts of the confessions which it wanted and rejected others, was now in a position to resurrect some of those parts which it had earlier rejected and make good use of them. The Crown could now say that the other car and the other roles previously filled by Anne Maguire and the rest were in fact filled by Dowd, O'Connell and the two girls and the other man they had refused to name.

Examining Guildford in detail, Lord Justice Roskill went over O'Connell's story of how he and Dowd, the two girls and the other man carried out the bombing and compared it with Dowd's. The two accounts agreed in detail except that Dowd's times were, as noted, an hour ahead of O'Connell's. In court Dowd had for the first time given details of the car in which he said the team of five had travelled, saying that it had been a white Escort hired from Swan National in the name of Moffat. A hiring for that date in the name of Moffat was to be confirmed by the manageress of the Victoria branch of Swan National who was called as a witness at the appeal. She said the car had been a yellow Cortina. It looked as if Dowd had become confused in the long interval, mistaking a yellow Cortina for a white Escort. Such faulty recollection after such a long period during the early part of which many similar type operations had been conducted, and much of the latter part of which had been spent in solitary confinement, was not perhaps all that surprising, though Lord Justice Roskill made the most of the discrepancy.

He then went similarly over O'Connell's account of the Woolwich bombing and again compared it with Dowd's. The Crown maintained that Dowd had in fact never gone to

Woolwich either on a reconnaissance or on the night of the bombing itself. A gap in the team was necessary so that it could be filled by Hill, who had already been convicted for being there. Roskill LJ had by his systematic discrediting of Dowd kept it open for them.

Yallop's point that the scientific similarities between the bombs used both at Guildford and Woolwich and those used by the Balcombe Street unit suggested a single identifiable pattern – a view confirmed albeit reluctantly by the Government scientists, Higgs and Lidstone – was dismissed as virtually irrelevant by Roskill LJ:

"There was no doubt that the bombings at Guildford and Woolwich were part and parcel of a larger terrorist campaign in the course of which similar weapons had from time to time been used. But that fact does not in the least assist to show who were or were not the guilty parties."

This was fair enough as far as it went. The vital question was certainly not whether Dowd and/or O'Connell had been at Guildford and Woolwich but whether the appellants had been there too. The crucial part of the new evidence was the unwavering assertion that they had not been there.

The Court attached much significance for general dismissal of the new evidence to the fact that on his arrest in July 1975 Dowd had denied any participation in the Woolwich bombing. But it is difficult to see why this should have been thought of as significant for, if O'Connell and the others had indeed been his companions on that occasion, they were then still at liberty and it could have been dangerously compromising if he had said anything about the expedition at all. Roskill LJ conceded that this was a "possible" explanation but nevertheless described the omission as "striking". As for the fact that Dowd had not disclosed to Logan, when the others were in custody, something which he disclosed in court, namely that he had participated in an abortive expedition to Woolwich the night before the actual bombing, this was taken as proof that Dowd was lying and that he had "belatedly concocted" the story to tie up with what O'Connell and the others had said. The failure of Dowd always to provide, when expected or required, a coherent detailed memory of events which even before his more than two years of prison life must have been something of a confused jumble of furtive illegal actions on a considerable scale, was consistently held against him. He had been in Lord Justice Roskill's words "a deplorable witness, giving the impression much of the time . . . that he was telling a story of events in which he had not taken part and the details of which he had but imperfectly and recently learned".

Further to discredit the new evidence and support the Crown's contention that, whoever else had been at Woolwich, Hill and Armstrong had been involved too, Roskill LJ drew attention to a letter which the police had found at an I.R.A. flat they had raided in West London. This bore the fingerprints of O'Connell, Duggan and Butler and contained a sentence to which he attached the greatest relevance.

"Get those two Belfast fellows home," it ran, "Clean them up a bit, change them a bit, send them singly through Glasgow unless you can think of something better . . . "

O'Connell admitted that the letter had been addressed to him and said that he had received it from Ireland in January 1975 – that is, after the arrests of Hill, Conlon, Armstrong and Richardson. For the Crown, Havers seized on the fact that there was no proof when the letter was received and, to substantiate his views that Hill and Armstrong had been involved in Woolwich, maintained that it had been received in November or December 1974 and that "the two Belfast boys" was a reference to them. Why it should have been thought to apply so specifically to Hill and Armstrong after Woolwich, why it should not also have been a reference to "two boys" involved in Guildford or other bombing and shooting incidents, and why there should have been no reference to the girl, Richardson, was not explained. Nor was it explained how, if they were guilty and if I.R.A. operators were under the fairly close control which the letter implied, Armstrong and Richardson should have been able to go on a carefree ten days' hitch-hiking trip round Britain between the Guildford and Woolwich bombings, in the course of which they had not hesitated to draw police attention to themselves when they needed help.* All Havers was anxious to explain was that Hill and Armstrong had somehow been involved in the Woolwich bombing. Lord Justice Roskill helped him.

O'Connell, pressed as to the meaning of the phrase in the letter, "clean them up a bit, change them a bit," said that "clean them up a bit" was simply another way of saying the same thing, that is, change or disguise them. But Roskill LJ was able to find this quite inconsistent with the use of "change them a bit" in the phrase which followed. "On the other hand," he added with sleuth-like perception, "if, as was the fact, Armstrong though not Hill had before his arrest been living in a squat, the phrase indeed has significance." This small detail alone of his judgment gives a good example of the selective technique he used throughout. If the phrase "clean them up" was significant as applicable to a person living in a squat (Armstrong) then that significance did not apply to a person living not in a squat but in a Catholic hostel (Hill). Yet Roskill LJ wanted its significance extended to Hill too. All in all his judgment amounted to an argument for the plausibility of the Crown case. The essence of this, in the light of the new evidence, was that, although only four people had been seen by witnesses at Woolwich, "there was nothing inherently improbable in seven or eight or even more being involved in an operation such as the Guildford bombings where two public houses were to be attacked at the same time, or that two cars should be used in such an eventuality". These were Lord Justice Roskill's own words. He did not add that thus could the embarrassing gap left in the "confessions" version of the Guildford bombing by the need to drop Anne Maguire, MacGuinness, Anderson and Colman be conveniently filled by the new claim that others were there, without having to drop Hill, Conlon, Armstrong and Richardson too. For Woolwich, Dowd's presence had to be specifically rejected to keep room for Hill. The dismissal of his "deplorable" witness performance, his "concocted" and "lying" story made this easy. At Guildford there was plenty of room once the proposition of a seven – or eight-man active

*See the Folkestone telephone box incident, page 42.

service unit and two cars had been accepted. Havers was prepared to say that Dowd had not in fact been at the Guildford bombing and that his account was false. He said he might indeed have taken part in a reconnaissance, which would account for his detailed knowledge of Guildford and the pubs, but that the only thing he could not have learned from an earlier visit was the presence of the two "old men". Knowledge of that "small detail . . . could easily have been acquired subsequently". It is of course possible that Dowd could have learned of the two old men from those who had taken part, in the months between the Guildford bombing and his own arrest, but the manner in which this detail had come up in the original interview with Logan does not suggest that it was a contrived memory. Dowd had had no contact with O'Connell at all in prison by the time he talked to Logan.

Lord Justice Roskill was prepared to be marginally more credulous of Dowd on the question of whether he had been at Guildford. He could afford to be so without in any way prejudicing the Crown's case. "We see no reason," he said, "to decide whether O'Connell or Dowd took part in the Guildford bombings. We are content to assume that O'Connell's story of his presence and participation may indeed be true and that Dowd may also have taken part, not withstanding the doubts that we have on that latter point . . . " No doubt whatsoever hung over the main point he wished to make:

"Having wholly rejected as unworthy of credence their evidence that they did not know the applicants [Hill, Conlon, Armstrong and Richardson] and that those two men alone took part in the Guildford bombings with one other man and two women, the whole of the case in relation to Guildford insofar as it is based on the new evidence necessarily collapses." And he added categorically: "That evidence therefore gives rise to no lurking doubts whatever in our minds." All four applications to appeal on the grounds of it were thus refused.

As to "the lurking doubt" which he, or indeed anyone, might have had about Carole Richardson's guilt, on the grounds of her presence at the Elephant and Castle Pop concert on the evening of October 5, he seemed to have no difficulty in resolving it. It was a "false alibi" and had been concocted. Frank Johnson, he said, had "concocted" his evidence. (He also said: "Johnson admitted that the alibi had been concocted", a distortion of what Johnson in fact said.) He was untroubled by the thought that, if Carole had been the sophisticated terrorist she was held to be, her prepared "false alibi" bearing "all the marks of concoction" would have been available to hand instead of emerging in the muddled and piecemeal way in which it did. Perhaps as he was concerned to castigate "her pose as a young innocent" he saw this simply as an additionally subtle twist to that pose. Certainly if one thought of her as a young innocent, she was as he put it, now "demolished".

The failure of the Appeal can have come as no surprise to the appellants. Gerard Conlon had written to his mother as it proceeded:

"Well, I suppose you want to hear how the Appeal is going? First of all you have got to understand that the three judges who are doing our appeal are the exact same who did Dad's [of the Maguire Seven] Appeal and you know what happened to Dad's appeal, don't you? These judges seem to be ultra-friendly towards the Crown and very icy towards our counsel, they seem to doubt anything that indicates our innocence, but they seem to find no bother with what the Crown say, in fact you can bet that they are definitely bending over backwards to help them, they are definitely on their side . . . "

And so they had definitely turned out to be. But by the end of the year he was again managing to cling to a sort of optimism.

"Mum," he wrote from Wormwood Scrubs on December 30, 1977, "let us hope that 1978 will be the year when the truth finally comes out in the end, it cannot be locked away for ever, somebody will finally open the door where the truth has been hid and it will come tumbling out into the open where everyone can see it . . ."

16
Considerations of Substance

"Persons accused of crimes, however odious, must be . . .
tried calmly and dispassionately, and afforded all the safeguards against miscarriage of justice. If we fail in this duty,
the terrorist's bomb can do worse than maim and kill the
innocent. It will destroy the fabric of justice itself and of
the free society which it is our desire and duty to defend."

Sir Peter Rawlinson Q.C.

September 26, 1975

Early in 1986 an application by Carole Richardson for parole
was turned down on the grounds that as a terrorist prisoner
she cannot, under new Home Office regulations, be granted
parole until she has served twenty years. She will not be
eligible again until 1994 by which time she will have spent
more of her life in prison than out of it. Paradoxically the
cause of British Justice can be said to have been well served
by the decision. Her release on parole might have reduced
that sense of urgency with which all convictions that derive
from the Guildford pub bombings need to be re-considered.
Without such urgency conventional pride in British Justice

and in the values of the free democratic system which it is designed to uphold becomes hypocritical and a sham.

This is by far the most important reason to review all the eleven convictions. It transcends in importance even the need to alleviate the personal suffering which so many people have experienced directly or indirectly since the arrest by the Surrey police of Paul Hill on November 28, 1974 though this has indeed been terrible. As for the suffering of those who were bereaved or received injuries from the Guildford bombs this is actually mocked by the failure to re-open the matter. For two men who, the Appeal Court "is content to assume", may have been responsible for that crime, Brendon Dowd and Joe O'Connell in custody for more than ten years, have never even been tried for it.

Any attempt to re-open either the case of the Guildford Four or that of the Maguire Seven – and they are inseparable for all the formal pretence that they were distinct – meets a fundamental technical difficulty. It is a difficulty which if the Home Office chooses – and up to now it has so chosen – can be made insuperable. In both cases trials took place according to the proper forms of British law. In both cases a jury found the accused guilty. In both cases the proper procedure for re-assessing the convictions was applied. In both cases as a result of that procedure it was decided that the convictions were sound. The classic formal procedures have all been completed.

One further procedure remains, provided by Parliament as a sort of safety net. The Criminal Appeal Act of 1968 permits a Home Secretary to send back to the Court of Appeal "if he thinks fit" a case which has already been fully heard in the prescribed manner. Home Secretaries who at first interpreted the proviso "if he thinks fit" to mean only "if new evidence becomes available" have since widened it to include "or considerations of substance" as well. What constitutes "a consideration of substance" remains the decision of the Home Secretary. It is argued here that re-consideration of all aspects of these cases before, during and after the trials and appeal hearings provides in itself such a "consideration of substance" on a massive scale. Whether the Appeal Court itself or some

Conclusion

other process is the appropriate machinery for a complete review of both cases is a subsidiary question. There is one main question: is it "fit" that something should be done?

The only new feature of the cases since the convictions and their confirmation is that all those convicted have consistently continued to assert their innocence.* Striking as this is and unusual after such long periods of imprisonment, it cannot *of itself* be reasonably regarded as sufficient justification for a re-trial, for this would provide an easy opportunity for every sort of convicted person always to exploit. And yet there must come a point where the continued assertion of innocence by eleven people after such a long time becomes a consideration of some weight. There is no new evidence as such, nor, given the circumstances of the two cases, could there now possibly be unless either a police officer or a government scientist were to come forward and say that the evidence he or she gave at the time was incorrect. On what grounds, other than that the juries seem to have come to the wrong verdicts and the Appeal Court to have confirmed wrong verdicts, can it be argued that the cases should be formally reassessed? The simple answer is: no other grounds – just those. Under the 1968 Act every individual case is subject to re-consideration *on its merit* on this score. Possibly the Act should be widened to include provision for re-trials as well as reference to the Court of Appeal. But the intention of the Act is plain. The pursuit of truth is the end of all justice and, if the technical formalities of justice stand in the way of that pursuit, then the pursuit must take precedence over the formalities.

This broad principle has in fact long been properly recognised by the law itself and has been re-emphasised in our

---

*In an attempt to help secure his father's release, at least on bail, Gerard Conlon after conviction made a long statement to Surrey police in which he not only re-affirmed his original statement that he had taken part in the Guildford bombing but gave as much detail as he could think of about IRA activity of which he had had knowledge while living in the Lower Falls, Belfast. This statement was not taken under caution. He withdrew it again when he realised he had done nothing to help his father and, while admitting to a life of burglary in London, has steadfastly continued to deny involvement in the Guildford bombing ever since.

own time by judges in the Appeal Court. For example, Lord Justice Scarman (as he then was) in a case in 1975 cited and concurred with the following judgment delivered in the Appeal Court in 1909:

"In my opinion this Court ought not to consider itself bound by any hard and fast rule never to allow further evidence to be called when the fact that it was not called was due to the mistaken conduct of the case ... If it was plainly made out that justice required it, I think this court would interfere."* (Further – not necessarily new – evidence.)

Lord Diplock in 1983 made clear with reference to cases referred back to the Court of Appeal under the Criminal Appeal Act of 1968 that "... since it is the whole case that is referred this must include all questions of fact and law involved in it", and in speaking of such instances where the grounds for appeal had previously been unsuccessfully relied on, he said:

"... the court that hears the reference will give weight to that previous judgment from which it will be very slow to differ, unless it is persuaded that some cogent argument that had not been advanced at the previous hearing would, if it had been properly developed at such hearing, have resulted in the appeal against conviction being allowed ... "*

The fact that the Appeal Court would understandably be "slow to differ" with its own previous decisions when asked to do so has been advanced by some as a good reason for thinking that reference to that court of cases of such magnitude and significance as those of the Guilford Four and Maguire Seven would be inappropriate. Hearings before a Special Commission of Investigation might well be better or even some sort of re-trial of the previous trials and hearings at which a jury could pronounce its verdict.

One of the ironical aspects of both the Guildford and the

---

*Per Walton J. In R v. Perry & Harvey (1909) 2 Cr. App. R. 89, 92 – see Archbold 42nd Edn. p. 884. For Lord Scarman's concurrence see R. v Lattimore & others 62 Cr. App. R. 53.
*Regina v. Chard (1983): 3 All E.R. p. 637 at page 641.

Conclusion

Maguire cases is that pointers to the innocence of the accused still lie in that very field of everyday commonsense judgment which does not take too much notice of legal niceties and which in the end it is the jury's right to assert. After two trials and two Appeal Court hearings the areas of unresolved doubt in both cases are to-day enormous.

For instance: would an I.R.A. Active Service Unit really have used as bombers a 17–year-old English shop-lifter and drug addict like Carole Richardson and her petty thief boyfriend, a rough Kilburn squatter from Belfast who had been on remand for a quarter of the year? Would not such a consideration lead any jury today to question whether their confessions could possibly have been true, whatever the police said?

Would such a pair, a fortnight or so after they had killed five people with a bomb in a Guildford pub, really have gone on a hitch-hiking tour of the south of England, ringing up the Folkestone police for help when in trouble and giving a correct name and address?

Were the confusions, contradictions and plainly untrue details in the statements of the four accused really a sophisticated example of skilled counter-interrogation technique or just a bewildered attempt to give the police what they seemed to want to hear?

How to account for those inconsistencies in the various statements which could serve no meaningful misleading purpose, such as conflicting versions of which of the four of them had planted the bomb in the Horse and Groom?

Might not the incongruous Pernod which Carole said she ordered for Paddy Armstrong in the Horse and Groom have something to do with her interrogators' knowledge that a Pernod had indeed been ordered from the bar before the bomb went off?

If Carole had really been an accomplice of Paddy Armstrong in the Guildford murders would she have been nonplussed when she heard the seriousness of the charge against him and immediately have told the police where he was?

If her alibi had been concocted would she not have had it

ready to hand instead of talking about a diary nobody could find?

Would she really have been driven from Guildford to the Elephant and Castle, after planting the bomb, in the amazingly short time in which a police car, breaking all the speed limits, had covered the distance?

And, if Carole Richardson's confession was false, what did that do to the statements of Hill, Conlon and Armstrong, in all of which she figured as if her confession were true?

Would the jury have been so prepared to accept these confessions as genuine if they had known that, only ten days after taking them, the Guildford police had obtained a confession on another matter after hours of interrogation but later had to admit that the man who made it was innocent? Or if they had known that, in yet another, quite different case, allegations of violence had been made against the Surrey Constabulary?

Did the transcript of the interrogations of Conlon and Armstrong – as opposed to the formal statements which were extracted from them – really make them sound guilty?

Or, if their early reactions are to be explained by their subtlety and sophistication as terrorists, did their demeanour in the dock, observable over many weeks, really suggest such qualities?

The same sort of objections on common-sense grounds can be raised even more powerfully against the "guilt" of the Maguire Seven. Here the doubts are overwhelming. Would Giuseppe Conlon, a devout Catholic, really have continued to insist, as he did, almost with his last breath, on his innocence, and have implored Gerry Fitt to clear his name after his death, if he had been guilty?

Why do all the others, so long after their sentences have been served, continue quietly to assert with as much determination as ever that the entire accusation against them was false?

Can their handling of nitroglycerine really be reconciled with all their other movements during the period in question?

Why was the bulk of the nitroglycerine from which the traces on their hands were said to have come never found?

Why was no sign of any other bomb-making equipment ever found?

Why was there no explanation of how they had managed to dispose of all this, except for the ludicrous one that it had been done while they were under police observation?

Would Paddy Maguire really have gone with enquiries to a police station during a critical period in which the nitro-glycerine was being handled?

If they had all been disposing of nitroglycerine as alleged would not Sean Tully have taken some away with him in his car when he left at the crucial time? How, then, when he was arrested, did all tests on him and his car prove to be negative?

Did not the astonished denials of all the Maguire Seven, when presented with information that their hands had been contaminated, ring disturbingly true? Could they possibly have given such confident and convincing denials had they been guilty, since they did not know then of the police failure to find any confirmatory bulk or other equipment?

Why, if Pat O'Neill had been a terrorist, did he not take advantage of the three days in which the police left him at liberty after swabbing his hands to try and leave the country or disappear?

Was there not perhaps something odd about the collaboration between the Surrey Constabulary and the Metropolitan Police? The search of 43, Third Avenue on the night of the arrests itself had not been very thorough, and the Judge had in fact commented on this. So did the Metropolitan Police really expect or not expect to find a bomb factory there? They were acting at the time not on their own behalf but that of Surrey. Was the main purpose at that time really to get hold of Anne Maguire, who at that time the Surrey police honestly thought had carried out the Guildford bombings? Was the real objective to get her to confess like Hill, Conlon and Armstrong and Richardson? Might not the appearance of nitroglycerine on the family's hands have been primarily useful a) as a means of holding her for longer than the seven days allowed by the Prevention of Terrorism Act, b) as an inducement to her to confess, and c) as a fall-back position should she not do so, and the murder charge thus have to be dropped?

Even accepting that the TLC test was a uniquely reliable indicator of nitroglycerine, was there perhaps something odd about an acknowledgedly inexperienced young laboratory assistant being put in charge of tests to be made on such an all-important issue? Would this not have provided a convenient reason for dismissing such tests as unreliable should the police not have wished to proceed with this particular charge of handling nitroglycerine unlawfully?

Was it in fact not odd that Vincent and Patrick were only charged with handling nitroglycerine unlawfully on the very day on which the charge against their mother Anne for murder at Guildford had to be dropped?

No question or consideration should be excluded from the thinking of jurors if it adds to the reasonable doubts which they examine on behalf of the accused. At the time of the trials many such proper considerations managed to become obscured, thanks to the undoubted forensic skill of Sir Michael Havers, to a certain lack of skill on behalf of the defence, and, in the Maguire case, above all to the blurring of the issue of the TLC test's reliability with that of the guilt or innocence of the accused. The latter tendency was much increased by what now may look like a selective summing-up on the part of the Judge, who did much to destroy the possibilities of doubt both on the specific scientific issue and other matters. An analogous effect was achieved in the trial of the Guildford Four by emphasis on the contrast of styles, between police denials of threats or violence to obtain the confessions, and the accused's insistence that such threats and violence were the only reason why the confessions had been made.

Over ten years later, in a different judicial climate, the awkward questions which were never properly asked before refuse to go away. One is overriding and it is one which British Justice cannot allow to remain open without damage to the British way of life. Was Justice seen to be done? That question has now remained open, doing damage, for over ten years. Only in the case of Giuseppe Conlon who died in custody in 1980 protesting his innocence is it too late to answer it.

The Maguires still live in west London. Their determination to survive the blow which tore their family apart for ten years has given them strength. Pat O'Neill and Sean Smyth live in Ireland; their family lives were destroyed. Paul Hill, Gerald Conlon, Paddy Armstrong and Carole Richardson sit in prison: their chances of ever having any family life probably depend on what happens to the Maguires' claim for justice.

On May 17, 1985 Gerry Fitt initiated a discussion of the Maguire case in the House of Lords in the form of an unstarred question. Anne, Paddy and Patrick Maguire watched from the Gallery. Lord Fitt concluded by quoting Anne-Marie Maguire who had been nine at the time of the arrests.

"My family, my father, my mother and my brothers, have all been convicted. A lot of years out of their lives have been taken away from them for no reason at all. Nothing will ever fill the gap that we have lost between each other. The truth has to come out because we are innocent and we will always keep saying that we are innocent. And if the truth does not come out while my Mum and Dad are still alive, then I hope that one day I will have children and my brothers will have children and they will keep continuing in this campaign until it has proved once and for all the total innocence of my family."

At the end of the discussion in which many Peers voiced their concern, Lord Glenarthur on behalf of the Government and the Home Office said:

"I should be the first to recognise the strength of feeling expressed this afternoon. I shall certainly draw the attention of my Right Honourable friend [the Home Secretary] to what has been said to-day and to the way in which it has been said."

No action on the part of the Home Office followed.

On January 31, 1986 Lord Fitt received a letter from the Home Office in reply to one he had written in October 1985 to the Home Secretary asking him to take action. The Under-

Secretary at the Home Office, David Mellor, replied politely and at length. His letter contained the phrase:

"Whatever action the accused may have taken in respect of the explosives they were found guilty of possessing, it remains the case that the jury was satisfied that there was evidence to show that explosives had been handled." He said he understood the wide interest and concern in the case but ". . . like the Home Secretary's predecessors, I do not find anything which offers ground for action to intervene in the case . . ."

In January 1986 an Early Day Motion was put down in the House of Commons in the names of John Wheeler, Conservative M.P. for Westminster North (the constituency in which the Maguires live) and a former Assistant Prison Governor, and Sir John Biggs-Davison who before Giuseppe Conlon died had campaigned on his behalf on the strength of private information. By the middle of 1986 that House of Commons motion had acquired over 200 signatories of all parties. The motion reads as follows:

"That this House notes the widespread concern felt in Parliament, by eminent scientists, by other responsible observers and by members of the public who have viewed programmes on the matter screened by Channel 4, that Anne Maguire, Patrick Maguire (senior), Vincent Maguire (then aged 17), Patrick Maguire (then aged 14), Sean Smyth, Patrick O'Neill and the late Giuseppe Conlon, sentenced in 1976 to long terms of imprisonment since served, now appear, despite confirmation of their convictions at the time by the Court of Appeal, to have been entirely innocent of the crime with which they were charged; further notes at the conclusion of a debate in the other place on 17th May 1975, the recognition by the Parliamentary Under Secretary at the Home Office of the strength of feeling on this matter in that House and his pledge to draw the attention of the Secretary of State for the Home Department to what had been said; and therefore earnestly urges the Secretary of State for the Home Department in the interests of the highest standards of British justice of which this country needs to feel rightly proud, to move without delay for a review of these convictions, either under the provisions of section 17 of the Criminal Appeal Act 1968, or by such other public process of review as he may deem appropriate to this disturbing case."

Sir John Biggs-Davison has regularly asked the Leader of the House for some Government action on the matter. There has been none.

Two former Home Secretaries, the leaders of the Liberal Party and the Social Democrat Party, and the Labour front bench spokesman on Home Affairs have approached the Home Secretary on the case. His reply remains constant:

". . . as yet nothing has emerged which might justify the Home Secretary in taking action with respect of their [the Maguire Seven's] convictions."

It has been stressed throughout this book that the cases of the Maguire Seven and the Guildford Four are inextricably interlocked for all the legally correct assertion that there was no connection between them. When considering however which case, as a matter of public conscience, calls for re-investigation first, there is a significant difference between them. The defence of the Guildford Four depended very largely on the allegations that their confessions had been obtained by improper methods of interrogation on the part of the police. But it must again be emphasised that all the police officers throughout the trial consistently and impressively denied all such allegations, and that their denials were clearly accepted as irreproachable by the jury and the judge, whose view was equally clearly confirmed by the Court of Appeal. In the case of the Maguire Seven allegations of improper interrogation were also made by the defendants and all such allegations were equally consistently refuted by all the police officers concerned and their refutations were accepted by jury, judge and the Court of Appeal. The difference lies in the fact that the allegations made in the Maguire trial were of no material relevance to the defence. With the marginal exception of Vincent calling a stick of chalk a candle, what they said under interrogation formed no significant part of the case against them. Re-investigation of the case of the Maguire Seven does not therefore immediately involve any need to re-open one highly sensitive area of evidence. This may spare the Home Secretary certain immediate difficulties.

However the Home Office attempt to spare the Home Secretary all difficulties, by sheltering him behind the perimeter of a formal need for "new evidence" in the Maguire case, merely increases the size of the problem he will have to deal with in the end and damages, every day it persists, the cause of British Justice. It is a time to recall the ancient precept: *Fiat justitia et ruant coeli* – let Justice be done though the heavens fall.

Index

Index

Index

Index

of bombings at 241–245; Magistrates
Court 8, 166; Mayor, 22; police
station 172; trial of Guildford Four
178–196; their Appeal, 238,
255–262; car park at, 240–1, 245; also
passim
Guinness, 79, 82, 219

Hailsham, Lord, 22–3
Hamilton, Anne (WRAC), 14, 16–18
Hampshire, 11
Harrison, Antoinette, Capt., 34
Harlesden, 45, 105; police station, 125,
130, 140, 155
Harrow Road
police station, 85, 91, 96, 101, 103–5,
206; St Mary's hospital, 100; also 82,
83, 89
Harrow school, 27
Hart, Robert, Builders, 51, 67, 70
Harvey, Detective Inspector, 114, 118
Havers, Sir Michael, 9, 22, 88, 185, 189,
198–200, 219, 222, 227–8, 237,
259–61, 270
Hayes, Dr., Government Scientific
Officer, 201, 206
Heath, Edward, 22, 27
Hendon, 138
Heysham, Lancs., 50, 78, 200
Higgs, Douglas, 105, 203, 206, 209, 213,
254–5, 258
Hill, Elizabeth, Paul's sister, 60
Hill, Paul, convicted 4; arrested 51, 53;
interrogation and statements 53–5,
59–63, 66, 69–70, 73, 102, 106, 122,
124, 127, 143; statement contradicts
Coulon's and Armstrong's 144; his
explanation of his statements,
53–56; and Gerard Conlon 57, 59,
63–66, 68, 72, 75–6, 102 and Anne
Maguire 70–71, 107; and Armstrong
128, 131; and Carole Richardson
132, 133, 156; charged with murder
147; trial 178–197; sentenced 196–7;
Appeal 255–262; also 145, 163, 173,
177, 227, 239–40, 249, 253, 255,
259–61, 264, 268–9, 271
Home Office, 25, 204 fn, 263, 274
Hope, Bob, "for President", 155, 157
Horton Hospital, Epsom, 78
Horse and Groom
on night of October 5 1974, 11–21;
also 23, 25–8, 49, 52, 56, 65, 68, 107,
139–40, 144, 170, 178–9, 185–6, 191,
196, 240–1, 243–5, 251, 267
Horse and Hound, 33
Horton, Detective Chief Inspector, 110,
111, 128
House of Commons, 24 & 24 fn, 272
House of Lords, 271–2
Housing Officer, 80
Howell, David, 22
Hughes, Maureen, 86
Hughes, Police Officer, 117
Hunt, Detective Sergeant, 96–7
Hunter, Detective Sergeant, 76, 89–90,
229–230
Hunter, John, 15, 17–18

Imbert, Detective Superintendent,
147–9, 198, 206, 239, 249, 254 fn
International Marxists, 26
Interrogation
see "allegations", Balcombe Street
and under named defendants
Internment night, 99
Ireland, 98, 128, 145, 247, 259
Irish Army, 78
Irish Guards, 12, 29
Irish Republic, 31, 183
Irish Republican Army (IRA)
Provisional, 4, 6, 8, 9–10, 24–26,
31–32, 35, 50, 55, 61 fn, 64–66, 92,
98, 100, 102, 117, 120, 123, 126–7,
130–1, 134, 140, 144, 146, 178–9,
185, 189, 192, 222, 227, 267;
condemned by Anne Maguire, 153;
"Balcombe Street" unit, 239–261
Official, 55, 127, 130
Irish Tourist Board, 25
Irvine, Sally, 152
Iverson Road, no 88 (Carole's mother's
house), 32–34, 36–7, 44–5

"Jack the Lad" (Pop group), 40, 166,
186
Jaguar, E-type, 128
Jailhouse Rock, 14
"Jane", 49
Jenkins, Roy, 22
Jermey, Detective Sergeant, 52–3,
56–9, 63–5, 71, 108, 113, 180, 192
John Moores, 97
Johnson's Air Freshener, 209
Johnson, Frank, 40, 154–5, 165–172,
183–4, 186, 262

278

Index

Index

in House of Lords, 271; also 52, 66, 76, 150–3, 161, 227, 229, 269

Maguire, Patrick (son),
convicted 4, 6 fn; on Tuesday December 3, 87, 89, 95–7, swab test 88, 105, 115; and mittens 105; released 105; interrogated in London 96–7; interrogated in Guildford 115–16; his allegations 118; released again 116; charged with handling explosives 2 months later, 160; trial 199–222; present in House of Lords, 271 also 52, 120, 151, 270–2

Maguire, Vincent (son),
convicted 4; on Monday December 2, 79–80; on Tuesday December 3, 81–2, 87, 89, 93–5, 97–8; swab test, 88, 105–6, 114, 115; released 105; interrogated in London, 97–8; interrogated in Guildford 114–15; and the "candle", 93, 114–16, 158, 201–2, 216, 220, 230, 237; his allegations 118; released again 116; charged with handling explosives 160; trial 199–22; also 52, 270, 272

Maguire Seven, 4–7; affected by Hill's statement 70; allegations 117–20; trial 199–222; Appeal, 228–238; also 262, 264, 266, 268–9, 272

Makos, Dr. Casimir, 138, 141

Malloyon, Roy Thomas, 195–6, 268

Maida Vale, 35

Manchester, 107

"Marion", 59, 61 and fn, 62–3, 67, 69, 70–71

Mark, Sir Robert, 163

Matthews, Sir Peter 23; on scatterbrains 24; 222, 227

Mellor, David, 272

Memphis Belle (Kilburn pub), 31, 34, 36, 40–1, 52, 165

Merrion square (Dublin), 43

Metropolitan police, 25, 62–3, 39, 123, 146, 163, 190, 269

Middlesex Crown Court, 36

Mildon, Arthur, Q.C. 180

Mills, WPC, 167, 181, 193

Mitchell, William, 166

Moffat, 257

Morris (car), 62–3, 69, 144

Mount Street, 197

Mulligan, Biddy, 47, 137

Mullin, Sean (15 Rondu Road) 43, 49, 52, 56, 62, 122, 158–9, 164

Munday, Detective Chief Inspector, 91–2, 100–3, 147; worried, 148; 149, 206, 222

Murphy's hut, 116

Murphy, Samuel, 12–13

Myers, Eric, Q.C., 180, 194

National Council of Civil Liberties, 184

Neville, Detective Chief Superintendent, 63, 249, 254 fn

Newmarket, 34

Newcastle, 40, 42, 165–167, 183

Nitroglycerine, 4, 7, 9, 50, 87–8, 110–11, 115, 117–118, 120, 123, 146, 200–1, 204–220, 227, 229, 230–8, 268–70

North Circular Road, 138

Northern Ireland, 31–2, 79

North Thames Gas Board, 78–9, 93

Nurse and Jones, 77, 81

O'Brien, Owen (Seven Stars Manager), 20

O'Connell, Joe (IRA, Balcombe Street), 239–40, 249–253, 255–261, 264

Odeon Cinema, 12

Old Bailey, 178, 213

Old Bell (Kilburn pub) 127, 131

Old men, two, 13, 15, 245

O'Leary, Mr, 95

O'Neill, Helen (wife of Pat), 84–5, 89

O'Neill, Jacqueline (daughter), 86, 89, 103

O'Neill, Jean (daughter), 86, 89, 103

O'Neill, Pat,
convicted 4; bitter, 6; telephones Maguires, 85; at 43, Third Avenue on Tuesday December 3, 86–7, 89–90; daughters 86, 89, 103; swab test 88, 103, 106, 115; interrogated in London 103; released, 103; arrested, 112; interrogated in Guildford 112–13, his allegations, 118; charged with possessing explosives 147; refused bail 160; trial 199–228; Appeal Court hearing 235; sentence reduced, 238; also 150, 152–3, 173, 227, 269, 271–2

O'Neill, Sharon (daughter), 86, 89, 103

O'Shea, Mrs, 83

280

Index

Index

Index

References

pp 74–76 Fifteen page Document in hand-writing of Gerard Conlon signed by him and handed to Alastair Logan, solicitor, on 23/1/86 at HM Prison, Long Larin.

p. 117 Central Criminal Court no 1649/R/1976 p. 80

p. 118 1649/R/1976 pp 77–8

p. 190 Central Criminal Court no 5291/R/75 pp 51–2, 54

p. 191 5291/R/75 pp 60, 64, 119

p. 193 5291/R/75 pp 68, 84–5

pp 193–4 5291/R/75 pp 86–9

p. 196 Surrey Daily Advertiser February 26–27, 1975, September 16–17, 1975

p. 202 Central Criminal Court no 1649/R/1976 pp 77–8

pp 220–1 1649/R/1976 p. 80